LANGUAGE IN DANGER

ANDREW DALBY

LANGUAGE
IN DANGER

ALLEN LANE
THE PENGUIN PRESS

ALLEN LANE
THE PENGUIN PRESS

Published by the Penguin Group
Penguin Books Ltd, 80 Strand, London WC2R 0RL, England
Penguin Putnam Inc., 375 Hudson Street, New York, New York 10014, USA
Penguin Books Australia Ltd, 250 Camberwell Road, Camberwell, Victoria 3124, Australia
Penguin Books Canada Ltd, 10 Alcorn Avenue, Toronto, Ontario, Canada M4V 3B2
Penguin Books India (P) Ltd, 11 Community Centre, Panchsheel Park, New Delhi – 110 017, India
Penguin Books (NZ) Ltd, Cnr Rosedale and Airborne Roads, Albany, Auckland, New Zealand
Penguin Books (South Africa) (Pty) Ltd, 24 Sturdee Avenue, Rosebank 2196, South Africa

Penguin Books Ltd, Registered Offices: 80 Strand, London WC2R 0RL, England

www.penguin.com

First published 2002
1

Copyright © Andrew Dalby, 2002

Set in 10.5/14 pt PostScript Linotype Sabon
Typeset by Rowland Phototypesetting Ltd, Bury St Edmunds, Suffolk
Printed in England by Clays Ltd, St Ives plc

ISBN 0-713-99443-6

CONTENTS

LIST OF MAPS

ACKNOWLEDGEMENTS

First I want to thank Cynthia Shelmerdine, Tom Hubbard and all my colleagues at the Classics Department at the University of Texas at Austin. In the spring semester 2001, as I worked deep into the evening at Waggener Hall or made a late-night visit to those lovely libraries, I had plenty of time to appreciate the opportunity that their invitation had given me to write as well as to teach. And then I must thank David Hill and Patricia Landy who, as graduate students, explored the languages of the Roman Empire with me: my lectures to them, with their questions and comments, formed the first draft of what is now Chapter 2. Thanks also to Erika Simon, with whom I shared an office and many dicussions. My involvement with the Institute of Linguists, over several years now, has helped to crystallize this book; it took its final shape at Austin.

But *Language in Danger* is really for my daughters Elizabeth and Rachel: for all you others who read it, but especially for them, for making a historian think about the future. In their generation, and in each generation that will follow after, the loss of languages will be an ever more urgent problem. I hope I have shown why.

79120 Saint-Coutant, France
12 December 2001

PROLOGUE

Languages are being lost, month by month, year by year. Does it matter? Will it matter if we eventually become a one-language species?

A couple of numbers will demonstrate, better than words, how rapidly we are discarding our languages. About 5,000 languages are now spoken as the first language or mother tongue of someone, somewhere. According to the best recent estimates, in the present century 2,500 languages are likely to be lost – which is what happens when the last living speakers turn to another language. A total of 2,500 languages in a hundred years is an average of one language every two weeks.

This is why it is happening. In almost every country, in increasing numbers, parents who are able to make the choice are no longer teaching minority languages to their children. Young people of school age are learning national and international languages and practising them with enthusiasm. Radio and television are honoured members of almost every family, and they speak the languages of mass communication. As a result, the number of speakers of the national languages of the world (fewer than 120 out of the 5,000) is swelling year by year. Not many minority languages will still be spoken in the twenty-second century.

There's more. In almost every field of modern life, English is in. You will hear foreign speech studded with English words (a German news broadcast, a French sports report, a conversation among Zulu teenagers). Or you will realize that an overheard conversation between two speakers of some other language (whether in a Singaporean software store or a corridor of the United Nations building) is, unexpectedly, mostly in English. Computer programs and manuals are in English, grudgingly translated into other languages. Easy as it is to put up Web pages in hundreds of languages, Web pages are predominantly in English and it is the English ones that get the hits. Statistics for all of this are hard to collect, but no one can doubt that the use of English world-wide is growing year by year, as is the demand for English language teaching.

It matters. The statistics are loaded with significance, not only for the old people who were usually the last living speakers of each lost language, but for every one of us and our descendants. This book will show that we need the knowledge that is preserved and transmitted in each of the languages of the world; we need the different and conflicting world views that each language gives us. And more: the language faculty, unique to the human species, allows us to communicate thought and innovation to one another – and it allows this because we have the ability to change and innovate in language. We need there to be interaction between a multiplicity of languages because it is this that catalyses language change. Some English speakers, even now, say openly that the multiplicity of languages is a nuisance and that the sooner everyone speaks English, the better. Once you have read this book, you will know why they are wrong.

In writing about the past and future of language, one must use language carefully. I have tried to do that here.

Languages are not entities and it can be seriously misleading to make them the subjects of active verbs. Even so, I have, for brevity's sake, allowed myself to say that languages 'spread', meaning that the use of what may be called 'the same language' extends over a wider area than it did before. For brevity, again, I have allowed myself to say that a language 'has' roles or functions, meaning that its users use it for these purposes. If I say that a language 'changes', I mean that users of 'the same language' are using it differently in some particular detail – as compared with the way that they themselves used to speak before, or the way that earlier users of the language spoke.

I have not usually said that a language 'dies'. The cessation of current use of any language is an event that is potentially disastrous to the shared knowledge and future abilities of our species, and an event that may be accompanied by the disappearance of a culture. Occasionally it may be linked with death – the violent death of all current speakers. More often the last speakers of any language have switched to another which meets their current needs, and occasionally (as we see in Chapter 6) a little of their former language may be incorporated in their new one. For an event with such varying consequences, an event that is defined in such different ways, death is not the ideal metaphor. Yet we are all losers when it happens. This is why I prefer to use the alternative term 'language loss'.

The word 'bilingual' is used in two ways in this book. A bilingual person is one who can and does use two languages effectively in daily life. That means using the languages adequately – well enough to get by – but not necessarily knowing both languages perfectly and not necessarily knowing them both equally. A bilingual community, whether a village or a whole country, is one in which two languages are used in daily life. That will imply that some people in the community (but not necessarily all of them) are themselves bilingual.

'Language shift' is an example of sociolinguistic jargon and a concept that is very important to this book: language shift occurs when people and communities change their linguistic behaviour, adopting a new language (for some purposes, or for all purposes) or ceasing to use a traditional language.

A 'national language', in this book, is one that is taught in schools and recognized as the everyday language of communication in any particular country. Many countries have constitutions in which a particular language is given this status officially. Whether this is the case or not, the concept of national language is important in every country, because the national language will be chosen by anyone who wants to reach the largest possible national audience in print, in television and on the Internet. Some national languages are shared by several countries, or are used world-wide: this makes them international languages, and, as such, it makes them an even better choice for reaching certain audiences.

The traditional term 'mother tongue' is used in this book for the first language that a child learns to speak.

Linguists and anthropologists have researched language spread and language loss in many parts of the world. The knowledge exists, but it is not as accessible as we need it to be. *Language in Danger* aims to offer a new perspective. It explores the linguistic world of the twenty-first century – language shift, the spread of national languages, the spread of English, the rapid disappearance of minority languages. We can predict the linguistic future. We do it, as this book shows, by making use of linguistic history – by exploring how languages have interacted in the past. In the case of the historical examples used here (such as the Roman Empire in Chapter 2) we know the final outcome. Working from known to unknown, we can discern a likely outcome for the language changes that are now under way. This book will, I hope, make it easier for people other than specialists to understand the likely future of the languages of today's world, and to understand in what ways we shall be poorer if the predicted future comes.

A sub-plot, reappearing at various points in this book, is the information recorded in each language about the natural world and its uses to human beings. The names of plants and animals will be frequently used as examples in discussing language change and language loss. This is why. Pure linguists, when asked what we lose when languages are lost, will often point to the enormous potential variety of linguistic structures, the rich library of possibilities (in sounds, word forms and syntax) whose existence we might not even guess if there were fewer languages to exemplify them. Some examples of such statements are quoted in the final chapter of this book. They are perfectly correct, but it is hard to persuade non-linguists that this issue matters. Ethnobiologists, by contrast, know that when cultures disappear – as peoples are assimilated or exterminated – knowledge of the natural world disappears with them. This knowledge may be important to our survival, as is shown in Chapter 6 with a few examples of major drugs whose benefits were first demonstrated by their medical use in traditional societies. Without these drugs, many readers of this book would be dead. This, you may agree, is a stronger argument than the purely linguistic one: we need the knowledge gathered over many centuries in cultures and languages that are now disappearing.

This is not an optimistic book. Drawing on anthropology, ethnobotany and cultural history, it shows what we shall lose as each language disappears.

LANGUAGE AND OUR SPECIES

The nature of language

It is agreed that the capacity for language is unique to *Homo sapiens*. Normal individuals of our human sub-species, *Homo sapiens sapiens*, if they begin to learn in infancy, can all learn a language perfectly. They can learn any human language with equal ease, and they can just as easily learn more than one, if they hear these languages spoken all around them.

Our sub-species supplanted another, *Homo sapiens neanderthalensis* or 'Neanderthal man', 35,000 years ago. Nobody knows whether Neanderthal people had language. Their mouths and throats would not have allowed the same range of speech sounds that we make; it is possible, none the less, that they did have languages, one or more than one, and if so it is probable that the shared structure of all of their languages was different from the shared structure of all of ours. No one knows whether it would have been easy or difficult for us to learn and speak such a language. It might even have been impossible. No one knows whether there was ever linguistic contact between that sub-species and our own.

Members of many other animal species communicate with one another, sometimes making sounds that are vaguely comparable with the sounds of our languages, sometimes not using their voices, sometimes not using sounds at all. No single species attains anything like the range of different sounds that is called for in our languages. And there is a deeper difference between animal communication and human language. No animal communication system has a grammar that allows one individual to make, and another individual to understand, a completely new statement, something that no one ever said before. All of our languages have such a grammar.

It is difficult to imagine that we could have made the progress we have made in investigating the world and understanding one another without, sometimes, saying things that no one had ever said before. No other natural communication systems so far known allow this. All of our languages allow it.

It is difficult for us to imagine that any extraterrestrial life form could have attained intelligence, and put it to use in science and technology, without a language that, like human languages, allowed novel ideas to be expressed and understood. However, extraterrestrial languages, if they exist, might not share any of the same underlying structures that all human languages share. So, just as with the hypothetical languages of the Neanderthalers, no one knows whether it would be easy, difficult or impossible for us to learn an extraterrestrial language, or for extraterrestrials to learn any of ours.

Let's look more closely at this unique communication device of ours. The language that we speak and hear consists of a range of sounds, a vocabulary of words made up of those sounds and a grammar of rules for combining the words meaningfully.

Our mouths and throats are capable of making a whole spectrum of sounds, from which about fifteen to seventy-five distinctive ones (called 'phonemes' by linguists) are in use in any one form of speech. The selection of sounds used, and the patterns with which they are combined in words, are astonishingly variable. Anyone can immediately tell Chinese from English by the tone pattern of a phrase or sentence, because every syllable in Chinese has a specified tone and that is not true of English. Anyone can immediately tell French from English by the special sound of *r* in French (uvular *r*, made at the back of the palate) – or by the occurrence of the sounds *th* and *h*, both of which are common in English and never used in French – or by the rhythm of sentences, because in English every major word has a stressed syllable and any word in a phrase can be given differential stress (*This is* my *book, you know* per*fectly well!*), while in French it is nearly always the last syllable of any phrase that receives the stress (*Mais c'est à* moi, *ce livre, tu le sais* bien!) Finally, even within English, the pronunciation of a single word such as *butter* will allow the listener to distinguish among United States, Canadian, London, West Country, Birmingham, Liverpool, Scottish, Irish and several other 'accents'. There are thousands of languages, some of which have hundreds of dialects. By its sound pattern you can distinguish any one of these from any other that you happen to know.

Any speaker commonly uses several thousand words. The list of words that you use will differ slightly from the list of words used by your closest friends and colleagues. You pick up new words throughout your life from conversation; in modern life you also pick them up from books, films and television. Some of these new words you will soon be using yourself. Until I was fourteen I did not know what a *computer* was; for some years after that I did not imagine that I myself would have any use for the word; now I seem to talk about computers all the time. So it is that you will find no immediate use for some of the new words you hear; but never mind that, because once you have learnt them you will understand them whenever you hear them. I have still not found a reason to say *proactive*, but I have it filed away.

Once you leave school, unless you work with languages or are fascinated by them, you may never have to think about the way words are put together in sentences. But whenever you hear an unpractised foreigner speaking English, you are reminded that there is more than one possible way to build sentences and that the way you first thought of is not the only obvious one. Every encounter with a different dialect of English is also a reminder that it is not only sounds and words, but also grammars, that differ.

Most of the time we are quite unaware of the making of sounds, the choosing of words and the applying of rules, yet this is how every sentence that we speak is made up, and this is how we understand the sentences that others say.

How do we learn to do it? The answer is that every child who learns to speak practises sounds, builds up a personal vocabulary and works out a personal set of grammatical rules.

This may seem a surprising statement. After all, if you had a traditional education, you spent a long time at school *learning* words and *learning* grammatical rules, as set out in textbooks and as retailed by teachers. But think about this: even before you studied grammar, you could say everything that you needed to say in your own first language,

3

and you could understand practically everything that was said to you in that language. With luck, your language lessons at school helped you to read, write and speak effectively, but they had very little effect on the way you spoke to your family and friends.

By the age of about seven, children are speaking their mother tongue well (and another language, if they are growing up bilingual). They know the words that they need to know, and they are still rapidly learning more as their experience widens. Between the ages of one and about seven, every child achieves all this independently. Parents, of course, correct their children's speech, but sometimes misguidedly, and unless they are linguists they do not do it by teaching rules. Unless they are linguists, they themselves are not conscious of the real grammatical rules of the language they speak. If they do try to give a rule, it may well be a false one.

Somehow, children can deal with all this. A parent says 'Don't say *teached*, say *taught*,' and the child obediently adds *teach* to a mental list of verbs whose forms must be separately learnt. A parent says, 'Don't say *could've*, say *could of*,' and the child ignores the instruction because people don't really say that.

The crucial fact is that every child is doing this afresh. Every child is sorting out a set of distinctive sounds, on the basis of the sounds that are heard in conversation, and will have them fully sorted out by the age of four or five. Every child is building up a dictionary, and will never stop adding to it. Every child is working out a grammar, and will be using it skilfully and consistently by about six or seven.

Parents and even teachers, if they try to explain the rules of the language they speak, soon become guiltily aware that their conscious knowledge of these rules is very hazy. Linguists have been trying hard but have never yet achieved a fully satisfying and complete statement of the grammar of English. No computer program so far devised can produce a full range of grammatical English sentences without any ungrammatical ones. Somehow, subconsciously, children have it all worked out. How can they do this?

The answer comes in two parts.

The first part is that all human languages, even if utterly different on the surface, have grammars that share many points of underlying similarity, 'linguistic universals'. The general consensus among linguists now is that linguistic universals are pre-programmed in the human brain. Children are to some extent attuned to human language (and they can as easily learn any language that is spoken around them, English, Chinese, Nahuatl) because all human languages are built on the same deep structure.

The deep structure is a framework on which, unconsciously, each child builds: because the second part of the answer is that children devote a massive amount of time and work to language, especially in those early years. Some of the activity is conscious. Children play with words; they conduct nonsense conversations; they remember, revise and imagine conversations; they memorize, invent and transform stories. All of this is serious linguistic work. They are doing it, almost full time, for years.

Beyond the linguistic universals, everyone's sound patterns, everyone's vocabulary and everyone's grammatical rules, are original. This is because each of us, as a child, worked out the rules afresh. Since we think independently, and are not clones of one another, everyone's language is very slightly but perceptibly different from everyone else's.[1] And all of us, throughout our lives, continue to adjust our speech as we listen and as we read.

This is how we learn to speak. This is how change and originality are built into human language.

How different is each person's language? That depends. If twins have grown up together, their language may be so similar that it is difficult for others to tell them apart by their voice and speech. Yes, each one worked independently at building up a sound system, a dictionary and a grammar, but they had so many contacts and experiences in common that the linguistic material they were unconsciously analysing was almost identical.

It can be a little difficult to tell siblings apart by voice. When my daughters telephone me, the words *Hello, Dad!* do not provide sufficient data to allow me to make a correct identification every time. They are three years apart in age, but they grew up in the same family, shared many friends and went to the same schools. The linguistic material they were analysing was very similar. It is important to realize that this has nothing to do with heredity: no one would fail to distinguish their voices from their mother's, or hers from her mother's.

It has everything to do with environment. 'With whom can he have lived?' asked Matthew Arnold rhetorically, when struck by the quaintness of F. W. Newman's use of English.[2]

Those living in a community interact most with others in the same community. So it is not difficult to see why everyday speech in any one community tends, over time, to diverge from that in others.

A new word, or a new use of an old word, becomes established among a particular group. The usage may never spread beyond a certain radius. Elsewhere, if the same meaning needs to be expressed, there may be a different way of saying it. What are called *sunglasses* in British English are *glare glasses* in Indian English. An Indian *pin code* is a British *postcode* is a United States *zip code*.[3] In the local dialects of England – soon to be forgotten – sparrows were *spadgers* in Gloucestershire, *hedge betties* in Cambridge, *dunnocks* in Cumberland; a *queer* fellow meant a Freemason in Barrow-in-Furness, a manager in Liverpool, a magistrate in old-fashioned thieves' cant. In the Gascon dialects of southwestern France a cock is *bigey* in the Gironde, *hazan* in the Landes, *pout* in Armagnac.

Pronunciation and grammar also tend to diverge. This is easy to show in the case of Indian English, whose typical pronunciation naturally shares some common features with the pronunciation of the major Indian languages: the typical Indian 'accent' is thus easily recognizable to speakers of British and American English. However, it also happens even if there is no external influence. In the modern world there are very few cases where we can be sure that language development has not been much influenced by neighbouring dialects or neighbouring languages. Here is one such example. The inhabitants of Tristan da Cunha lived almost wholly cut off from the rest of the world for almost 150 years, though with occasional departures and new arrivals. Outside influences were limited to these newcomers, along with schoolteachers and priests. Their isolation lasted until 1961, when they were briefly evacuated to England because the volcano became active. Their English speech, as recorded about that time, was a very distinct and fairly uniform dialect. Naturally it reminded linguists of the various British, United States and South African dialects that the original settlers had spoken; but Tristan speakers had already developed many special features of pronunciation and grammar, as exemplified by the word *wriss* 'wrist' with its plural *wrisses* 'wrists'. Tristan vocabulary had plenty of unique expressions. A *hardy* was a precipitous sea rock. The island's calendar included *berry time* when the *island berries* were picked, and *molly-egg time*, in late September and early October, when trips were made to Nightingale Island to collect the eggs of the *mollymawk*. Not surprisingly on an almost circular volcanic island with only one village, *east* meant 'clockwise' and *west* 'anti-clockwise': if you went *east* round the island, some of the time you would be facing 'west' in our terms. So, over that short period, the Tristan dialect had become unmistakably different from all other forms of English. It reflected the special ecology of Tristan and the way of life of its inhabitants: of course it did, since they had adapted it, gradually,[4] to suit the way they lived.[5]

We immediately notice such oddities in people's speech. We talk of the 'accent' or of the 'dialect' of those whose speech uses identifiably different sound patterns, different words or different grammatical rules – though still so close to our own speech that we can understand it easily. Until quite modern times, given that there was much less communication and much less population movement than there is today, such differences eventually became noticeable over very short distances. For that reason, very localized dialects still exist in many parts of the world. Within a 20-kilometre radius of where I write now, four local equivalents of the word *couteau* 'knife' are easily distinguishable, all of them quite different from the standard French form (but it is also said that young people no longer use the local dialects). Such differences do not take long to develop. Australian English and British English have become quite sharply distinct, both in pronunciation and vocabulary, in well under two hundred years.

We have seen that certain features of grammar are 'universal', common to all human languages. We have seen, too, that these linguistic universals are now widely believed to be built into the human brain. It may be claimed that the presence of these deep linguistic structures is the crucial difference – beyond mere size – that sets apart the brain of *Homo sapiens sapiens* from that of all other creatures. The general acceptance of this view is one of the major results of Noam Chomsky's work on language. It was prefigured in his 1957 monograph *Syntactic Structures*, in which an underlying structure and a

7

series of grammatical transformations were already exemplified: the 'deep structure' and 'surface structure' of languages were being explicitly distinguished. With continuing research it would become clear that deep structures were to be equated with linguistic universals. Chomsky later became aware that the so-called Grammar of Port-Royal (Lancelot and Arnauld 1660) was an early attempt to identify linguistic universals.[6]

Beyond the universals, then, children have to analyse the language spoken around them in order to learn it. Why is it so? If some language is built into the brain, why isn't it all built in?[7] Surely, if language were fully built into the brain, the massive computing power that young children currently use, over several years, in observing the language that is spoken around them, devising a sound pattern, constructing a vocabulary and grammar and thus gradually expanding their own linguistic skills, could be put to some other use. It could be used, surely, in exploring the world; and presumably the result of that would be swifter scientific advance, more rapid human development?

The answer is crucial to the subject of this book. The answer is that, however new and penetrating they may be, ideas are useful only to the original thinker – they are useless to humanity as a whole – unless they are communicated.

Now, as we have just seen, the part of language that is not universal is original to each of us in turn: that is how it comes to exist, and that is how it varies and changes.

With the part of language that is universal, the opposite is true. The universals are embedded in everyone's grammar. They are its basis and framework; they are taken for granted and do not change when each of us in turn, in early childhood, develops a personal grammar. They are there in the background of every language, unchanging, unchangeable. If language were totally inborn or 'hard-wired' – which would mean that it consisted entirely of universals – then we could not vary it, individually or as a group, any more than in speaking to one another now we can vary the universals that lie behind our grammar. Which is another way of saying that if language were totally inborn we would not have the ability to innovate in speech.

Let's set it out step by step. As things are, the inborn language universals provide only a basis, a framework, for human language. To complement them, we individually need, and have, the ability to build a grammar and dictionary on their framework. We do it on the evidence of the language we hear around us, a different sample or corpus for each of us; so each of builds a new, original grammar and dictionary (very much like those of our closest relatives and friends, but not quite like that of any one of them). The ability to do this is the ability to innovate: because the way it works is that, more or less consciously, we choose our words and our style of speech as we please, from among all the things we hear or read or half-remember or even invent (as we said above, children's playing with words is all part of the same language faculty). Because we innovate – because each of us produces and uses an original grammar and dictionary – language varies and changes. Humans beings, like other species, are lazy. We use this unique faculty, this ability to make and understand innovative language, to make our lives easier. Words for old-fashioned and dis-used things are gradually forgotten: I often saw my father light a *gas-mantle*, but I have not used the expression for many years, and it is probably not in my daughters' mental dictionary. It would take me a sentence or two to explain to them what a gas-mantle was. Handy, brief expressions come into use for activities once unknown but now commonplace: my father would have been able to understand the processes involved in getting a text from my computer's hard disk on to paper, but it would have taken some explaining. But I do it often, almost without thinking about it, and I use for this complex ritual the handy word *print*, a word which he certainly would not have used in this way. In the same way, words for completely novel concepts and technical breakthroughs are devised as soon as needed, explained with ease and absorbed with scarcely an effort by all who need them. This ability to innovate in language is crucial to every scientific advance, to our intellectual curiosity, to our originality as human individuals, because it is crucial to our ability to communicate new ideas and discoveries.

Well, we have this ability because it is one half of our human language faculty: the other half is made up of the language universals. Now if language were all inborn, universal, one ready-made pro-gramme, children would not have to spend all those years on language work and language play – and they would not need this powerful ability to devise a grammar and dictionary of their own, the ability to innovate in language. Evolution (to put it informally) is just as lazy as individual species are: if the ability were not needed in order to implement our language faculty, we would not have it at all.

But if we didn't have the ability to innovate in language, there would be no way to talk about something for which we had not inherited a word – no way, that is, until the mechanism of genetic change (which is what has produced the universal part of language in *Homo sapiens sapiens*) acted again to introduce new structures or words into the single human dictionary. There would be no way to shorten an expression that we found we needed to use many times a day. There would be no 'recycle bin' for words we might never want to use again.

The problems we would then encounter are well demonstrated by some of the artificial languages that people have invented for special purposes – because these, like the universal part of natural human language, are fixed by rule and unchangeable until the next edition of the rules comes out, a procedure whose slowness, when contrasted with the amazing rapidity of innovation in natural language, may reasonably be compared with the slowness of genetic change. The result is that these artificial languages appear almost reluctant to accommodate new ideas. Take botanical names, for example. You cannot add a botanical name to the accepted list, or alter a botanical name that does not agree with your current views, until you have published the change in botanical Latin in the prescribed form and so gained acceptance for it:[8] this can take years. Again, take programming languages. You cannot add an expression to a programming language until your new version of the language has been accepted by the industry leaders and is likely to have been installed on all computers that might encounter it: the frustrations are indescribable.

Animal communication systems demonstrate the same limitation. Some of them are quite varied – but none of them offers the potential for one individual to express, and for another to understand, an innovative idea.

All human language would be like this if it were totally inborn. As things are, in your own everyday language you can make innovations whenever you need to – because your everyday language is not totally inborn and fixed, but contains a large element that is variable and is built afresh by each of us. Each of us has the ability to innovate. That includes the ability to use a word or phrase or even a new grammatical form that no one has used before; or to use technical terms or foreign words that our audience will not have heard before.[9] The corollary of this is that each of us has the capacity to learn and accept into our vocabulary words and forms of expression that no one has used till now, or that we have never heard before.

And that is why, when discussing their new ideas with one another, even botanists and software people don't use their artificial languages: they use their own everyday language.

At this stage in the exploration of language it is worth taking a glance at the story of Babel, which gives the biblical explanation of human language variation. Here is the story:

Once upon a time all the world was of one language and of few words. As men journeyed in the East, they came upon a plain in the land of Shinar and settled there. They said to one another, 'Come, let us make bricks and bake them hard;' they used bricks for stone and bitumen for mortar. 'Come,' they said, 'let us build ourselves a city and a tower with its top in the heavens, and make a name for ourselves, or we shall be dispersed all over the earth.'

Then the Lord came down to see the city and tower which mortal men had built, and he said, 'Here they are, one people with a single language, and look what they have begun to do. After this, nothing they have a mind to do will be out of their reach. Come, let us go down there and confuse their speech, so that they will not understand what they say to one another.'

The Lord dispersed them from there all over the earth, and they left off building the city. That is why it is called Babel, because there the Lord confused the language of the whole world.[10]

At Babel, so the story tells us, we lost our universal language: free intercommunication among all humans, which we had taken for granted since the Garden of Eden, was no longer possible. At Babel we lost that universality of communication.

Well, we have found that we can get around the Babel problem. Many human beings, quite possibly the majority of all human beings, have been able to speak at least two languages; at Babel we became multilingual. After Babel, our languages have more words: the new diversity in human language meant that our languages were able to influence one another and to grow and change under this mutual influence. We gained the ability to innovate, the capacity to say the new and unexpected.

We failed to finish the Tower of Babel, but we have achieved some other things since then. Human language since Babel – human language as it really is, embodying not only the universals but also the elements that are continually re-analysed and continually renewed – is the most indispensable item of equipment in the continuing development of *Homo sapiens*.

How languages grow apart

In the days when many people lived all their lives in a single community, travelling little and seldom meeting outsiders – until very recently, in fact – any language, if it had once spread across several communities, steadily differentiated into distinct local dialects. We have already seen this process at work in the development of the English dialect of Tristan da Cunha. We have seen that Indian English came to have its own sound pattern and its own vocabulary.

If the process continued freely, the dialects eventually became so different that speakers of one could not understand speakers of another.

This point has almost been reached with some of the forms of speech that we group under the name of English: some Scottish dialects, the Geordie dialect of Newcastle upon Tyne, and some dialects of the southeastern United States, are really difficult for the average listener from southern England. Yet, with a few hours' conversation and good will on both sides, such difficulties disappear. Unlike these, the *patois* or country dialects of central and southern France are truly incomprehensible to the average Parisian. *Plattdeutsch* or 'Low German' of the country districts of northern Germany cannot be understood by most speakers of standard German. A 'language' is often defined as a group of mutually comprehensible dialects. Most linguists would therefore say that the traditional dialects of southern France and northern Germany are not French or German, but belong to different languages. The languages concerned are generally called Occitan or Provençal in the one case, Low German in the other.

The ultimate result of gradual dialect differentiation is well demonstrated by the fact that great numbers of very different languages, each with small numbers of speakers, tend to be found in mountainous districts where communications are difficult. In the Caucasus, at least five independent language families are represented, three of them unique to the region; dozens of sharply different languages are spoken, many of them by only a few hundred speakers.

We need to know a little more of the way this process of language differentiation works in practice. Let's explore it by way of a single example – an example that matters to all speakers of English.

Two thousand and several hundred years ago, a certain language was spoken in northern and central Germany and in southern Scandinavia. The population that spoke it had gradually expanded outwards. Individual communities remained in touch over this large area, though they were divided up among fairly small political units. This language, now called proto-Germanic, is unrecorded. Proto-Germanic was one of several related languages that are recognized as offshoots of a much earlier, also unrecorded, language known to us now as proto-Indo-European.

Two thousand years ago proto-Germanic was already splitting into dialects. A distinct dialect boundary was marked by the southern shore of the Baltic Sea. North of this were the North Germanic dialects: still represented in early medieval times by the single written language known to us as Old Norse, these have gradually separated into five modern languages, Swedish, Norwegian, Danish, Faroese and Icelandic. In spite of their very wide geographical range – they now extend into the Arctic Circle at the far northern point of Norway, as well as westwards to Iceland and Greenland – they have never differentiated very much from one another. Modern Icelandic is famous for having altered very little from the language of the medieval sagas, written down in the thirteenth century. Faroese seems, in some ways, even more conservative than Icelandic; actually both Icelandic and Faroese are written with consciously old-fashioned spelling rules, and the medieval language will have sounded rather different from these two modern ones. Speakers of modern Danish, Norwegian and Swedish can all understand one another without difficulty: in fact, by one of the usual definitions of language (as explained later in this chapter), these are not really three separate languages. They are always regarded as such, none the less, because each of the three has its own standard written form and its own literature.

There was a sixth North Germanic language, Norn. This was spoken in the island groups of Shetland and Orkney, both of which were colonized by Scandinavians at the same period at which they were settling in the Faroes and Iceland. Shetland and Orkney eventually passed under Scottish rule in 1472. Norn continued to be spoken for some centuries longer: it disappeared from everyday use only in the eighteenth century.

South of the Baltic shore was a second large section of dialects, classed by linguists as West Germanic. A central group of these occupied the low-lying north European plain, from northern Belgium eastwards, eventually extending as far as East Prussia (which is now southern Lithuania). These are the Low German dialects, but those at the western end of the range are regarded as making up a separate language, Dutch. South of the Low German dialects, Germanic speakers spread in later Roman times along the middle Rhine valley, southwards into Switzerland and eastwards into Bavaria and Austria. These migrants' speech is the origin of the High German dialects which form the basis of modern standard German. In early medieval times the seagoing people of the northwestern edge of the Low German dialect area, in the Frisian islands and along the neighbouring coast, developed a lingua franca,[11] whose local descendant today is Frisian, a minority language of the Netherlands and northern Germany. The 'Angles, Saxons and Jutes' who invaded Britain must have communicated with one another using this early Frisian of the seaways, because English, the modern form of their language, is more closely related to Frisian than to any other Germanic language.

There are offshoots of various West Germanic languages all over the world (including the many forms of world English). Some of these scattered languages are thriving, like Afrikaans, which originated as the language of Dutch settlers in South Africa. Some of them are unlikely to survive long, like Yiddish, a variant of German once spoken and written by millions of Jews living throughout eastern Europe. We shall see more of the present position and likely future of Yiddish.

To complete the survey: as a result of migrations at the end of the Roman Empire, Lombard and Frankish – two early West Germanic dialects – left their mark on the development of French and of Italian before disappearing. And East Germanic once existed as a third subdivision of proto-Germanic, originating somewhere on the Baltic shores, where the Goths, its speakers, are still commemorated in the name of the island of Gotland and the Swedish district of Götaland. With these adventurous migrants the Gothic and Burgundian languages were carried across the Roman Empire (but were soon forgotten there) and also to the Crimea, where Gothic was still spoken in the seventeenth century.

We needed this nutshell history of the Germanic languages to get a clearer idea of the variations that can occur as languages grow apart. Some linguists like to assume that language change happens randomly and at a regular rate of change per hundred years. It doesn't; there is no reason why it should,[12] and every reason why it shouldn't. Regular contact between communities will mean that their dialects will tend to remain similar. If politics and geography create a sharp dividing line between communities, the dialects on opposing sides of the line will tend to become gradually more different. If one community goes through a prolonged period of contact with a quite different language – if, for example, over a certain period, many speakers are bilingual in that other language – the community's dialect will reflect this and will differentiate quickly from the others in the group. And that is probably the commonest case.

So we can easily explain the close similarities among Danish, Norwegian and Swedish. There has been no strong external influence on any one of them. Short- and long-distance contacts, including sea travel, have held the three linguistic communities together. The national boundaries separating them have shifted and sometimes disappeared.

Why have Icelandic and Faroese remained so similar to the medieval form of North Germanic, while the three continental Scandinavian languages have changed rather more? Because of trade and cultural links, these three have collectively been influenced by other languages around them – notably Low and High German, French and English.

Faroese, meanwhile, was influenced by its close relative Danish, but by other languages very little. Icelandic is the language of a community that has been almost continuously isolated from all others.

Notice the circumstances in which languages spread. Iceland and the Faroes were uninhabited, except perhaps for a few monkish hermits, when speakers of old Norse first settled there. In Britain the speakers of West Germanic dialects were sufficiently numerous or influential to assert the use of their new language over an extensive, well-settled territory where British Latin and British Celtic had previously been spoken (more about this later). Lombard and Frankish, although they also were the languages of conquering peoples, disappeared from use within a few generations. Gothic, too, was spoken by conquerors and kings. It was once thought so important that a script was devised for it and the Bible was translated into it; but Gothic has disappeared too.

Of all the major Germanic languages in our survey, English can be seen to have changed most from the proto-Germanic type: although the links between English and Frisian are still obvious (a few examples below), modern Frisian now looks much more like the neighbouring languages of the north German plain than English does. There are two reasons for this. The first is that after the initial Anglo-Saxon migrations, England gradually drifted away from close contact with the other Germanic-speaking countries. The North Sea, naturally enough, became a linguistic boundary. Frisians, meanwhile, have been in continual contact ever since with neighbouring communities where Dutch and Low German were spoken. The second reason is that English was nearly always under foreign influence from quite different sources: at first from the Latin and Celtic speech of the previous inhabitants of England; later from the Norman French dialect and the French culture of the Norman kings and their followers. In fact, French influence on English has continued ever since. At the end of a thousand-year symbiosis, English contains so much French – so many words that still resemble their French equivalents, so many turns of phrase that have exact French parallels – that to English speakers nowadays French is a much easier foreign language than German.

The way that dialects and languages gradually differentiate has often been compared to family relationships. Family trees can be found depicting proto-Germanic as a grandparent, West, East and North Germanic as parents, the modern languages as children. The comparison is occasionally handy, but it is clearly imperfect. The most obvious point is that (except in extremely unusual cases) languages cannot be said to inherit material on an equal basis from two parent languages. More deeply, the comparison doesn't work because languages are not autonomous entities like human beings. We can't give a date when proto-Germanic 'died' or a date when English 'was born', as we might in a real family tree. The linguistic practice of speakers has gradually shifted, through the generations, so that whereas two thousand years ago some people were speaking in that way, now some people are speaking in this way.

An alternative comparison is also popular. Since Darwin developed the theory of evolution, linguistic relationships have often been likened to the relationships among biological species, genera, families and orders. Now it's true that some species may remain close to an ancestral form, while others may evolve rapidly, over the same period of time, and this phenomenon may be superficially compared with the development, say, of Icelandic and English from proto-Germanic. But we can now see that this comparison, too, is seriously misleading, because it only tells one side of the story. A glance at the history of English will show how unhelpful it really is. How can the multifarious origins of English words ever be fitted into a genetic model of language change?

How languages come together

By some counts, over half the English vocabulary may be traced to French, Latin and Greek, and a good deal less than half to proto-Germanic which, on the family model, is the parent language of English. English speakers through the centuries have included in their language huge numbers of words and phrases from distantly related languages that they happened to know.

English owes its origin to migrants who crossed the North Sea and settled in the Roman provinces of Britannia. The traditional date of the invasion is 449. By about 600 Anglo-Saxon kingdoms covered most of what is now England. So the formative influences on Old

English – whether or not their contributions can now be traced – are the various Germanic dialects that the migrants had spoken before their departure; the early Frisian that became their lingua franca; and the two languages that were already spoken in England when they arrived. These were British Celtic (a practically unrecorded language, but Welsh and Breton are the modern descendants of its western dialects), and British Latin, a regional variant of the Latin of the Roman Empire.

Frisian predominated. We are certain of this fact because Old English eventually resembled Old Frisian more than any other Germanic language. The Angles may possibly have been a sea-going people who already used a form of Frisian; the Jutes and Saxons did not, but would have understood it without difficulty. Among the many Germanic words still heard in modern English are *arm*, *eye*, *heart*, *daughter*, *cow*, *plum*, *eel* – a few examples among thousands. The basic number words are also Germanic in origin (in modern Frisian these are *ien*, *twa*, *trije*, *fjouwer*, *fiif*, *seis*, *saun*, *acht*, *njuggen*, *tsien*). Most of the place names of England are Germanic, because the 'Anglo-Saxons' or their successors devised the names: *Bristol* 'bridge town', *Oxford*, *Clifton*, *Aldborough* 'old fort'. These words and names can reasonably be taken as representing the inherited part of the English vocabulary.

Words that came from the Celtic of Britain include *dad* and *mam*, *ass* 'donkey', *bin*, *bogey*, *bullace*, *cradle*, *creel*, *cross*, *dun* 'brown', *hog*, *iron*, *peat*, *pick*, *prod*, *wan*.[13] *Street*, *port*, *wall*, *kale* 'cabbage', *fennel*, *box* 'kind of tree' and perhaps *cup* and *cockle* came from Latin.[14] Plenty of other Celtic words can be found in the western and northern dialects of English. Some of these, including *brat*, *cairn*, *crag*, *combe*, *glen*, have eventually become familiar to speakers of standard English. Others have remained regional words, like *bannock* 'cake', *Beltane* 'May day', *brock* 'badger', *caddow* 'jackdaw', *caird* 'tinker', *carr* 'rock', *coble* 'fishing boat', *crowd* 'violin', *pill* 'tidal creek', *tor* 'hill', *whinnock* 'milk-pail'. A number of originally Celtic and Latin words were once familiar in English but have now fallen out of use: examples are *bragget* 'honeyed ale', *bodkin* 'dagger, pin', *capul* 'horse' (from Latin *cavallus* by way of Celtic), *chester* 'walled town' (direct from Latin *castra* 'fort'), *cirisbeam* 'cherry tree' (a compound made up of Latin *cerasus* 'cherry' and Old English *beam* 'tree'), *cod-æppel* ('quince', made up of Latin *cotoneum* 'quince' and Old English *æppel* 'apple'). British Celtic, directly or by way of Latin, was the source of many familiar place-names, including names of rivers. Some originate as Celtic common nouns. One of these is the widespread river-name *Avon* (Middle Welsh *avon*, Modern Welsh *afon* 'river'): the word was adopted as a Latin river-name *Abona*. Another Celtic noun (compare Welsh *dwr* 'water') lies behind the name of the river *Dore*. Other modern river-names were already proper names in Celtic, such as *Calder*, which will have meant 'swift water'. The names of the earliest towns of southern Britain derive from the Latin versions of even older Celtic names: these names were adopted by the Romans at the time of their conquest, like *Londinium*, modern *London*. In the form in which they were learnt by the Anglo-Saxons, some of these names included the Latin label *castra* which was also the source of that now-forgotten word *chester*. *Wroxeter*, for example, comes from the originally Celtic town name *Viroconium* plus the label *castra*, all passed on in a wrapped parcel to the Anglo-Saxon invaders by Britons who evidently spoke some Latin as well as Celtic.

After the Anglo-Saxon settlements came the Viking invasion of eastern England. It is because of the Vikings that English has a strong element of Old Norse words. This was a Germanic language, like Old English, but its forms were already quite distinct. Some of the Norse loanwords still exist in modern English as 'doublets' (meaning that the same Germanic word already existed in Anglo-Saxon with a slightly different sense). We use both the Anglo-Saxon word *shirt* and the Norse word *skirt*; both the Anglo-Saxon *ship* and the Norse *skip* 'boat-shaped container'. Here are a few more of the numerous Norse loanwords in English: *window, husband, wrong, steak, knife, crave*. Northern and eastern dialects of English have even more Norse loan-words than standard English does: examples are Scottish *gain* 'direct', Yorkshire *lake* 'play' and *gate* 'street', Isle of Man *clet* 'rock' and *burrow* 'hill'.

Next came the single most powerful influence on English, that of French. The long-term linguistic effect of the Norman Conquest was the incorporation of hundreds, even thousands of French loanwords in Middle and Modern English. Many of these are semantic doublets of existing Germanic words, with essentially the same meaning but with a cultured or elevated nuance: *clean* from Germanic, *pure* from French; *song* from Germanic, *chant* from French; *bed* from Germanic, *couch* from French; and the familiar example, *sheep* from Germanic, *mutton* from French. They are so well established in English that we long ago stopped thinking of them as French words – but they make the break between English and the other Germanic languages, which will often have only one, native, word to cover the senses for which English has two. Many words of French origin in English suggest social development, specialization or polarization: examples are *engineer*, *surgeon, nurse, master, mistress, serf, slave, venison* (originally 'meat from the hunt'). Others denote southern fruits and vegetables like *chestnut, pear, peach*, fine foods and spices like *sugar, mustard*, and cultural novelties like *romance* ('fictional tale').

Latin, once the scientific language of Europe, has for many centuries been the source of new scientific and technical terms in English, some of them based ultimately on Greek or Arabic. English as spoken and written today is full of Latin words like *science, medicine, architecture*; Greek words like *technology, astronomy*; Arabic words like *alkali, azimuth*. In recent centuries English has drawn new words from languages of every part of the world: *chocolate* and *chilli* from Nahuatl (Aztec), *curare* from a Cariban language of northern South America, *albatross* from Portuguese (the original word was *alcatraz*), *curry* from Tamil or Kannada, *bandicoot* from Telugu, *juggernaut* from Oriya (the name of a Hindu god, *Jagannāth*, under whose wheels celebrants were sometimes crushed), *gecko* and *orang utan* from Malay, *kangaroo* from Guugu Yimidhirr, the Australian language encountered by Captain Cook, *taboo* from Tongan, *anorak* and *kayak* from Inuit (Eskimo), *springbok* from Afrikaans. Closer to home, English speakers have continued to learn from the other languages of the British Isles: *flannel* and *gull* came from Welsh, *trousers, clan, bard, ptarmigan* and *slogan* from Scottish Gaelic, *pillion, phoney* and *Tory* from Irish.

Genetic inheritance and biological evolution are nothing like this, and that is why they are so unsatisfactory as models of language change. Species are the product of genetic variation on the basis of a single earlier species, or occasionally of hybridization between two very closely related species. They cannot, consciously or unconsciously, take into their own genetic pool features of interest from another source.

With languages, this is what is always happening, and we can now see why. Whatever the reason for which people may come into prolonged contact with speakers of a different dialect or language, the contact will result in linguistic changes of this kind.

And people do. They have to travel, or simply to mix with speakers of other dialects and languages, in order to study, and to trade, and to find work. People move from region to region, or from country to country, as refugees, as emigrants, as businessmen, as administrators and indeed as conquerors.

Will they take their own language with them initially? Will they retain it later? The answers will depend entirely on circumstances. Imperialists, whether of the political or the economic kind, take their own language for granted: they do not at first give much thought to the effect on others of the way they speak. It is completely different with many millions of ordinary people, year by year, who for some reason find that they need to present themselves in a new environment. They may be schoolchildren, university students, examination candidates, job applicants, junior employees, new managers, salesmen, politicians, preachers. All these need to make a good impression on the people around them, and this means that they have to give a great deal of thought (consciously or unconsciously) to the way they speak. They have a message to get across, even if the message is as simple as 'Choose me!' or 'Do what I tell you!' Language is crucial to their success.

It isn't that they must immediately change their speech so that it is identical with that of the people around them. Only spies need to do that, and rather unusual linguistic abilities are demanded of spies. In most contexts it is expected that those who come from a different region will speak with a different accent. It is expected that those who are learning a language that is new to them will make mistakes and will need help. But, as quickly as possible, these outsiders need to limit the extent to which their accent or dialect or language, their choice of words, even their tone of voice, will distract others from taking them seriously.

Here is the converse of the language differentiation that we discussed above. In this second process of language change, both children and adults continually adjust their speech to their hearers' expectations. They do it in the interests of getting their message across – however crucial, however trivial the message may be.

21

In this way people pick up new words, new phrases, new tones of voice or a whole new language, from those around them. They imitate not only others who are speaking 'the same' language, but also those who are speaking a different dialect (perhaps a more prestigious one, the dialect of a capital city or a university), or indeed a completely different language (perhaps the language used in government or in the army or in business).

Languages in competition

So far we have talked of what individuals do when they find themselves in new linguistic surroundings. But the process can eventually make for drastic changes in the language of a whole community.

One obvious case is a large-scale political shift. We'll take three examples: case 1, the 'Anglo-Saxon' invasion and conquest of the lowlands of Britain, begun in 449; case 2, the Norman conquest of England in 1066; and case 3, the period of British rule in India which ended in 1947. In all three cases, the migrants retained their original language, in the sense that they did not abandon it in favour of the languages that were spoken around them (British Celtic and Latin in the first case, Old English in the second, Hindustani and the regional languages of India in the third). But soon it was no longer their original language.

The English used in India began immediately to differ in vocabulary from British English. Some words were introduced in the course of administrative business, to handle practices and problems that were unfamiliar in England: *competition-wallah* 'officer chosen by competitive examination', *Durbar* 'visiting court', *sepoy* 'Indian soldier in European uniform'. Some arrived by way of the household. Intermarriage was not the usual background to these borrowings, because in the highly stratified society of British India intermarriage was rather uncommon: the usual context was interaction with tradesmen, cooks and other servants. Such words are *pyjamas* 'informal trousers', *tiffin* 'lunch'. Some reflect other aspects of India, its life and its trade: *lakh* '100,000', *viss* 'weight of about 3 pounds', *godown* 'warehouse', *bund* 'embankment', *thug* 'member of robber caste', *munshi* 'language consultant'. Many of the words that were originally special to Indian

English have now spread more widely – sometimes taking on slightly different meanings: *pyjamas*, *curry* and *bungalow* are among words that have spread in this way.

The early Anglo-Saxon speakers, likewise, needed new terminology in their newly conquered territories, and we have already seen examples of the words they adopted. Some came from observing unfamiliar surroundings. These include *street*: paved roads, such as the Romans built in Britain, had been unknown in northern Germany.

The speakers of the Norman dialect of French who came to England in 1066 were not slow to introduce new words to their language. Anglo-Norman is the name of the new form of French (or new language) that resulted. Documents written in Anglo-Norman are full of English loanwords: *alderman*, *agys* 'haggis', *ande* 'hand (measure of 4 inches)', *ayle* 'ale'.

In all such cases, the initial context is of two or more languages spoken side by side. The immediate results are bilingualism and powerful mutual influences among the newly neighbouring languages. What are the long-term results?

During British rule in India many English speakers who worked there learnt Hindustani and other Indian languages, and many Indians learnt English. We know the political outcome: British rule ended at the independence of India and Pakistan in 1947. But we do not yet know the linguistic outcome: although that period in India's history came to an end fifty-five years ago it will be a long time yet before the relative status of English, Hindi, Urdu and the other languages of the subcontinent is stabilized. Premature attempts to settle this question have failed, resulting only in fierce controversy. What is certain is that all the languages of the region now contain numerous English loanwords and loan phrases.

In the case of the Anglo-Saxon invasion, we know both the political and the linguistic outcomes. The migrants became the new rulers; in parallel, their speech ousted spoken Latin and Celtic from the British lowlands. Before they adopted the new language, or migrated westwards or to Brittany (as some did), the original inhabitants and their children left their visible mark in the formation of Old English, though it seems far smaller in proportion than, say, the English element that is now to be found in Hindi.

In the case of the Norman invasion, too, we know the outcomes. The Norman conquerors in 1066 became the new rulers of England, initiating a period of intense cultural exchange between elites in England and France which lasted for two centuries. For all that time the Norman dialect of French and the French of Paris were administratively and culturally supreme in England, alongside Latin, the language of scholarship and the Church. But finally Anglo-Norman and even Law French have been forgotten.

These three cases are chosen from many others, some of which will be explored later in this book. In case 1 the original language of the country ceased to be spoken; in case 2 it survived, profoundly altered; in case 3 the outcome lies in the future. We suspect from cases 2 and 3 that bilingualism can continue for a long time, and from cases 1 and 2 that it will eventually end. In all three cases the linguistic situation is rather more complex than can be set out in a single paragraph, but it is by comparing these and other examples that we shall eventually find the way to predict linguistic futures with a greater measure of confidence.

Languages in the world

At the beginning of this book I gave an estimate of five thousand languages currently spoken. I was repeating the figure that I gave in 1998 in the *Dictionary of Languages*, and I must now justify it.

In his enumeration of the languages of the world – as complete as his Observatoire Linguistique can make it, more systematic and in many ways more complete than any other available source – David Dalby (in *The Linguasphere*, also published in 1998) arrives at the much higher figure of 13,720 for 'inner-languages', to use the Observatoire's terminology.[15] In this listing, to give one example, 27 inner-languages are counted within the entity usually defined as English; they are grouped into 3 outer-languages, corresponding to (1) Scots with Northumbrian English, (2) English of the rest of England, and (3) English of the rest of the world.

Here is the list, omitting historical forms of English and the numerous dialects and sub-dialects included in the *Linguasphere*.

Northumbro-Scots :
Scots
Northumbrian

Anglo-English :
Midlands-Anglo-English
Southern-Anglo-English

Global-English :

Standard-English
British-Colloquial
Cambrian-English
Hiberno-English
Canadian-Traditional
Northern-States-Traditional
Midland-States-Traditional
Southern-States-Traditional
Talkin-Black
Northamerican-General
Hispanic-American-English
Caribbean-English
South-Atlantic-English
Mediterranean+Middle-East-
    English
West-African-English
East-African+Indian-Ocean-
    English
Southern-African-English
Euro-South-African-English
Antipodean-English
Oceanian-English
South-Asian-English
East-Asian-English
Transnational-English

These 'inner-languages' would be regarded by many others who are engaged with language statistics as dialects and linguistic variants rather than languages, and the same applies to thousands of other inner-languages not just under the heading of English but throughout the *Linguasphere*. Apart from the 13,720 inner-languages of the world, as listed by the Observatoire, David Dalby also gives a figure of 6,000 million 'voices' in the world, corresponding of course to its estimated total population. There is much truth in this, for a reason that will now be clear: each person's language is unique. In fact you would have to give a higher figure still, because many – who knows how many? – of these people are bilingual or multilingual.

But there is some value, after all, in trying to get it clear how many forms of speech there are in the world that are mutually exclusive, or, as linguists often put it, mutually incomprehensible (meaning that a monolingual speaker of one such language will not be able to understand any of the others). This correlates with one of the usual definitions of a language – a group of dialects, or a collection of 'voices', that are mutually comprehensible (meaning that their speakers can understand one another). So how many languages, in this sense, are there? The Observatoire Linguistique has calculated that there are 4,910 'outer-languages', in its own terminology, and by that term it means 'largely interintelligible . . . idioms'.

It is true that many linguists give higher figures. Estimates of between 6,000 and 7,000 languages are commonly accepted, and the latest version of another authoritative language list arrives at the figure of 6,703. This is *Ethnologue*, a regularly published survey linked with the Summer Institute of Linguistics and the Wycliffe Bible Translators.

Why is it so difficult? There are three reasons. One is that dialects, because they differentiate from one another gradually and almost imperceptibly, eventually form mosaics – perhaps across a wide geographical area – in which all neighbouring dialects are mutually comprehensible, but speakers of the dialects at opposite corners of the mosaic cannot understand one another. This might well be true, for example, among English dialects if we take Scots at one corner and the dialects of the southeastern United States (Southern-States-Traditional, in the list quoted above) at another. So how many languages do we count for English – one, two or (as listed by the Observatoire Linguistique) three? There are many such cases, and the way we count in each case will have a very big effect on the final total. When you look closely at *Ethnologue*, to take that listing as an example, you find that many of the languages tabulated are in fact mutually intelligible variants of one another.[16]

A second reason why it is really difficult to give a definite figure is that there is more than one definition of a language. The word 'language' can mean a group of mutually intelligible dialects. It can also mean a standard form of speech and writing adopted by the speakers of several dialects – a standard form which often has some official status in a national context. This was why Swedish, Norwegian and Danish are regarded as three languages. They are to a high degree mutually intelligible – speakers of any one can understand the other two without much difficulty – but each is a standard literary language and each is an official language. In fact, in this sense, many would count Norwegian as two languages, since two forms of Norwegian have official status and are used in literature. Some African standard languages, such as Tsonga and Ronga, or Ewe and Fon, differ from one another far less than do the local dialects of a language like English: yet, since there seemed to be no overall literary or political unity, and colonial frontiers crossed the language map on no logical principle, the people (usually missionaries) who first devised the written forms of these languages had no basis on which to develop a single standard language covering several dialects. Indeed, some who attempted to do just that found their efforts wasted and the resulting artificial standard rejected. So, if 'language' is defined as a standard or national or official language, each of those groups counts as several languages, and that is in fact precisely how they are usually counted. With English, however, everyone who learns the language, all over the world, is taught to use a form of it closely resembling what is called 'Standard-English' in the table above (long ago Scots used to be officially taught, and used to have a significant literary output, but its status is very tenuous now). So, using this second definition of 'language', Standard English and just possibly Scots are the only two languages in the table above: the other items listed would count as dialects.

The third reason for the difficulty is that we have not yet finished finding out about the languages of the world. In Brazil and New Guinea, and even occasionally elsewhere, small communities still turn up, year after year, speaking languages that were until that moment unknown to the outside world.

These various problems of definition and calculation are, I think, sufficient explanation why I was happy to find my own rough estimate of 5,000 languages approximating so closely to the Observatoire Linguistique's calculation of 4,910 outer-languages. And that is why this conservative figure of about 5,000, the liberal figure of about 7,000, and even as generous a figure as 13,720, are all, in their way, true.

It is even more difficult to say how many families the languages of the world belong to. I will sketch the beginning of an answer here – but I will not take it so far as to give a precise figure. You'll see why.

A language family, in the terms used in this book, is a grouping of languages that have been shown to be related to one another. All members of a language family are known to originate from one earlier language. Therefore the count of language families depends on the state of historical linguists' knowledge. If a researcher shows that two language families, previously without any identified wider links, are related to one another, then the count of language families goes down by one. In these terms, a 'language isolate' (a language which has not been shown to be related to any other) counts as a language family; again, if it is shown to relate to an established family or another isolate, the total count goes down by one.

That's fine. But there are seven language families represented in Europe (Indo-European, Uralic, Altaic, North Caucasian, North West Caucasian, South Caucasian and Basque) and well over a hundred in South America. Let's look at the nature of this contrast. It's partly because the languages of South America are really extremely varied; but it's partly because the languages of South America have been much less intensively studied, and some of them are still very poorly recorded or not recorded at all: thus not enough possible lines of research on their interrelationships have yet opened up or been explored.

Now a few researchers have tried to link Basque with one of the Caucasian language families (admittedly at such an amateurish level that it is hardly necessary for them to specify, or for others to ask, *which* Caucasian family they have in mind). If this case were proved, or if it were proved (as some others claim with better evidence) that North Caucasian and North West Caucasian are related, then the total count of language families would go down by one. Meanwhile one of the doyens of language relationship studies, Joseph Greenberg, has claimed that all the indigenous languages of South America are related, along with most of those of North America. He has not proved it – it would take a great deal more work to prove it – but, given what we think we know about human history in South America, it must be accepted as possible and it might eventually be proved. If it were true, the number of language families in South America would drop from 117 to 2 (Indo-European and Greenberg's Amerind): and the total count for the whole world would fall by 116.

South America is not the only region where such huge uncertainties exist. The languages of central America are almost equally varied. 'Splitters' allocate them to about fifteen families, while 'lumpers' such as Greenberg bring them all together in two, the same two as for South America. North America (the United States and Canada) may have sixty-two language families[17] or it may have four: two of these four would be the same as those of Central and South America, and another one has been linked by enthusiastic lumpers with Sino-Tibetan or alternatively with Caucasian again. This one is the Na-Dené family, whose membership is itself controversial. The great island of New Guinea is a linguist's paradise, a place of many language families that few have yet tried to lump, but New Guinea is spanned by what the *International Encyclopedia of Linguistics* often calls 'the controversial Trans-New-Guinea Phylum', which is either one big language family or a bundle of almost numberless unrelated smaller groups and isolates.

Enough, I think, to demonstrate that no one should yet try to count the language families of the world.

Language spread and language decline

Next we must look at the number of speakers of each individual language. This, too, is a difficult figure to give. Often national censuses provide a precise total – but what are they measuring? What question was asked? How did the respondents, or the census-taker, understand the question? Does the census record all the languages that each person speaks, or only one – and who is to choose whether that will be the 'mother tongue', the first language of childhood, or the language currently used most, or the one that the government prefers? If there are questions as to whether dialects should be counted as separate languages or not, how will the census resolve these questions? The only answer is that all censuses are different, and all are intended to provide information towards government planning, which is not at all the primary aim of most linguists.

In some countries there is a cachet in claiming to adhere to a minority language which is actually on the way to being lost. In Ireland the Irish language is a national symbol, as we shall see. A million people say they know it, but only a few thousand use it every day, and hardly any children learn it as their mother tongue. In highly nationalistic countries it may be unwise to claim to speak a minority language.

Therefore census figures for languages like Greek and Turkish are unrealistically high. Some governments are so fearful of minority cultures that they outlaw languages or pretend that they do not exist. Many small minorities in many countries are not reported in censuses because their language has never been noticed by those who designed the census. Such languages may have no official name, or no listing on the census form. Some people have never been reached by any census. Some censuses, such as the Belgian and French ones, usually keep off the linguistic questions. Hence it is impossible to know the number of speakers of Breton and Occitan (for example).

Therefore all such figures are to be taken with a pinch of salt. Some quite large minorities in Asian and European countries would not exist at all if censuses were to be believed. In all such cases, and wherever census information is inadequate, the linguist can only rely on personal observation or on extrapolation from sample surveys. This may result in estimates that are wildly high or low. Given all these reasons for uncertainty, it is not surprising that published figures of the number of speakers of any particular language can vary by thousands or millions.

It matters crucially with the smaller languages.

With these we don't just want to know how many people are speaking them, or can speak them; we want to know what is the age pattern. As we look at North American and Australian languages we shall see, over and over again, the depressing refrain that these languages are 'not being taught to children'. We know this because enough linguists are now exploring the tattered remains of these language communities to give us a good idea of their demographic state. Elsewhere in the world it is not so, and we rely on anecdotal evidence – which is now also singing the same refrain. A language of tens of thousands or hundreds of thousands of speakers (such as Scottish Gaelic or Romansch) will just as surely disappear from use as one with two hundred speakers if it is not being taught to children.

With the smaller languages we also want to know how intensively they are used – whether speakers use them all the time or only in limited contexts; whether within their own communities there are migrants with whom they have to speak the national language, or some families who still consider themselves to belong to the ethnic group but don't speak the language any more. This may matter, to the prospects for the survival of a language, much more than how small the community is.

Far easier than to say how few people are speaking any particular minority language is to say how many millions are now using the mass languages of the world. Here we are sketching a situation that is quite new in world history, one that will have devastating implications for human linguistic and cultural diversity.

These are the great mother tongues of the year 2002. Of the people of today's world, 800 million learnt to speak the Chinese of Beijing (Mandarin or Putonghua) at home; 350 million learnt English; 350 million learnt Hindi or Urdu; 315 million learnt Spanish; 170 million learnt Bengali; 165 million learnt Russian; 165 million learnt Arabic; 160 million learnt Portuguese; 125 million learnt Japanese; 90 million learnt German; 75 million learnt French. In total, nearly half the people in the world learnt one of only eleven languages as their mother tongue.

Here are the great languages of mass communication of 2002. A thousand million people use Chinese – most of them in one country, China; 550 million people use Hindi or Urdu – most of them in two countries, India and Pakistan; 200 million use Malay (Indonesian and Malaysian) – in four countries; 180 million use Portuguese – in five countries. But the real international languages are the ones that follow: 130 million use French; 180 million use Arabic; 290 million use Russian; 450 million people use Spanish. And the number using English is growing so fast that statistics vary wildly, but it has been estimated that nearly 700 million speak it fluently and 1,800 million can handle it competently.[18]

In the last two paragraphs twelve languages are named. What's in a name? If you understand Serbian, you also understand Croatian and Bosnian. If you understand Hindi, you also understand Urdu. If you understand Indonesian, you also understand the Malaysian of Malaysia and the Malay of Singapore. These forms of speech are separated by law, national pride, culture, religion or script, but to linguists and to listeners they are 'the same' language. Just twelve languages used by about two-thirds of the people in the world.

It has never happened like this before. To any who look on languages as a medium for superficial communication, this strange new world should appear very promising. So many people can understand one another without even needing a translation. If they can understand one another, isn't that the first step towards universal friendship?

Sadly, easy assumptions on this topic are not borne out by the events of modern history.[19] The fact that in the twentieth century a greater proportion of the people in the world could communicate with one another, using English or just a few other languages, appears not to have stopped any wars, nor to have reduced the frequency with which wars have broken out, nor to have made the wars that have broken out less brutal. In fact, several murderous wars have been fought recently among people who speak 'the same language' in real terms: that applies to the civil war in Rwanda, to the Iraqi invasion of Kuwait, to the war in Bosnia and to the endless stand-off between North and South Korea.[20] On the basis of this information, it would be possible to argue that if everybody spoke English (or Chinese or Esperanto for that matter) everybody would be at war even more often.

So much for the present. What of the number of languages there will be in the world in the future? To learn this we need the perspective of the past: we need to ask whether the number of languages in the world is definitely in decline, and, if so, how rapid a decline this may be.

It is, admittedly, impossible with our present knowledge to write anything resembling a full linguistic history of the world. We do know part of the history of the languages spoken in Europe and much of southern and eastern Asia over the last two or three thousand years. In these areas written records exist in plentiful supply – but those records do not cover all the languages that have been spoken, or even necessarily mention them all. So even here there are surprising and very large gaps and uncertainties. Look first at the British Isles. What languages were spoken in Britain and Ireland before Celtic speakers arrived there? We cannot name them or relate them to any other known language. When did Pictish and Cumbrian cease to be spoken in Scotland and northwestern England? We do not know. Look at southeastern Europe. Was Ancient Macedonian (the native language of Alexander's kingdom) a dialect of Greek or an entirely different language? Where exactly were the speakers of Romanian during the thousand years that followed the collapse of the western Roman

Empire? To neither of these questions, politically charged as they now are, can linguists give a certain answer. And what were the relationships of Etruscan (spoken in Tuscany before the spread of Latin) or of Linear A (spoken in Minoan Crete before Greek)? If we could understand these languages and answer the question, we would know much more than we do about the prehistory of the Mediterranean. Can Basque (of the western Pyrenees) or Sumerian (the ancient language of southern Iraq) be related to either of these or to any other known language? There might be a relationship, but in the present state of our knowledge it cannot be demonstrated.

On the other hand, history does allow us to interpret the language map of Europe and southern Asia with greater confidence than we can usually muster in other parts of the world. For example, we can effectively deconstruct the language map of the Balkans, relating the current apparently random patchwork to a series of successive movements of peoples and cultures. Albanian and Greek, now very different from one another, are the two remaining representatives of the Indo-European languages that have been spoken in the region since before historical records began. Romanian and Aromunian (Vlach), as descendants of Latin, are a record of the incorporation of the Balkans in the Roman Empire and of the spread of Latin there in the first four centuries AD. Slavonic languages were not spoken at all in this region until they were introduced in a series of invasions and migrations from the northeast, beginning around the fifth century: the modern languages resulting from these events are Bulgarian, Macedonian, Serbo-Croat (or Serbian, Croatian and Bosnian, as people say now) and Slovene. Finally, Hungarian was introduced to parts of Transylvania and the Hungarian plain in the ninth and tenth centuries by a conquering people who had made a truly epic migration from somewhere near the valley of the Ob, in western Siberia, where two languages related to Hungarian are still spoken by small minority groups.

For a good deal of the rest of the world, including Australia, New Guinea and large parts of the Americas, we can write no linguistic history at all except by using internal evidence – the interrelationships and borrowings between languages. One thing we can say with confidence is that the history of languages in those three regions must have been complex in the extreme to explain the patchwork of language relationships that now exists on the modern language map. Although people, when migrating, sometimes adopt new languages, it is still true that complex patterns of languages must also reflect complex movements of peoples.

If you study them on maps of a uniform scale the world's languages show a distribution that is anything but uniform. In some areas will be found very large numbers of languages, strongly differentiated from one another, each with relatively small numbers of speakers. Elsewhere a single language may spread over an extensive area; or a group of related languages, each one differing slightly from its neighbours, may cover a whole region. The effect is not random, but it has more than one cause.

Language distribution depends partly on the way human beings exploit their environment. If they are mobile – naturally – they spread across the map. So, in Siberia, in the Central Asian steppes, in the Western Desert of Australia, in the Sahara and the Kalahari, languages are to be found that have a fairly small number of speakers but vast geographical distribution: they are spoken by people with a nomadic lifestyle who range widely across those relatively inhospitable environments.

It also depends on historical movements, principally migrations, sometimes conquests. Languages of the Bantu or Sintu group, all clearly related to one another, are spread in a patchwork across the whole of central and southern Africa, because (linguists and archaeologists suppose) of a series of expansionary migrations that began, probably in the grasslands of northwestern Cameroon and northeastern Nigeria, well over two thousand years ago. In an even more complicated pattern, Indo-European languages spread (from what original 'homeland' is controversial) across southwestern Asia and most of Europe, beginning several thousand years ago. In just the same way English and Spanish have spread across large parts of the Americas, in the last few hundred years, because of conquest and migration.

Thirdly, language distribution depends on the frequency of travel and communication, and the need for such communication, among essentially sedentary communities. Chinese has more speakers than any other language because for many hundreds of years it has been the administrative and cultural language of a highly organized and centralized state. Over most of this period, many Chinese in all parts of the country have needed to communicate with the capital, to travel to it and back again, to speak its language, to study and to pass examinations in this language. Although in earlier Chinese history communication was less intense – which is the historical reason why there are other Chinese languages, such as Cantonese and Hokkien, in the south of the country – centralizing forces have in the last millennium been consistently more powerful than centrifugal forces.

China came in here as the first example, but in fact all the extensive, stable empires that you can remember have left a linguistic legacy. Aramaic, administrative language of the Persian Empire (559–330 BC), remained a lingua franca in the Middle East for centuries afterwards and survives tenaciously even now among minorities in Syria and Iraq. Quechua, administrative language of the Inca Empire (fourteenth century to AD 1535), is still spoken by millions from southern Colombia to western Bolivia. Latin, having been spread around the western Mediterranean at the time of the Roman Empire, still thrives in the form of Portuguese, Spanish, Catalan, French, Italian, Romanian and several minority languages of southern Europe. Arabic was simply one of the languages of Arabia (and Arabia was never a very populous country) until, after Muhammad, it became the language of Islam and the lingua franca of the conquering Muslim armies. Even the short-lived Mongolian domination of Asia has left a legacy on the linguistic map of the world in the form of the modern Mongolian languages, which stretch from the north shore of the Caspian almost to Beijing.

So, if the typical lifestyle is sedentary, with a fixed home; if there is no current large-scale migration; if there is no especially intensive communication among geographically separated communities, then whatever the existing relationship among neighbouring languages, they will tend, slowly but surely, to grow further apart. That's linguistic change. And it means, as dialects gradually differentiate into languages, that the number of languages in the world will gradually increase. Which is the single overriding reason for the large number of languages that existed in the world until, say, a hundred years ago.

Take the first two of these three independent constraints on the geographical extent of languages, and thus on the number of languages that will be found in a specified geographical area, or in the whole world: the use of the natural environment, and the fact of migration and conquest. We can sometimes estimate the force of one or other of these constraints at certain times and places in the past. But we cannot calculate the effect they have both had, world-wide, over an extended period.

Now we may imagine (as the writer of Genesis did) a certain far-off period in the past when the few existing members of the human species formed, as yet, only one community and spoke, as yet, only one language. Whether such a situation really existed depends on how we suppose the language faculty to have developed among the immediate ancestors of *Homo sapiens sapiens*. In any case, because evolution is lazy, it is incredible that the language capability should have arisen and should be inherited uselessly; so it must have been used, by whichever first communities possessed it, and ever since without inter-ruption. So their language or languages are certainly ancestral to all of ours. If there was ever one single language that may claim that position, we don't know how long ago it was spoken. It was surely at least as long ago as the lifetime of 'Eve', the woman whose DNA is claimed to be ancestral to every present human inhabitant of the earth. The date of 'Eve' has been estimated as 140,000 years BP ('before the present', as palaeontologists like to express it).[21] A time when there was only one language could hardly be more recent than that; but it might be even longer ago. There might at that moment have already been many other human females whose lineages, by chance, have since died out; there might already have been many communities or groups of humans, and many languages, and Eve herself and the man or men privileged to impregnate her might have been multilingual, like so many of her descendants.

Over the intervening 140,000 years we do not know, at any single moment in time, how many languages there were; nor do we know the relative effect exerted on the simple differentiation and multiplication of languages at any particular time either by the current prevalence of migration, or by the ways in which human communities used their environment – whether they ranged over extensive territories or exploited small areas intensively. At any single time, therefore, we do not know the base figure for numbers of languages, and we do not know whether it was tending to increase or decrease.

Now take the last of those three constraints, that of the frequency of and need for communication among communities. This seems to be linked with the presence of one of two preconditions. The most obvious one is the development and persistence of large political units – large states and empires. These, if they are going to last for any length of time, depend on communication, but they also depend on various technological capabilities that humans have developed relatively recently. An empire doesn't have to have a tick in every box – most people would list writing and wheeled vehicles among the prerequisites of empire, yet the Incas managed perfectly well without them – but large empires without *any* of the technological skills that the last ten thousand years have given us can scarcely be imagined. The alternative precondition is the presence of frequent links of exchange or trade. This is essentially why certain languages have been spreading so rapidly in central Africa in the past century. Swahili, from its base in Zanzibar and Pemba and the facing mainland coast, has not only become a national language in Tanzania, Kenya and Uganda but is also widely spoken in the whole eastern swathe of Congo (Kinshasa) and in northern Mozambique and Madagascar, thus effortlessly crossing the colonial boundaries between German, British, Portuguese, French and Belgian territories – boundaries which have been continued in the frontiers between modern national states. Sango in the Central African Republic, Kongo and Lingala in western Congo (Kinshasa), and others, have likewise spread in trade with only secondary help from colonial and national governments. But regular long-distance exchange requires some social development – the traders have to specialize, and so do their suppliers – and we cannot find evidence of that kind of social development beyond a few thousand years ago.

So although we counted three constraints on the differentiation of languages, we may judge that this third constraint did not operate in the distant past. Those technological skills did not exist; specialization did not exist; therefore large centralized states and long-distance trade did not exist. We may guess – and we shall gather some evidence to support the guess – that one of the two preconditions, the emergence of large states, is what tipped the balance. From the time when large

37

states began to be a widespread feature of human society, the total number of languages in the world has definitely tended to fall.

We need only glance forward to one familiar example to see the potential scale of the process. By the time the Roman Empire was in decline (see Chapter 2), Latin and Greek, its two ruling languages, had supplanted six of the seven other languages formerly spoken in Spain, all of the sixteen or more additional languages formerly spoken in Italy, all of the fourteen languages formerly spoken in Anatolia, all but one of seven or more languages formerly spoken in the Balkans, and more too.

Here is a hypothesis, then, to be refined or replaced after further investigation: large centralized political units (both the old-fashioned empire and the all-modern nation state) cause the total number of languages in their territory to decline. In so far as the world goes on being apportioned among such units, the total number of languages in the world will go on falling.

'However, things may change,' writes R. M. W. Dixon, on reaching a similar stage in his discussion of the declining number of languages in the world.[22] But he gives no reason to suppose that they will. I see none either. There is no sign that large political units are about to disappear.

2

LANGUAGE AND CHANGE

The Roman Empire: Latin conquers Europe

So what is it about empires and nation states that makes their inhabitants turn to a new language? Since, in modern times, global communications and intrusive governments also have a hand in language shift and possibly confuse the issue, the best way to answer this question will be to look at a period in history when global communications and intrusive governments scarcely yet existed. That is why most of this chapter is a case study of the Roman Empire and its languages. As we shall see, this was a critical episode for the languages of Europe and the Mediterranean. A great number of local languages ceased to be spoken and disappeared for ever, supplanted by Greek and Latin. This happened in the absence of printed books, journalism, television, the Internet, official educational policies and much of the government-inspired paperwork – all those influences that conspire to force modern minority peoples to use national and international languages.

Around 100 BC the lands that surround the Mediterranean were crowded with peoples speaking numerous languages of several different families. Southern Europe and southwestern Asia formed a language patchwork quite as colourful as that of west Africa or Mexico today. Within six hundred years, around AD 500, the Mediterranean language patchwork was disappearing almost totally, leaving Latin and Greek as almost the only languages still in use as mother tongues in the region.

In this chapter we shall explore why it happened, how it happened, what effect it had on the later language history of Europe, and what the implications are for our own linguistic future. Based on the picture

PICTISH

E. IRISH

BRITISH

WEST GERMANIC

G A U L I S H

NORIC

DALMATIAN-PANNONIAN

ILLY

BRESCIAN
LEPONTIC

RAETIC

VENETIC

A. GALICIAN

A. ASTURIAN

VASCONIAN
(E. BASQUE)

I B E R I A N

LIGURIAN

ETRUSCAN

ITALIC DIALECTS

NORTH
PICENE

MESSAPI

CELTIBERIAN

NORTH
LUSITANIAN

SOUTH
LUSITANIAN

TARTESSIAN

A.
SARDINIAN

LATIN

OSCAN

ELYMAIC

SICAN

SICEL

P U N I C

M A S S Y L I A N - N U M I D I A

LOCAL LANGUAGES OF THE ROMAN WORLD

·········· Extent of Roman rule c.106–115

A. = Ancient (language with the same name as modern one, but not related to it)

E. = Early (early form of language still spoken)

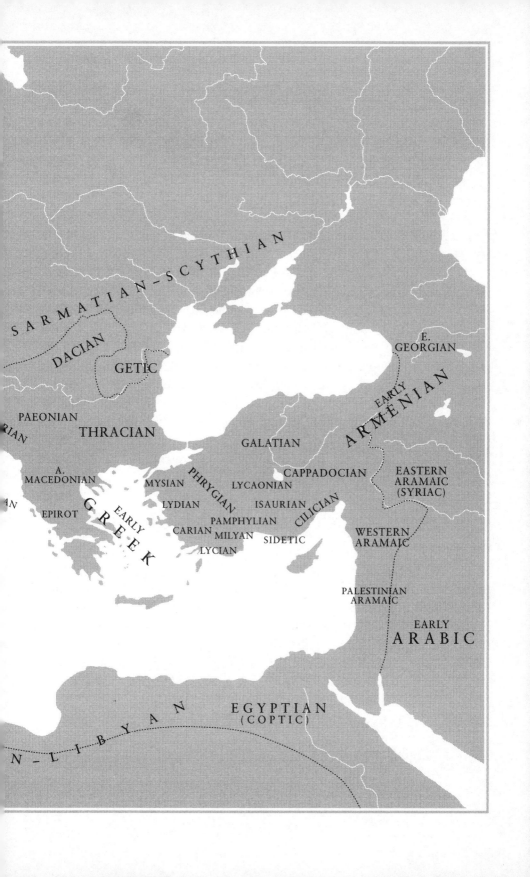

of language shift that we are to reconstruct here, we cannot help making modern comparisons. Here we stand, just five hundred years after the way was opened for European colonialism to spread across the world thanks to the discoveries of Christopher Columbus (in 1492) and Vasco da Gama (in 1498). In the year 2100, will the whole modern world be as uniform linguistically as the Mediterranean lands were in AD 300?

No two scholars agree on the precise number of languages that were spoken where Latin and Greek were destined to spread. It's partly the problem we have already encountered – when do two dialects become two different languages? – and that problem becomes all the more acute when the dialects are no longer spoken. There is no one around to answer the crucial question of whether they are mutually intelligible. In addition, many of these languages were not usually written, so there are no full records of them – perhaps only a few tombstones, or a few words quoted by Latin or Greek authors. Such quotations would surely tend to be inaccurate, because most people cannot reproduce accurately the words or sounds of a language that is unfamiliar to them. Finally, some of the languages were never written at all. In these cases, all we have to go on are place-names and personal names which *might* belong to the language in question or might have quite different origins, impossible to pin down.

Still, here goes. Our quick linguistic tour of the ancient Mediterranean begins with the Spanish peninsula. At least ten languages were spoken there. Greek and Punic (the language of Carthage) were spoken in scattered towns and cities on the southern and eastern coast. Iberian, the best-known language of the hinterland ('best-known' is to be taken relatively: there are inscriptions, but they have not yet been fully deciphered), was spoken over a wide area of the south and east: it also extended along the Mediterranean coast into southern France, perhaps as far as the Rhône valley. Surrounding Iberian were the speakers of Tartessian (around modern Cadiz and Córdoba), Vasconian (which survives as Basque) and five other languages. Most of the ten languages of ancient Spain were completely unrelated to one another.[1]

In southwestern France there were Aquitani – again apparently speakers of early Basque – extending as far north as Bordeaux and the Gironde. To their east and north were Gaulish-speaking peoples in the Massif Central and the Rhône valley and northwards throughout the remainder of France; the language of most of Britain was closely related to Gaulish. It is usually called British Celtic, and is the direct ancestor of modern Welsh and Breton. Related Celtic languages had spread into northern Spain, northern Italy and along the Danube valley. But, to return to southern France, Greek was spoken in Marseille and several smaller coastal towns. Ligurian was spoken across Provence and further east into the region of Italy that is called Liguria today.

North of this, in the Po valley and extending eastwards as far as modern Slovenia, was a series of five little-known languages apparently unrelated to one another. One of them, Raetic, was recognized in ancient times to be a northern offshoot of Etruscan, the language then spoken in modern Tuscany. Etruscan is known from many brief inscriptions. It seems to be unrelated to all other known languages (as the ancient Greek historian, Dionysius of Halicarnassus, already asserted two thousand years ago) and has not been deciphered. Latin was the language of the lower Tiber valley and Latium (modern Lazio); its most important dialect was that of the city of Rome. Latin speech was already spreading across Italy, as Rome's influence grew and as cities were founded or re-founded under Roman dominance. With two obscure exceptions, the other languages of peninsular Italy were distantly related to Latin. These 'Italic' languages made up a dialect chain from Umbrian in the north to Oscan in the south.

Ten languages can be counted in the Danube valley and the Balkans; one of them was the ancestor of modern Albanian. South of these again, the Greek peninsula, the Aegean islands and the western rim of Asia Minor (modern Turkey) together formed the homeland of Greek, which, as we have already seen, had also become the language of many ports and harbours around the Mediterranean. In the remainder of Asia Minor there were as many as fourteen languages, six of them related to the long-extinct Hittite, which, written in cuneiform on clay tablets, had recorded – a thousand years earlier – the history and mythology of a now-forgotten empire.

In Syria and Palestine we can easily distinguish four current lan-guages, with dialect subdivisions that there is no need to list here. All belonged to the Semitic group and were closely related to one another: Phoenician along the coast (called 'Syrian' by most ancient writers), traditional western Aramaic (including the speech of Palmyra), eastern Aramaic (notably the dialect of Edessa, Syriac, destined to form a new literary language in Roman times) and the colloquial Aramaic of Palestine and Syria (which had replaced Hebrew as an everyday language, and is itself usually called 'Hebrew' in ancient sources). Arabic, another Semitic language, was spoken in Nabataea (in northwestern Arabia). Ancient Egyptian, the language of Egypt, was distantly related to these; in Roman times Egyptian, now strongly influenced by Greek, began to be written in an alphabet of Greek style: in this form it is known to us as Coptic. Throughout Asia Minor, Syria and Egypt Greek was widely spoken: after the conquests of Alexander the Great it was the language of government, the armies and the cultural elite.

Several hundred years earlier Phoenician speakers had founded their great western colony, Carthage (near modern Tunis). The language of Carthage, its hinterland and its coastal colonies, at first scarcely distinct from Phoenician but gradually becoming more individual, is called Punic. The inland peoples of north Africa retained their own language. There was apparently only one, extending (no doubt with dialect variation) from the Atlantic to the oases of the Western Desert of Egypt. Known variously as Libyan, Numidian and Massylian, it was ancestral to modern Berber and thus distantly related to Egyptian and the Semitic languages. It was eventually written, in an alphabet that survives in modern use in the arid mountains of the central Sahara: the name of this script (*Tifinagh* 'the Punic') correctly suggests that it was developed out of Punic letter forms.

Back to Greek and Latin. Greek, an Indo-European language, is first recorded when it was written in 'Linear B' script on clay tablets in the accounts offices of the Mycenaean palaces of southern Greece, about 1300 BC. The real beginning of recorded Greek history – for this was indeed the earliest European language to be used for written poetry and history – comes around 600 BC, at which time Greek was spoken across southern and central Greece, on the Aegean islands, along the facing coast of Anatolia and already in many colonies across the Mediterranean, as far away as Massalia (Marseille), Cyrene on the Libyan coast, Byzantium (Istanbul) and at many points around the Black Sea. With the conquests of Alexander the Great (died 323 BC) Greek expanded eastwards as well. Alexander's own ancestral kingdom of Macedon had adopted Greek at court: the ruling family regarded itself as Greek. Alexander's conquests imposed Greek-speaking nobility and elites on almost the whole territory of the former Persian Empire.

The area under Greek-speaking rulers gradually shrank in the following three centuries. For all that, when Roman rule spread eastwards in the second and first centuries BC, Greek was the language of government and culture almost everywhere that it touched. In the western Mediterranean, too, Greek was seen as the language of rich culture and of a myriad pleasures. The Roman Senate might disapprove, expel Greeks from Rome and outlaw Greek practices; the rulers of Carthage no doubt did the same. It made no difference.

Thus the eastern half of the expanded Roman Empire never had to change its everyday language. Romans respected Greek, even admired it. Latin was more practical, but Greek was more versatile. It stayed. Although high provincial officials were Roman citizens, and communicated with Rome in Latin, local administration was carried out largely in Greek. It was only when St Paul addressed a Roman army officer unexpectedly in Greek that the officer was prepared to believe his prisoner was a respectable citizen.

When about to be taken to the barracks Paul said to the tribune:

'Might I say something to you?'

'You know Greek?' said the other. 'I thought you were the Egyptian who started a revolt some while ago, the leader of those four thousand bandits in the desert?'

'I am a Jewish person of Tarsus of Cilicia,' said Paul, 'a citizen of no mean city. I ask you to let me speak to the people.'

He agreed, and Paul stood on the steps and held up his hand to the people. When it was quiet enough he addressed them thus in Aramaic:

'Brothers, fathers, listen while I defend myself to you.'

Hearing him speak to them in Aramaic they became quieter. He said:

'I am a Jewish man, born in Tarsus of Cilicia and brought up in that city at the feet of Gamaliel, strictly educated in the ancestral law, a zealous servant of God, as you are all today . . .'[2]

And meanwhile what had once been the local language of a growing town on the banks of the lower Tiber became a vehicle of Empire –

for, whatever the cultural influence of Greek, Latin was to be the language of the Roman Imperial court and the institutions of government. It would be the language of army command and surely the lingua franca of most army units, across the whole of that vast Empire. Rome's rise to power, already under way in the fifth century BC, had led the city in the second and first centuries BC to control of the whole Mediterranean basin. The next four hundred years constitute the only period in history during which all the coasts of the Mediterranean were subject to a single political power. Travel, trade and migration were relatively free across this whole vast region.

Latin spread with Roman power. Rome was (as one of its enemies described it) a 'many-headed' state, one in which individuals of varied origins were in practice able to attain wealth and to reach positions of power. But the political institutions of Rome used Latin; citizenship was best exercised in Latin; the army, a very large employer, used Latin. To attempt to prosper under Roman rule, Latin must have been almost a prerequisite.

I count sixty languages around 100 BC. You could make it fifty-eight or sixty-two, but sixty is a good round number. Five hundred years later, in AD 400, the whole region that we have just surveyed had been subject to the Roman Empire for about half a millennium. How many languages had survived?

The answer comes as something of a shock. Ten languages were in vigorous use and and were destined to continue to flourish in the long term: Latin (which would live on in the form of Italian, Spanish, French and the other Romance languages), Greek, Coptic, Syriac, Arabic, Aramaic (which survives as a minority language in modern Syria), Libyan (surviving in the modern Berber languages), British (which would live on in the form of Welsh, Cornish and Breton), early Basque and whichever language (most probably Illyrian) was the ancestor of modern Albanian. It is true that at the cut-off date of AD 400 two other languages were still to be heard: Gaulish, regarded by Latin authors of the middle Empire as being still in common use; and Punic, which was familiar to St Augustine and his contemporaries as late as the fifth century. But Gaulish and Punic, vigorous as they still appeared, were soon to disappear without further trace. Only ten out of the sixty languages – less than 17 per cent – were destined for survival.

Multilingualism in a world empire

So far we have treated the language map of the ancient Mediterranean as if it were a simple patchwork – a succession of sixty geographical blocks where sixty different languages were spoken.

It was not so, of course. In those days Mediterranean peoples were probably at least as likely to be bilingual or multilingual as they are now. One of the earliest writers of Latin literature, Quintus Ennius, who lived about 150 BC, 'used to say that he had three hearts, because he knew how to speak Greek, Oscan and Latin'.[3] Bilingualism will be important in our investigation of the present and likely future of minority languages today: so why did people become bilingual in the ancient world? What would their second and subsequent languages be, and how would they use them?

Ennius, we can be confident, learned Oscan at home because he was born in the Oscan-speaking region of southern Italy. He learnt Greek either as a young child, if it was a second language in his family, or, if not then, soon afterwards. At that time and place Greek was the language of the big cities and the language of culture. If he did not learn it from those around him, he would have learnt it at school. He learnt Latin probably as an adult, when, as slave or dependant of a Roman nobleman, he eventually settled in Rome. Many other Romans, known and unknown, will have had a very similar range of linguistic experiences. One other whose personal history we happen to know is Lucius Apuleius, author of a marvellous work of fantasy fiction known as *The Golden Ass*. Apuleius, a native of North Africa, grew up (about three hundred years after Ennius) in a family in which Punic was the everyday language. Some members of his family – his stepson, for example – never spoke any other language fluently, but Apuleius learnt Greek and then travelled to Rome where he taught himself Latin. Both Ennius and Apuleius wrote their works of literature in Latin, their third language, which both of them learnt as adults. In some of their writings, as it happens, they were adapting and transforming existing works of Greek literature. Scholars can enjoy searching for the stylistic influences of Ennius' and Apuleius' first two languages, clearly discernible in the highly individual way in which they wrote Latin.

Most cities of the Empire must have been multilingual. The scale of this multilingualism has to be estimated by gathering the limited explicit evidence available on the subject, and then considering the pattern of languages set out above. For example, Varro, writing in the first century BC, observed that 'the people of Marseille are trilingual: they speak Greek, Latin and Gaulish'.[4] No doubt he was right – but Marseille, a centre of Greek culture, stood near the point where the linguistic territories of Gaulish, Iberian and Ligurian met, so it will certainly have had communities speaking the two latter languages also. Syrian and Jewish traders would soon settle there (if they had not already done so in Varro's time), bringing two additional languages with them. The greater the city, the greater its linguistic profile. Rome was surely the most multilingual of all. Several Latin and Greek writers evoke this aspect of their capital. In their eyes it was a microcosm, a 'world city'. Some wrote specifically on the voices and accents to be heard in the crowded streets of Rome. The philosopher Seneca heard from his study 'a patissier's varied cries, and a sausage-vendor and a confectioner and all the proprietors of cookshops selling their wares, each in his distinctive accent'.[5] In the first century AD we know specifically of 'Hebrew' and Oscan-speaking communities among others, and we know that these and others were sufficiently distinct and identifiable to merit the production of plays in community languages under the emperors' patronage.

It may surprise us now to realize how multilingualism was built into the structure of the Roman Empire. In this feature it was not at all unusual in the ancient world. Take the Persian Empire, which flourished from 559 to 330 BC. Its everyday administrative language was Aramaic, but it also produced documents centrally in three other languages. Babylonian was a form of Akkadian, another early Semitic language, used by preceding empires including the Assyrians. Old Persian was the Indo-European language of central Iran, a dialect very close to the Avestan in which, around this same time, the earliest Zoroastrian scriptures were being recorded. Finally Elamite, possibly related to the Dravidian languages of modern southern India, was spoken in southwestern Iran and happened to be the local language of the Persian imperial family. Additionally, Greek, Phoenician and Egyptian were important languages in the empire's western reaches.

The kingdom of Pontus, eventual successor to the Persian empire in the lands around the Black Sea, presented even more of a linguistic challenge to its rulers, a challenge one of them at least was ready to meet.

Mithridates, the celebrated king of Pontus and Bithynia, the one who was defeated in war by Pompey, was fluent in the languages of the twenty-five peoples whom he held under his sway. He never spoke to the men of all those peoples through an interpreter; whenever it was necessary for him to address any one of his subjects, he used the man's own language and oratorical style with as much skill as if it were native to him.[6]

The linguistic complexity of Persia is echoed by that of the Roman Empire. Elamite and Old Persian were the languages of Persia's heartland (and no doubt of the royal palace), but the empire-wide culture demanded Aramaic. Latin was the language of Rome's heartland (and of the Senate and the army), but all serious education was in Greek. Everything we can learn from the early and middle centuries of the Empire assures us that, as you went through a full course of Roman education, you studied Greek and *then* you studied Latin. Even in the far west, hundreds of miles from the nearest historic centre of Greek influence, and as late as the mid-fourth century, it was still so. The poet Ausonius, in his *Memorial of my Father*, sets out for us the linguistic background of a local professional man from a small town south of Bordeaux. In this extract it is the poet's father who speaks, and his mother tongue, though he does not tell us this specifically, is likely to have been Aquitanian (early Basque).

> Nomen ego Ausonius, non ultimus arte medendi
> et, mea si nosses tempora, primus eram.
> Vicinas urbes colui patriaque domoque
> Vasates patria, sed lare Burdigalam . . .
> Non opulens nec egens, parcus sine sordibus egi;
> victum, habitum, mores semper eadem habui.
> Sermone impromptus Latio, verum Attica lingua
> suffecit culti vocibus eloquii.

My name was Ausonius. I was not the last among medical men: if you consider only my own times, I was the first. In two neighbouring cities I was born and resided: Bazas [Gironde] was my origin, Bordeaux my hearth . . . I was neither rich nor poor; I lived sparingly but respectably; I never altered my food, my dress, my way of life. I was unready with Latin, but Greek words came to me easily enough for educated speech.[7]

To back up the personal evidence of the families of Apuleius and Ausonius we can look to the educational theorist of ancient Rome, Quintilian. His aim was that young men should be brought up as active citizens, ready to take a full role in politics and the Roman legal system, for both of which purposes persuasive public speaking in Latin would be required. This is how it was done: 'I prefer a boy to begin with the Greek language rather than the Latin, because the latter is so widely used that he will imbibe it whether we wish him to or not; also because he must learn the Greek arts and sciences first, since they are the sources of ours.' Quintilian does however foresee the problems that may arise if this approach is pushed too far. Perhaps he is foreseeing the beautiful but very un-Latin eloquence of Apuleius. He is surely remembering the strange, barbaric compound words that the reader would encounter in the poems of Ennius. It was a fact that Greek was a 'free-compounding' language (as modern linguists might say) in which any speaker might naturally create new compound words, a facility that Greek writers used freely and Latin authors imitated at their peril: there are examples to prove it in the story told by Aulus Gellius below. At any rate, Quintilian continues: 'I do not like this course to be followed so religiously that the pupil speaks and learns nothing but Greek for any length of time. It is true that many people do precisely this, but the result of it will be to introduce a great many faults of pronunciation and grammar into his Latin . . .'[8]

Until about the time of Ausonius Greek had been not only the first language of a general education throughout the Roman Empire, but also, and especially, the language of philosophy, science and all kinds of specialized trades and pursuits. If you were to qualify as a physician, or indeed as a cook, you had no choice but to do so in Greek. This is why colloquial Latin, the language of slaves, other lower-class speakers and technical experts of all kinds, was soon full of Greek words:

philologia 'literary studies', *poeta* 'poet', *epigramma* 'short poem', *mimus, pantomimus* 'actors', *chirurgus* 'surgeon', *stomachum* 'indigestion', *horologium* 'clock'. You recognize these: all but the last have become essential European words, re-borrowed in some form from Latin into English, while that last word is familiar in French (*horloge* 'clock'), where it still survives in direct line of descent from the colloquial Latin of the Empire.

Greek words, as Quintilian foresaw, crept into upper-class Latin as well, though on a slightly smaller scale. Its speakers had had their lessons in Latin as well as Greek; they had been taught to choose their words carefully, and if Greek words did slip in they might think it best to apologize as if for a slip of the tongue. This is exactly what the emperor Tiberius did in the course of a speech in the Senate when he used a Greek word *monopolium* 'monopoly' because there was no Latin one. However, these speakers had had the opportunity to compare their two languages intelligently. Those who had become fully at home with both, as many evidently had, were able to assert that some things, easily said in Greek, could only be expressed in Latin with the greatest difficulty. The learned Aulus Gellius – allowing himself a modicum of quiet pride in his confident handling of two very different languages – argues exactly this, recalling a chance encounter at a library enquiry desk. At least, I think that is the setting. His story may as well be quoted in full at this point: it will be important to us again at a later stage.

It has often struck me that there are quite a few ideas that cannot be expressed by a single word in Latin, though they can in Greek. Indeed, even a long Latin sentence may still not be as apt as the single Greek word. Recently I sent for a Greek book by Plutarch and when it arrived I read its title, *Peri Polypragmosynes*. A man standing by me who could not understand or read Greek asked me who wrote the book and what it was about. I could answer the first question, but I found I was at a loss to explain the topic. It would not quite do to translate it as *De Negotiositate*, 'On Busyness' . . . I racked my brains for a Latin word that would match the Greek. I could not think that I had ever come across one, and any word I might invent out of *multitudo* 'large number' and *negotium* 'business' would be an absurd and ugly expression, like *multiiugus* 'manifold' or *multicolor* 'many-coloured' or *multiformis* 'many-shaped'. It would be just as awkward as if you tried to translate into a single Latin word those Greek terms *polyphilia* 'the condition of one who has a lot of friends', *polytropia* 'the state of entities that are of many kinds' and *polysarkia* 'fleshiness'. After pondering for a moment, I said that I did not think any single word would express the idea, and I would try to do it with a sentence: 'Being involved in a great many things and being busy with them all at once is what the title means, and that's what the book is about.' 'So Plutarch encourages his readers to get down to business and get things done? A cardinal virtue,' said my monolingual companion. 'No,' I said in frustration, 'the Greek word denotes a vice, not a virtue, and Plutarch doesn't encourage it, and I didn't mean to say that he did. I take the blame for your mistake: even using all those words of Latin I was unable to get across to you what is expressed elegantly and clearly in one single Greek word.'⁹

How local languages died

If we are to find out why the local languages of the Empire disappeared we must look for traits that they shared or that they jointly lacked – features that somehow mark them off from the few that survived.

We can begin with a striking fact about Gaulish and Punic – both of which survived longer than the majority, but were destined to disappear none the less. They were once languages of power. Both were spoken by peoples who were politically dominant, over an extensive region, immediately before the spread of Roman rule. The Gauls, without any long-term formal political unity, had established their rule from mid-Spain to inland Asia Minor. Carthaginian settlement and trade, along with the Punic language, extended from southern Spain through the islands of the western Mediterranean and along the north African coast as far east as modern Libya.

Gaulish and Punic were two of the languages that retained a high profile even after the Roman expansion. If, as a time traveller engaged in a market survey, you asked a Roman administrator what languages were spoken in the Empire, he would hardly bother to name most of the others just listed in our linguistic tour. He would certainly name Latin, Greek and maybe one or two others, and Gaulish and Punic were likely to be in the list. I can prove this by quoting a Roman lawyer. The great jurist Ulpian, wishing to make it clear that verbal bequests made in any language were equally valid, put it like this: 'They can leave a bequest in any language, not only Latin and Greek, but also Punic or Gaulish or that of any other people.'[10] Elsewhere he discussed a comparable question, whether a formal verbal contract could be made bilingually – in Latin, Greek and perhaps other languages of the Empire: 'Do we also include Punic perhaps, or Assyrian or some other language? Sabinus writes – and this is evidently true – that every language may accommodate a verbal agreement, provided that each party understands the language of the other, either directly or through an interpreter.'[11]

So, on the one hand, Gaulish and Punic – like 'Assyrian' or Aramaic, which did not disappear – were significant everyday languages of a large part of the Empire. They are the ones that would occur to Ulpian when he reached out for examples of languages potentially spoken by the kind of people whose business or family interests might come to a lawyer's attention. But, crucially, Ulpian is discussing the spoken word. Powerful though the spoken word might be, a great deal of the business of Roman law, trade and government depended on writing. In similar debates concerning the validity of written documents, Roman practice allowed the use of Latin and sometimes Greek, but not of any other languages of the Empire.

In this context there is an instructive contrast to be drawn between Gaulish and Aramaic. In both of these languages there was a formal and elaborate system of education. Josephus, a first-century AD figure who wrote a history of the Jews in Greek (and was not distinguished for his modesty), claims to be 'distinguished for my native learning. I also took up the Greek course of education and studied that language,' he adds, 'though our traditional system has ensured that I pronounce it inaccurately.'[12] The Greek author Lucian, a few decades later, was helped to understand a Gaulish religious icon (or so he says) by someone who had been through both Gaulish and Greek educational systems. 'There was a Celt nearby, well educated in our system (as he made clear by his fluent Greek) and a philosopher, I believe, in their native system. "I'll solve the riddle of this picture for you, stranger," he said.'[13] Not everything that Lucian says in his essays is true, but, as usual, he has done his research and chosen his words well. It is a fact that the traditional Druidic educational system of Gaul taught 'philosophy' in the broad ancient sense of that term. 'The Druids . . . give rulings on all religious questions. Large numbers of young men flock to them for instruction,' said Julius Caesar,[14] writing of the period during which he himself conquered Gaul, in the 50s BC. The geographer Strabo, who wrote after Caesar's death but sometimes used earlier material, outlined Gaulish intellectual culture thus: 'There are three castes who are specially honoured, the Bards, the Seers and the Druids. The bards are praise-singers and poets. The seers are magicians and scientists. The Druids cultivate philosophy as well as science and ethics: they are considered the most just.'[15]

Now it is well known that the traditional Jewish course of education, in Roman times and indeed today, is firmly based on the written word. 'To be thought wise among us, you must know the Laws and be capable of interpreting the Scriptures,' so Josephus puts it. Gaulish learning, on the other hand, had a distinctive feature – again noted by Caesar – in which it differed totally from that of the Jews.

It is said that pupils have to memorize a great number of verses – so many, indeed, that some of them spend twenty years at their studies. The Druids believe that their religion forbids them to commit their teachings to writing, although for most other purposes, such as public and private accounts, the Gauls use the Greek alphabet. But I imagine that this rule was originally established for other reasons – because they did not want their doctrine to become public property, and in order to prevent their pupils from relying on the written word and neglecting to train their memories; for it is usually found that when people have the help of texts, they are less diligent in learning by heart, and let their memories rust.

So the Gauls had an educational system, but writing had little part in it. The Jewish educational system relied heavily on writing. What of Punic? While theirs was still an independent and powerful state the Carthaginians had had a literature and were distinguished for their skill in technologies including agriculture and irrigation. Their libraries, however, were broken up after the Roman conquest in 146 BC. In the hundred years following that turning-point, one or two authors in Greek and Latin show some familiarity with what had been written in the old Punic texts. After that, they are forgotten totally.

Under the Roman Empire, both Gaulish and Punic eventually disappeared, while Aramaic survived. The presence or absence of a broadly based written culture seems significant, especially when set beside those legal opinions given by Ulpian. We must regard these details not simplistically but as providing evidence on questions that frequently arise elsewhere in this book, questions that may be crucial in the survival of a minority language. In how many fields of daily life is this language still of practical use? In how many fields of daily life are speakers compelled to use the majority language?

Certain languages, then, retained a written culture throughout the period of the Empire. At the end of the period we are discussing there was a written literature in three languages that were very widely known and used – Aramaic, Greek and Latin – but also in two languages that were used only in a single restricted area, Coptic (in Egypt) and Syriac (in Edessa and its neighbourhood). You could even say that these two literary languages did not exist at all until some time in the Roman period. That statement cannot pass, however. Coptic inherited the literary status of Egyptian, which, in its Late form and its Demotic script, survived an independent Egyptian-speaking government of Egypt by hundreds of years. Egyptian literacy did not die; it was rejuvenated in Coptic. As for Syriac, it belongs in the multi-dialectal literacy of the classical Near East, with a history of over three thousand years if we begin with Ugaritic cuneiform and Biblical Hebrew.

Now there had once been a written literature in Tartessian, Etruscan and Oscan, before the regions where these languages were spoken fell under Roman rule. But in all three cases local literary culture collapsed, apparently quite early in the Roman period. There is no better way to state this than by saying that all three cultures and languages were swamped by that of Rome. The southern Spanish province of Baetica, where Tartessian was spoken, was an area of intensive settlement after Rome took it over from Carthage around 200 BC. Two centuries later the geographer Strabo, after recalling that the local people 'are ranked as the wisest of the Iberians: they use writing, and they have records of their ancient traditions, poems, and verse laws, six thousand years old so they say', brings the story up to date by adding that they 'have quite gone over to Roman ways, not even remembering their own dialect any longer'. Strabo links this change with the intensive Roman colonization of the region.[16]

The heartland of Oscan was relatively close to Rome, and it appears that Roman culture was beginning to dominate the region even while it retained some political autonomy. Plays were written in Oscan, but major playwrights and poets were already choosing to write in Latin in the second century BC. The last gasp of Oscan was the Social War, fought by Rome's erstwhile Italian allies in 90–89 BC for a fairer share of status and power: Oscan was (as we would now say) the 'official language' of the allies. In the event, Rome conceded their principal aims, but only after defeating them in war. The defeat meant the end of Oscan coinage, Oscan legislation and (to the extent that this had existed) Oscan-language education.

Etruscan, language of a confederation of cities of Tuscany, mean-while – more peacefully – became a thing of the past. Long ago the Etruscan cities had dominated Rome, and it was said that Romans had once gone to school to study Etruscan language and literature as they later studied Greek. Etruscan had been a language of theology and science. But by the first century BC, if an Etruscan wanted to move outside his local orbit, whether in business or in politics, he could not expect to use his local language. Around that date even Etruscan tomb inscriptions begin to be bilingual – a strong indication that families and local communities, too, were bilingual. In one specialized field, none the less, Etruscans were the Roman Empire's acknowledged experts. No one could reliably predict the future, by inspecting sacri-ficial entrails or observing the flight of birds or the incidence of thunder-bolts, as Etruscans could. As late as AD 365 the last pagan emperor, Julian the Apostate, had Etruscan experts with him on his invasion of Persia. As successive omens threatened the well-being of the expedition they consulted their 'military books' and their 'thunderbolt books' and gave wise advice, which Julian, disastrously, ignored.

In addition to Tartessian, Oscan and Etruscan, several other lan-guages of the Empire were written when their speakers wanted to write them. Venetic and Messapian, from northeastern and southeastern Italy respectively, were used in brief inscriptions until about the first century BC. The various languages of Spain were written in several alphabets, as Strabo rightly observes. Gaulish could be written in the

Greek alphabet, said Caesar (quoted above): he noted that it was used for accounts, and we also know that it was used in inscriptions. Punic continued to be used on tomb inscriptions, centuries after people had stopped (so far as we know) writing Punic literature. Libyan had been an 'official' language in the north African hinterland, which became the Roman Empire's southern edge. It was used alongside Punic on inscriptions and coins. Arabic is visible in the background of the local Aramaic inscriptions of Nabataea. Phrygian was the most prominent of the local languages of Asia Minor in Roman times, found on inscriptions even from the third and fourth centuries AD. Phrygian, Gaulish and later Arabic were of importance to the spreading Christian church. Bishop Irenaeus, appointed to the diocese of Lyon in the late second century, modestly made this an excuse for his straightforward Greek. 'I live among the Gauls and put my efforts into their barbaric language. Do not expect style, because I have not learnt it, or power of expression, because I do not aim at it, or beauty of words, or persuasiveness, because I am not capable of them.'[17]

As evidence of when these languages ceased to be spoken we have little more than the clues offered by tombstones and occasionally other inscriptions and graffiti. There are problems with dating them accurately (dates were not a feature of tombstones in ancient times), but the general pattern is clear. Inscriptions continued to be made in the first two or three generations after the Roman takeover; many of them are still in the local language; some are bilingual. After that the local language simply disappears from view. In the west of the Empire, it is Latin that takes the place of the local language. In the east, it is Greek. We cannot expect to learn from such evidence precisely how long it took the local languages to disappear. All over this vast region, most people were too poor, too unambitious or – in their own or their neighbours' view – too insignificant ever to merit a record inscribed on stone. Those are precisely the people who will have been the last to feel the impulse to shift from their local language to Latin or Greek. Those are the people who will have been the last to choose to bring up their children speaking not the local language but Latin or Greek. The fact remains that, quickly or slowly, nearly everybody eventually made that decision. By the time the Roman Empire itself crumbled away, which as far as the western Mediterranean is concerned means between

AD 400 and 476, most of the local languages were long forgotten and even Gaulish and Punic were doomed.

Of the languages discussed in the preceding five paragraphs, only two survived: Arabic, destined to be the language of Islam and to spread with this conquering religion across the Near Eastern world; and Libyan, as the parent, or one of the parents, of the modern Berber languages. We shall return to deal with them, alongside British, below.

We still have to deal with the languages that were never or hardly ever written down. This includes at least four languages of western and northern Spain, Aquitanian and Ligurian in southern France, British, Noric, Pannonian-Dalmatian and all the languages of the Balkans, the minor languages or dialects of central Italy, the local languages of Sicily, and finally most of the local languages of Asia Minor.

These are the languages for which there is the smallest amount of evidence – for two good reasons. First, because they were not written, few or no inscriptions survive for us to read (or fail to read). Second, because they were less prominent in culture, even locally, writers of the Roman period never or hardly ever mention them. On the language map of the Empire that accompanies this chapter, several of these languages are listed without a proper name or with a stopgap name, a reminder that we don't even know what their speakers called them, or what any Romans who heard of them would have called them. In these circumstances, we cannot expect to know much more than *whether* these languages survived the Roman period into medieval and modern times. If they didn't, it may be difficult or impossible to say *when* it was that they ceased to be spoken, and in what circumstances.

As regards the survival of the languages of this last group, the minor and unwritten languages, we can put up two hypotheses. First: the languages that disappeared should be those whose speakers became dependent on Roman or other neighbouring cultures for their survival or prosperity. After all, this is why Etruscan disappeared, literate though the Etruscans were; it is even more likely that a language with no written culture, whose speakers are surrounded by literate peoples and require literacy to prosper, would disappear in such circumstances. If we hear anything of such languages in their last days, it will be of some residual use – something which would now be described as folkloric or worse – rather than of a fully rounded linguistic culture.

Second: the languages that survived should be those whose speakers, perhaps because of remoteness or inaccessibility, held aloof from Roman culture or had no chance, while they remained where they were, to share in Roman wealth. Now to test these hypotheses.

The first is about languages that disappeared. We start, then, by looking at a few of these languages for evidence of their last known uses.

In western Asia Minor, we are told by a Roman geographer, most local peoples had already lost their languages after just a century of Roman rule. In Lydia, for example, though it was once a kingdom powerful enough to challenge the Persian Empire and rich enough to awe the classical Greeks, the Lydian language was no longer to be heard at all, unless you attended the rituals at Hypaepa at which magicians chanted special words (which *might* be Lydian) to kindle fire on the altar. Gaulish was the language in which a 'Druid woman' was said to have prophesied the military uprising in which the emperor Severus Alexander died in AD 235; Gaulish is also the language of spells that must be chanted by doctors while compounding or administering drugs – no doubt Ausonius *père*, best of doctors in his own time, had learnt how to do this – as set out in a fifth-century medical textbook. *Marcellus De Medicamentis* is all in Latin (not 'good' Latin, but the Latin of provincial Gaul, studded with Greek loanwords) apart from these Gaulish spells. We have just seen how Etruscan experts were called on to interpret their magic books for Julian the Apostate. Not far from the Etruscan homeland were other magic-makers, whose language was one of the Italic dialects between Umbrian and Oscan:

The Marsi ... knew how to send snakes to sleep by charms, and rob a serpent's tooth of its venom by simples and spells. They say that Angitia, daughter of Aeetes, first revealed magic herbs to them, and taught them to tame vipers, to drive the moon from the sky, to stop the flow of rivers by their incantations, and to call the forests down, leaving the mountains bare.[18]

It's necessary to emphasize a point here. It seems unimportant and obvious to ancient historians but it is loaded with significance to linguists who specialize in disappearing languages.

These glimpses of Lydian, Gaulish and Etruscan are our last. Nothing had been heard of Etruscan for three hundred years – since about the time when Claudius, emperor and antiquarian scholar, wrote his Etruscan history – until the priests turn up in Julian's camp with their magic books. Had Julian not been personally dedicated to reviving pagan 'philosophies', this incident might never have occurred or been reported. In any case, from this moment Etruscan disappears from the record. Nothing had been heard of Lydian for several centuries, before the Greek traveller Pausanias mentions the ritual at Hypaepa; and that's the end of Lydian. Gaulish was much more in evidence than these two during the early centuries of the Roman Empire, but in this case too it happens to be a fact that the spells in *Marcellus De Medicamentis* (and some other spells of about the same date) are the very latest Gaulish texts now known.

In the cases of Lydian and Gaulish magic the speakers did not need to understand the words involved. They simply had to be able to repeat them as prescribed. Bystanders did not need to understand what was said either. In fact it was much better if they did not understand, because they would then be more easily impressed by the speakers' abstruse knowledge and the supernatural power it conferred. Even in the case of the Etruscan books we, as readers of the ancient historian's narrative, are allowed to be sceptical – to ask whether the priests still did understand their ancient language, or whether their own intelligence prompted the cautious advice which they gave and Julian ignored. In fact these incidents are strangely parallel to certain other cases in which ancient magic was made by the use of languages that were counterfeit or wholly imaginary. In a magic ritual in the fourth-century AD *Eighth Book of Moses* the angels are addressed in so-called hieroglyphic, hieratic, Egyptian, Hebrew and then also in bird-glyphic and the language of baboons and falcons. It is promised that they will reply in the same languages, the falconic response being '*Chi chi chi chi chi chi chi tip tip tip tip tip tip tip*'.[19] To sum up, these are not real, mainstream uses of language. As we shall see in Chapter 3, they are exactly the type of language use that can still be observed and recorded when to all intents and purposes the language has already been lost.

The second hypothesis is about minor languages that survived beyond the Roman period. Let us look now at these.

Of the languages that survived the Roman Empire only two (apart from Latin and Greek) were spoken relatively close to the Empire's geographical focus, well removed from its land frontiers. These two are Illyrian (if that is the ancestor of Albanian) and Aquitanian-Vasconian (if that is the ancestor of Basque). Basque and Albanian are both spoken in difficult mountain districts that display, as far as archaeologists can see, relatively sparse signs of Roman influence. We are allowed to guess that the speakers of the ancient forms of Albanian and Basque retained more than average self-sufficiency under Roman rule. Unless they emigrated, they had less than average opportunity to participate in Roman trade and prosperity.

The same is certainly true of some of the speakers of British, those in the Welsh mountains and on either side of the Pennines. It is a significant detail that both British and Basque were spoken not only in the highlands but also across wide areas of good, level agricultural land: British in the lowlands of southern and eastern England, Basque in the plains of Aquitaine. It is in precisely those lowland regions that British and Basque did not survive; though one must be honest and add that it is not clear whether it was in Roman times or later that the two languages retreated from the lowlands. It is certainly true that in these lowland regions Roman-style agriculture spread, and with it, evidently, the use of Latin. Basque survives in the western Pyrenees, British in Wales.

By contrast with Basque and Albanian, British was a language of the borderlands of the Empire; its speakers extended across the usual northern frontier – which was Hadrian's Wall – as far as the lowlands of Scotland. The same is true of Arabic and Libyan: Arabic was spoken in most of the Arabian peninsula, Libyan probably far across the Sahara as the Berber languages are now. Regular cross-border contact with communities that spoke the same language but were independent of Rome and not subject to Roman influence will have influenced the survival of these languages on Roman territory – and in two of the three cases we know for certain that regular contact, in the course of trade and nomadic pastoralism, took place. The speakers of Libyan and Arabic, and the mountain-speakers of British, were also less accessible than most other Romans to Empire-wide cosmopolitan culture. They were under special forms of government at arm's length from Rome. Nabataea was, for much of its history, an autonomous buffer state, a kingdom usually under Roman suzerainty but with its own sources of wealth from long-distance trade that Rome did not control. The Libyans of the northern edge of the Sahara, and the Britons of Wales and the Pennines, were wild peoples governed by local tribal rulers responsible to Roman provincial governors.

It is worth emphasizing how little we know of most of the languages supplanted by Latin. Even when they were written down, what was written is mostly lost.

Except for a few brief references by Greek and Latin writers, we know nothing of what once existed in Punic literature. The Roman Senate thought it worth saving and translating only one book, Mago's manual of farming. There are rumours of one manuscript of Mago having survived on Cyprus as late as the twelfth century,[20] but it is lost now. Because Punic is close to Phoenician, and that in turn is close to other Semitic languages in which there is plenty of literature, we can understand Punic tomb inscriptions pretty well, but they hardly represent a whole language.

We can make out some Gaulish, because this language was related to Welsh and Irish. But the few texts we have, the inscriptions and the spells, are not all clear to us. We can make very little of Etruscan, in spite of the attempts of generations of scholars and crackpots. Those who aim to decipher lost languages of the ancient past need lengthy, coherent, varied texts to work on. In Etruscan such texts did once exist. There were the military books and the thunderbolt books that were taken on Julian's Persian expedition. There were the histories or annals from which Claudius worked (whether he read them himself or used an Etruscan amanuensis) when he wrote the history of Etruria. There were the philosophy and cosmology texts that Roman writers thought the Etruscans had written. But they do not survive: once a language is forgotten, only the occasional antiquarian has any interest in the survival of records that have become unreadable. In Gaulish, meanwhile, texts of that kind existed only in oral tradition and were not written down: other sources agree with Caesar, quoted on p. 54, that it was contrary to Druidical rule to commit them to writing. The 'philosophical' or cosmological poetry, the praise-songs and the epics of ancient Gaulish are mentioned briefly by classical writers from the second century BC onwards: they are entirely lost, as is the oral poetry of ancient Galician. All we know is that these literatures existed.

We would suppose from Caesar's statement that in Gaulish culture the spoken word was highly valued. More evidence of that fact comes from several Latin authors who stress that eloquence – the ability to make good use of rhetoric – was a Gaulish trait. 'Most of Gaul cultivates two arts most actively: warfare and rhetoric,' said the elder Cato as early as the mid-second century BC. Further detail on Gaulish oral techniques comes from a Greek author of the following century:

When [the Gauls] meet they converse with few words and in riddles, hinting darkly at things for the most part and using one word when they mean another; and they like to talk in superlatives, to the end that they may extol themselves and depreciate all other men. They are also boasters and threateners and are fond of pompous language . . .[21]

This convincing sketch surely emanates from a careful observer – one who, if he did not himself speak Gaulish, was prepared to listen critically to those who did. He did not admire their skills, however. The pejorative tone of this report does not prepare us for the favourable way in which later Latin authors habitually refer to Gaulish oratory. Since few native Latin or Greek speakers ever needed to learn Gaulish, this special skill – if it truly existed, as we are repeatedly assured it did – could only have been observed by most of them in the way that people from Gaul used Latin and cultivated Latin oratory. And it was not unique to the Gauls. Latin speakers of Iberian and African origin are also often picked out for their skill and persuasiveness in public speaking. 'Go to Gaul, or better still to Africa, nurse of lawyers, if you want your tongue to earn you a living,' said the cynical poet Juvenal in the early second century AD.[22] The emperor Septimius Severus (died 211), like Apuleius, came from a Punic-speaking family. Severus' sister and nephew never spoke anything else but Punic – which was a severe embarrassment to him when they visited Rome – but he himself was eventually trilingual. 'He was competent at Latin letters, an educated speaker of Greek, but readier with Punic eloquence, naturally enough, since he was born in Lepcis in the province of Africa,' so one Roman historian was to summarize the matter. The linguistic nuances are interesting. Still more interesting, as we learn from another memoir, are the first steps that Severus took in Punic eloquence. 'In his early childhood, before he had learnt his Latin and Greek letters . . . the only game he enjoyed with his friends was to play at judges.'[23] Did you often play judges when you were a child? I didn't. If Juvenal and other Rome-centred littérateurs found something worth praising in African eloquence, the games that were played by children in the great Libyan city of Lepcis help us to understand why. Romans, understandably, characterize this ethnic trait as 'Punic eloquence'. But that is perhaps shorthand. Its origin is to be traced less to the Carthaginians (though political oratory must have had its place in their constitution) and to their Phoenician forebears, more perhaps to the Libyans, speakers of an early Berber language. Lepcis itself had been a place of mixed culture, of Phoenician law and culture but of Numidian (Libyan) language, when it first became part of the Roman Empire. The evidence, as far as it goes, is quite consistent: the three cultures of the western Mediterranean that were noted by Romans for their verbal eloquence were, at the same time, the three greatest that lacked a written literature, Gaulish, Iberian and Libyan.

Whatever was said in Gaulish, Iberian and Punic, however memorable, is now forgotten. Since the recording of Berber traditions did not begin until the thirteenth century, the Libyan eloquence of early Roman times is also wholly lost. The nearest we can come to sampling any of the lost literatures of the western Roman Empire is, strangely enough, in Britain. Praise-songs (whether in British or in Latin) once flattered the petty kings who ruled Britain soon after the Romans had said goodbye to their foggiest province. Their exponents will have been colleagues of the Bards of Gaul, who specialized in praise poetry. Gildas, in the sixth century, knew their work well and cordially hated it. 'Your excited ears' (he addresses one of those petty kings) 'hear not the praises of God from the sweet voices of the tuneful recruits of Christ, nor the melodious music of the church, but empty praises of yourself from the mouths of criminals who grate on the hearing like raving hucksters – mouths stuffed with lies and liable to bedew bystanders with their foaming phlegm.'[24] Although this poetry, too, is lost to us, we may easily imagine its resemblance to the very oldest Welsh poetry: the *Gododdin* in origin is a poem of current politics, a lament for those who fought and fell in battle against the English at the battle of Catterick.

That is the case, too, with some of the languages just across the Empire's borders. Already in the first century AD we know that the peoples of Germany recorded their traditions and their heroic history in oral verse: we are assured of it by the great Roman historian Tacitus, whose youthful pamphlet *Germania*, though based entirely on his reading, is a fund of moderately reliable information about the Empire's northern barbarian neighbours. We can guess that the tradition continued unbroken to the fifth century and beyond, when there were Germans in large numbers in the lands of the Empire. By then, historians such as Jordanes had begun to write on German history and legend and were able to base themselves directly on German tradition. We can guess that the same traditions continued to be retold till around AD 800, the time of the emperor Charlemagne. Conscious of his Germanic ancestry, Charlemagne instructed that the epic poetry of his people was to be written down in a book – a book that no longer survives. The verse forms of German heroic tradition (and we can guess that it was still the same tradition) certainly provided a model for the poet who wrote the Old Saxon poem *Genesis*, a paraphrase of the biblical story, on the instruction of Charlemagne's successor Louis the Pious. Finally, we can guess that the same tradition lies behind the old Germanic geography, genealogy and mythology that appears in Anglo-Saxon poems such as *Beowulf* and *Widsith* and the Old Norse poetry of the elder *Edda*. It is absolutely certain that Germanic oral poetry is reflected in all these sources: the only guesswork is as to whether the tradition was continuous, but it is not a very risky guess. Just as the earliest Welsh poetry gives us a clue as to the praise-songs that Gildas so heartily disliked, so these various sources, though mostly post-Roman, give us clues as to the oral poetry of Germany in Roman times.

The triumph of Greek and Latin

Anyone in the Empire who learnt Latin as mother tongue had a head start on others: there were circumstances of everyday life, and certainly of law and politics, in which a confident command of Latin was decisive. Any such person who additionally learnt Greek, at home or school, might be regarded as having a more rounded culture and would be better able to hold his own in cultured circles, in which people dropped Greek words and phrases into their speech and informal writing. You needed to know when to do this and when not to. It was an affectation, implying that Latin could not supply the *mot juste* but that Greek could, and thus also implying that the writer had a perfect command of Greek. The orator Cicero, contemporary of Caesar, eventually assassinated at Mark Antony's orders, demonstrates how an educated man kept his Latin/Greek balance. In his personal letters, not written for publication although they were published after his death, he often slipped Greek expressions into his Latin – and more so when he was writing to a close friend, such as his lifelong confidant Atticus. Publicly, however, in the context of Roman politics, Greek culture had no such high status: it was conventionally branded weak, even effeminate, unworthy of Roman tradition. So in his public speeches Cicero hardly ever introduces Greek except with malice afore-thought – as when he is careful to give the Greek name, *authepsa*, of the cooker on which his opponent Chrysogonus had spent so much money.[25]

Even more than Latin speakers needed to learn Greek, Greek speakers needed to learn Latin. It was true that the 'academics', whether professors of oratory, physicians or philosophers, could choose to bypass their Latin studies. If once successful, they would then only need to interact with Latin speakers who were anxious to practise their Greek and to learn more. Those with a more varied curriculum vitae had more varied linguistic needs, and Latin would certainly help them. Such people include the second-century writer Plutarch. He had been a professor of Greek; later he was involved in politics in his native Greece, while his researches included Roman history and philology. He has this to say of his knowledge of Latin:

When I lived in Rome and other parts of Italy, my public duties and the number of pupils who came to me to study philosophy took up so much of my time that I had no leisure to practise speaking the Latin tongue, and so it was not until quite late in life that I began to study Roman literature . . . To be able to appreciate the beauty and the pithiness of the Roman style, the figures of speech, the oratorical rhythms and the other embellishments of the language would be a most graceful and enjoyable accomplishment. But the study and practice required would be formidable for a man of my age, and I must leave such ambitions to those who have the youth and the leisure to pursue them.[26]

Well below Plutarch on the social ladder we can see the imaginary young man, planning to take a position as tutor in a wealthy Roman family, to whom the Greek satirist Lucian writes an amusing sketch of advice, and warns him that he will be 'the only person in all that Roman throng who wears the incongruous cloak of a scholar and talks Latin with a villainous accent'.[27] How could this be? Surely many of the slaves in such a household would have Greek as a language of child-hood and Latin as a second or third language? The young gentleman is unlucky because – although a full Roman education included plenty of Greek – a full Greek education included no Latin. He, like the real Plutarch, would have to pick up his Latin for himself, as an adult. A skilled or well-travelled slave in Rome was likely to have begun his Latin (perforce) much earlier in life, and to speak it much better.

This same imaginary young man helps us to see how it must have been concerning the other languages of the Empire. He would need Latin, after all, even though his chosen profession was to 'sell' his knowledge of Greek. Speakers of all the other languages of the Empire, if they had anything at all to offer to the speakers of Latin or Greek (and that was where the money and the privilege resided), needed to offer it in Latin or Greek, because, as we concluded above, 'few native Latin or Greek speakers ever needed to learn Gaulish' or Punic or Aramaic, still less any of the minor languages of the Empire. In general, whether we are speaking of ancient or modern times, relatively few of those who who happen to speak a language of high status as a mother tongue find it necessary to learn one of lower status later. Some do: bishop Irenaeus did. But we are not surprised to hear of no others like him.

As it spread across the former Persian Empire, Greek was to become a very different language. We don't find strong influence from any one identifiable underlying form of speech. There is perhaps more from Aramaic than from any other, but this may be less because Aramaic was the lingua franca of the Persian Empire, more because Aramaic was the mother tongue of several authors of the New Testament, whose writings in a slightly Aramaicized Greek had great influence, in their turn, on later Christian Greek. Aside from the influence of individual languages, Greek changed rapidly and decisively. The former tonal accent became a stress accent. All diphthongs were reduced to simple vowels; the distinction of vowel length (i.e. between long and short vowels) disappeared; the aspirated stops, *ph, th, kh*, became fricatives that sounded like English *f* and *th* and German *ch*; the consonant *h*, a relatively rare sound confined (except as part of these aspirates) to word-initial position, disappeared. The dual number disappeared, leaving only singular and plural; the perfect tense of verbs disappeared, leaving the aorist and imperfect to cover all past senses.

Once Greek speech had undergone these fundamental changes, largely between the third century BC and the first century AD, changes thereafter came less frequently. Apart from the addition of new words – see below – Greek appears in fact to have been rather stable and unchanging through the later centuries of Roman rule. Literary Greek, incidentally, does not reflect these changes, or at least not in any consistent way: we know of them from non-literary papyri and various other types of evidence.

Latin was to undergo its own fundamental changes, around the first century BC. Although literary Latin, during that period and for a long time after it, continued to look very largely the same, spoken Latin was changing rapidly. All diphthongs were reduced to simple vowels; the distinction of vowel length disappeared, and the number of vowel sounds increased from five to seven. The consonant *h* disappeared: it was still part of 'standard Latin' but uneducated speakers did not know when to use it, any more than they knew when to use the *ph, th* and *kh* sounds adopted in learned Greek vocabulary. 'It is a mark of rustic speech to misplace aspirates,' a Latin scholar tells us,[28] and a poem by Catullus satirizes a badly educated speaker who does just this. Noun and verb forms began to be simplified; of the six 'cases' in a Latin noun declension, eventually only two survived. These changes are to be observed in some less-literary and less-educated Latin texts, including inscriptions and graffiti; they are also known to the extent that they are reflected in all the modern Romance languages, which descend from Latin.

Having undergone these changes, Latin, like Greek, seems to settle down. The rate of subsequent change, between the first century AD and the ninth, when we are able for the first time to read texts in the Romance languages, is comparatively slow. One important sign of the slowing of linguistic change is the fact that it is very difficult to identify local geographical variation in Latin of the Empire. Scholars would like to identify the initial stages of the separation of the Romance languages in the Roman period, but there seems to be little to find. A similar uniformity, over a very wide geographical area, was observed in American English in the eighteenth century.[29]

The reason for these phenomena is clear enough. Both Greek and Latin changed extremely rapidly at the time when each language was spreading extremely rapidly to new speakers. To a certain extent the type of change was the same in both cases, and in both cases there was a tendency to eliminate rare and complex forms. The Greek dual, and the Greek perfect stem, were not especially easy to form, were less used than other noun and verb forms and probably had fewer direct equivalences in the languages of those who were newly shifting to Greek; in spoken Greek these forms ceased to be used at this period. The sound *h* was of restricted use in early Greek and early Latin and is not one of the commonest sounds in languages generally; it was eliminated at this period from both languages. The distinction of vowel length creates difficulties for foreign learners of many languages in which it is found; it too was eliminated from both languages at this period.

Very large numbers of people were beginning to speak Greek and Latin as adults because the languages had suddenly become crucial to their survival and prosperity. We may postulate that already at those periods large numbers of children were learning Greek and Latin as mother tongues, though their parents' own mother tongues had been different. The changes observed in Greek and Latin in these crucial centuries cannot quite be described as 'dumbing down'. The new speakers were no less intelligent that the old, but they brought with them many different linguistic traditions. The changes had thus placed 'Koine Greek' and 'Vulgar Latin' (as these new forms are usually called) a little closer to a notional linguistic common denominator; they had become temporarily easier for non-natives to learn.

When we compare the results of their periods of expansion, there is a significant difference between Greek and Latin. There were about five centuries, from, say, 100 BC to AD 400, during which we can show administrative and economic reasons why people should change to Latin in the Western Empire. With the exception of the wild and remote speakers of Basque, British Celtic and Albanian, they all did. There were about nine centuries, from, say, 300 BC to AD 600, during which people in the Levant and Egypt had similar reasons to change to Greek. They did not, or not so as to make the difference: Coptic, Syriac and Aramaic survived in those regions, while Greek eventually disappeared from them. Only in Asia Minor (modern Turkey), where Greek was the language of rule for over a millennium, did the old local languages disappear.

The relatively rapid expansion of Latin is closely linked with an unusual constitutional feature of ancient Rome. In the typical Greek city, citizenship was rather seldom granted to outsiders. It belonged to those whose ancestors had been citizens. The new 'Greek' cities of the Greek kingdoms of the East certainly did incorporate citizens of local origins, but in their hinterlands there were many who still had no hope of citizenship and little chance of self-improvement. Rome's practice was different. It was from the beginning somewhat inclusive: we may or may not believe the story of Rome's origin as a settlement of vagrants and runaways, all equally new citizens, but it fits with what followed. As Rome's power spread across Italy, some land was seized and occupied, but many existing occupants remained, became Roman and eventually attained citizen status. Thus Roman citizenship spread with Roman power, not quite step by step, but not far behind. The same happened as Rome took over control of Sicily, southern Spain, southern Gaul and then various additional provinces. Again, the result was a combination of colonization, subjection and the bestowal of municipal and eventually citizen status. Service in the Roman army was in principle a citizen career: in practice, many non-citizens served, to be awarded citizenship and a grant of land on retirement.

All this is extremely important for the spread of Latin. Citizenship was attainable: you could become Roman. To exercise citizen rights, and certainly to aim at a political career, you needed Latin. One route to citizenship was army service, and in serving in the army you would use Latin. Admittedly, by the time the emperor Caracalla awarded citizen status to all free inhabitants of the Empire, in 212, the privilege in itself meant little: but Latin remained the route to whatever political, social and economic privileges were to be had. There was every reason for parents who could manage it to bring up their children to speak Latin rather than their local language.

Not only did the local languages of the Empire gradually shrink away. In their later forms these old languages give evidence that they were gradually submitting to Latin influence. This can be seen in the latest inscriptions of the soon-to-disappear Punic and Gaulish: it can also be seen in surviving Latin loanwords in the languages of the edges of the Empire, languages that just managed to survive. The names of the days of the week, still very much as they were listed in later Latin (*dies Lunae, dies Martis, dies Mercurii, dies Jovis, dies Veneris, dies Saturni, dies Solis*), are now to be found in Welsh (*dydd Llun, dydd Mawrth, dydd Mercher, dydd Iau, dydd Gwener, dydd Sadwrn, dydd Sul*). The Latin month names (*Januarius, Februarius, Martius, Aprilis, Maius, Junius, Julius, Augustus, September, October, November, December*) survive to this day in Berber languages such as Tashelhet (*innayr, xubayr, mars, ibrir, mayyuh, yunyu, yulyuz, ghusht, shutam-bir, ktubr, nuwambir, dujanbir*). Plenty of other Latin words are now to be identified in the languages that were formerly spoken on the Empire's frontiers. There are names for vegetables and fruits that spread to the frontiers and beyond under Roman cultivation: Latin *pirus*, Berber *ti-fires-t* 'pear tree'; Latin *ceresia*, German *Kirsche* 'cherry'; Latin *persica*, German *Pfirsich* 'peach'; Latin *radice*, German *Rettich* 'radish'. There are names for the most admirable achievements of Roman technical skill: Latin *vallum*, German and English *wall*; Latin *puteus*, German *Pfütze* 'well'; Latin *vinum*, German *Wein*, English *wine*; Latin *caseus*, German *Käse*, English *cheese*. This category also includes such apparently simple matters as the structure of a stone-built house: Latin *murus*, German *Mauer* 'house wall'; Latin *fenestra*, German *Fenster* 'window'. There are names for concepts connected with government and the army, in both of which subject areas Rome's achievement could not be ignored: Latin *Caesar*, a name which became an Imperial title, is found in German *Kaiser*. Finally there are names for Christian concepts, some of them originally borrowed from Greek into Latin, transmitted by Latin to the languages of the frontiers: Latin *episcopus* 'bishop' (originally Greek) is to be found in English *bishop*, German *Bischof*; Latin *ecclesia* 'church' (originally Greek) is in Welsh *eglwys*.

Using this approach it is evident that Greek exerted a similar and very powerful influence both on languages within the borders of the eastern Empire and on those beyond. Again, it is more interesting here to quote examples from one of the languages that survived. It has been estimated that about a fifth of the vocabulary of Coptic is of Greek origin, including terms such as *martyros* 'witness' (Greek *martys*, genitive form *martyros*), *diakon* 'deacon, attendant' (Greek *diakonos*), *axiou* 'pray' (Greek *axioun*), *halkin* 'copper coin' (Greek *khalkion*, colloquial *khalkin*).

In outlining what happened as the Roman Empire shrank away, we can begin with the Asian and African provinces. These remained very largely under Roman rule – which means rule not from Rome but from the new Roman capital of Constantinople (Istanbul) – until the sweeping Islamic conquests of the 630s.

At that point Greek was the language of government; Syriac and Coptic flourished as spoken and literary languages; Aramaic, too, must have had a considerable local population base, and was also in more general use as a language of literature and communication among Jews. It is not wholly clear whether Punic was still spoken in North Africa or had finally been squeezed out by Latin and Libyan (Berber), which were certainly both in use. In Asia Minor Phrygian was probably the last of the old local languages to disappear, and Greek was spoken throughout as far east as the linguistic frontier with Armenian and the Iranian languages (represented by modern Kurdish and Zaza).

From the 630s onwards the ruling language was Arabic, as it still is, from Syria and Iraq westwards to Morocco, down to the present day. Berber is still spoken by large numbers, from coastal Algeria to the middle Niger valley and from Mauritania to the western desert of Egypt, but in all this vast region Arabic is the language of prestige. Coptic and Syriac are no longer in current use and Aramaic is a minor local language of Syria, threatened with extinction. In Asia Minor the eventual ruling language was to be Turkish. Greek was still quite widely spoken in Turkey till early in the twentieth century, but most

Greek speakers were expelled in 1923 after the Greek invasion. A Greek-speaking majority remained in Cyprus.

The Germanic invasions, though a major contributing factor to the disappearance of the Roman Empire in Europe, had very little linguistic effect as compared with the Islamic invasions in Africa and Asia. From Spain and Portugal in the west to the Balkans in the east, Latin went on being spoken. Basque survived, and survives, in the western Pyrenees. Albanian, descendant of one of the ancient languages of the southern Balkans, also survives. Gaulish and all the other languages of western continental Europe were gone.

Only in Britain was the immediate sequel different. Whether Latin or British Celtic predominated in the lowlands, both were replaced by the language of the Anglo-Saxon invaders, usually known now as Old English. In the hills, British Celtic became Welsh and Cornish and had a third offshoot as the emigrant language Breton.

In the Balkans a north–south linguistic frontier had separated Latin from Greek; Greece itself, both mainland and islands, spoke Greek exclusively. The Slavic migrations of the fifth century and after effected great changes here. The modern languages that result from the migration are Bulgarian, Macedonian, Slovene and Serbo-Croat (which is now officially three languages, Serbian, Croatian and Bosnian). The Latin of the Balkans eventually almost disappeared, except for the small southern enclaves of Aromunian (Vlach) and the large, coherent, more northerly territory where Romanian is spoken. The territory where Greek was spoken also shrank.

Since the European provinces of the former Empire – again contrasting with the area of Islamic conquest – were to be politically fragmented from now on, there was no particular reason why the Latin that was their everyday speech should remain a single language. If the Church, still governed from Rome, might have constituted such a reason, it was an insufficient one. Latin gradually split into dialects, which by about the ninth and tenth centuries were beginning to be felt as sufficiently different from the fossilized Latin of Church and education to be regarded as separate languages. Until this point, if the local Romance dialects are on record at all, it is because they were written by mistake. Careless or unskilled scribes intended to write correct Latin and failed, or made notes of the failures of others. Now, however, people began to write their vernacular languages intentionally, and to this period can be traced the earliest written forms of some of the Romance languages which are the modern representatives of Latin. These, incidentally, are Portuguese, Galician, Spanish, Catalan, Occitan, French, Italian, Romansch, Ladin, Friulian and Romanian. Others, from Sardinian to Aromunian, may be added to the list but are seldom written.

Thus, largely because of later events (and principally the Islamic conquests), Greek is now merely the language of two rather small states. By contrast, the extensive reach of the Romance languages remains as a long-term reminder of the speed and apparent inexorability with which Latin spread across western Europe in the few centuries of the Roman Empire.

Languages and families

The Roman Empire was not nationalist or chauvinistic about language. Nationalism hardly existed as a concept. No one is recorded as saying that inhabitants of the Empire ought to speak Latin or Greek, or that minority languages ought to be abandoned. It is indeed true that senators were expected to know Latin, because Latin was the language in which senatorial debates were held; it is true that lawsuits were heard in Latin or Greek. But for people who had no political ambitions and avoided lawyers, life went on and nobody demanded Latin.

In this way Rome differed very strongly from modern empires and nation states, in most of which some particular language is favoured in all kinds of official ways. So why was it, finally, in spite of the lack of official persuasion or compulsion, that nearly all the local languages of the Empire were supplanted by Latin and Greek? To begin to construct an answer we need to look at the language situation of the Empire as it would affect an individual family.

Under the Roman Empire, when speakers of minority languages found themselves to be a part of a larger society and economy in which Latin dominated, they had more than one course of conduct open to them. They might decide to have nothing to do with the new language. But then they would be cutting themselves off from possible income and possible betterment: it would soon be obvious that trade and employment would be offered in Latin, or might eventually demand the use of it. If they failed to respond to this prompt, it would fall to the next generation to do so instead. They might on the other hand try to talk in Latin, whenever necessary, to the customers or employers who arrived using Latin, in which case, with practice, they would eventually be able to speak it adequately for everyday use.

From that point on, these people also had more than one course of conduct open to them when bringing up children. They might insist on using their native language alone. This would be an easy option, but it might disadvantage their children: it would be clear, sooner or later, that more opportunities would open to youngsters who spoke Latin. If they failed to respond to this prompt, the next generation would in due course be faced with the same decision. Or they might teach their children Latin, as well as they could, and encourage them to learn more.

Those children would grow up more or less bilingual. They would find the old native language used at home and among neighbours, Latin needed in trade and perhaps in employment (including, for example, in army service). Since the Empire encouraged (or at times enforced) considerable population mobility, it would be much more likely than in preceding generations that they would marry someone of a different mother tongue.

When the young people of this new generation become parents themselves, they have an option that was probably not open to *their* parents. If a mixed marriage, they may already speak Latin at home; if not, they are in any case bilingual. They can choose freely in which language to bring up their children. One choice will represent the old, local community, the old people, their more limited outlook, their inability to travel and find new opportunities; the other will represent the Empire and its money economy. They can, of course, choose to ensure that their children learn both (or all three) of their languages – but without a certain level of cultural awareness they are not really very likely to make this choice consciously. They will tend to use one language habitually with their children, and will leave to chance, or to later teaching, the question whether their children will learn others too.

If in those children's upbringing there is already an emphasis on

Latin, each successive generation in turn will have less opportunity, and less incentive, to learn the old local language. Soon there will be no incentive, and the old language will have been forgotten.

Working with the Roman example it was necessary to set out the issues for families as a series of hypotheses. It had to be done this way, because we have no record from Roman times of the process of 'language shift' (in a family or in a community) actually taking place. But there is nothing in the least hypothetical about any of it. From the Roman evidence, we know exactly *what* happened. Most of the local languages ceased to be used in writing by the end of the first century AD. Almost all of them had disappeared completely by the fifth century, and many of them well before that. We are now beginning to see exactly *how* it happened.

Finally we can look within the family unit to see whether women were less likely than men to shift to a new language. Some believed this to be true, including Cicero, the most eloquent of Romans, who wrote as follows:

I myself, when I listen to my mother-in-law Laelia – of course women more easily keep the old fashions unaltered, because however many people's speech they may encounter they always retain what they first learnt – so, when I listen to Laelia, I seem to be listening to Plautus or Naevius. Her speaking voice is so correct, so plain, that no artificiality and no imitation could possibly be present, and I feel sure that her father and her ancestors spoke just so.[30]

This seminal observation, written in 55 BC, deserves careful reading. Cicero assumes that others will agree with his general view about language change – that the older form of speech is the more correct one. His assumption is pretty well justified: it's a view that many people, at many times, have taken, even if scientific linguists don't. He also takes for granted readers' agreement with what he says in general about women's language – 'of course women more easily keep the old fashions unaltered, because … they always retain what they first learnt' – even though it might not have occurred to his readers till this moment that by listening to women's speech one could hear all over again the language of a past generation, as Cicero goes on to suggest (Plautus and Naevius are playwrights of the previous century). His ideas must not be dismissed as simply sexist, as embodying an invalid assumption that women in general share a more conservative pattern of thinking and learning. Why not? Because plenty of modern studies of language in families (in some societies though not in all) support Cicero's observation. In those societies women *do* tend to be still using the older, traditional language; men are rather more likely to have shifted towards the newly introduced, external language. This is so because, independently of external observers' views on the matter, in traditional societies women's activities are more likely to centre on the household and its surrounding land; men are more likely to travel further and to interact more widely. Language is a highly practical ability. If language is changing in the wider community, then, owing to the nature of their traditional activities, men are more likely than women to encounter the change first and to reflect it in their own speech habits. They need to. Women don't.

Cicero is not talking about bilingualism in any usual sense of the word: two slightly different forms of the same language, Latin, are in question. He means that among Latin speakers you heard an older variety of the language – and one that was proportionately less influenced by foreign ways of speech – when you listened to older women. A possible reason for this might be that Cicero's mother-in-law had not followed a course of education that included the study of Greek (as men in the family probably would have done): thus her Latin would not have been influenced by classroom Greek, as Quintilian, quoted earlier, complained that boys' Latin might be. Yes, we can offer that as a simple explanation, but it is not the one that Cicero had in mind. Educational influence would have been irrelevant if, as Cicero says, 'however many people's speech they may encounter they always retain what they first learnt'. In fact, there is plenty of evidence that women of the elite were able to read Greek and enjoy Greek poetry – all too enthusiastically, so some men believed, because, by comparison with Latin, Greek poetry tended to be sensual and erotic.[31]

Bilingualism in its usual sense is not involved – but we can see the possible implications of Cicero's observation, backed up as it is by some modern research, for communities and families where there is bilingualism. The older community language may be in more active use among the women of a typical family, and among women in the community, than among the men. Such creative tensions within families and communities may actually be crucial in keeping the older language in use over a longer period than would otherwise be the case. In the Aromunian community of Albania, studied during the 1920s, the men were multilingual – speaking Albanian and Turkish as well as their local dialect of Aromunian – while the women spoke only Aromunian. The result, observed by the Romanian linguist Th. Capidan, was an effect just such as Cicero had noticed. Men and women spoke their dialect with a distinctly different accent and vocabulary. A similar slight difference was observed in the 1920s between men's and women's Yiddish speech.[32]

But the linguistic differences between men and women of the same community cannot be forced into any simple general pattern. One of the most challenging cases is that of the Island-Carib speakers formerly inhabiting Dominica in the Lesser Antilles. Their unusual sociolinguistic behaviour was reported (though he didn't call it 'sociolinguistic behaviour') by Fr. Raymond Breton in 1647. Although, structurally, the language of men and women was the same, the two sexes had vocabularies that were extensively different. Breton explains matters thus:

Ils ont diverses sortes de langages. Les hommes ont le leur et les femmes un autre, et encor un autre pour les harangues et traittés de conséquence, que leur jeunes gens mesme n'entendent pas bien . . . Ils chantent ce qui leur vient à l'esprit sans ryme et bien souvent sans raison, spécialement contre leurs ennemys . . . Ils ont un baragouïn ou langage corrompu, dont ils traittent avec nous, qui est espagnol-françois-caraïbe pesle-meslés par ensemble.

They have several different forms of speech. Men have theirs and women have another; there is yet another for speeches and formal debates, a form of speech that even their own young people do not understand fully . . . They sing whatever comes into their heads, with no rhyme and often no reason, especially against their enemies . . . They have a jargon or corrupt language with which they do business with us: it is Spanish-French-Carib all mixed together.[33]

Naturally, men and women both understood both forms of speech: but what is really unusual is that each sex, in the proper circumstances, *used* both. Fr. Breton makes this clear in his Latin report to his superiors:

Karaïbumque lingua iterum duplex, alia vulgaris, alia politior, qua in rebus seriis utuntur, juvenibus ignota. Vulgaris vero alia virorum alia mulierum; ridiculumque inter eos cum mulieribus mascula lingua loqui et vice versa.

The language of the Caribs is of two kinds, one for every day and another, more elaborate, not known to the youngsters, which they use for political debate. The everyday language, meanwhile, is different for men and for women, and to speak the men's language when talking to women, and vice versa, is to invite ridicule.[34]

This is perfectly credible, since it is precisely the way that the politeness registers work in Javanese and several other languages. Everyone who grows up in the culture knows all the registers, and uses all of them in the proper circumstances. But so far as I know no other case is on record in which this pattern of use applies to men's and women's linguistic registers.[35] Why had it happened? Because, some generations earlier, warriors from the South American mainland, speaking Mainland Carib (a quite different language, though with a similar name), had invaded the Antilles, killed or put to flight all the men of Dominica and some other islands, and taken over their settlements, their women and their children. The men's vocabulary, as linguists have since demonstrated, was what remained of the Mainland Carib language that the invading men had originally spoken.

And we know what happened next: although no such language is now spoken on Dominica, a later migration took it to Belize and it survives there. Nowadays there is scarcely any difference between male and female registers: the women's language is the one that has survived. In this case, then, it was the men who were holding on to a disappearing language, the Mainland Carib that their ancestors had brought to the island.[36] Incidentally, the importance of food culture is signalled in the preponderance of food terms among the mainland words that the men of Breton's time had retained. They are still noticeable among a couple of dozen words in modern Island-Carib, as spoken in Belize, that are traceable to the old Mainland Carib of five hundred years ago: *maina* 'garden', now meaning 'manioc field', *ouloui* 'cashew', *ouekou* 'cassava beer', *areba* 'cassava bread'.

The history of Cornish, the lost Celtic language of Cornwall, provides another case in which men, rather than women, held on longest to a disappearing language. It is true, on the one hand, that in the eighteenth century a group of old women of Mousehole in Cornwall were the very last people who spoke Cornish habitually with one another. So, when Dorothy Jeffrey or 'Dolly Pentreath', the last survivor of them, died in 1777, the Cornish language might be thought to have died with her. Logical enough, and most reference books give it as a fact. And yet the very last speaker who learnt some Cornish in early childhood was not Dolly Pentreath or any other of the fishwives of Mousehole. It was John Davey of Zennor, who died in 1891. He learnt Cornish from his grandfather (who also must have lived some years after Dolly Pentreath's death, unknown to any antiquarian of that period).[37] So the last known speaker of Cornish was a man, and it was from a male relative that he learnt the language; and in fact we can find plenty of cases to set against Cicero's observation, cases where the last recorded use of a soon-to-be-forgotten language is among men, and where women are the first to change.

A recent survey at Valkenswaard, near Eindhoven in the Netherlands, found that women consistently used (or admitted to using) fewer dialect words than men: their speech was closer to standard Dutch. When it was a question of dialect words used in baby talk and relating to children's play, the difference between men and women was still greater: women used the old local words even less. In Brittany, it is reported, Breton is more used among men in cafés and in the fields; in bars and in other places where both sexes congregate, French has made more rapid inroads.

It is surprising and interesting that a similar observation has recently been made concerning the so-called 'Pennsylvania German' or 'Pennsylvania Dutch' spoken by Amish and other Anabaptist religious groups in their numerous scattered settlements in North America. The Amish have held on to their ancestral language (in origin a dialect of Low German) much longer than most other immigrant peoples in the United States and Canada, for the obvious reason that their religious beliefs led them to retain a traditional, agricultural lifestyle and to restrict their interaction with outsiders. Amish tend to learn Pennsyl-vania German as their mother tongue and pick up English as soon as they go to school if not before (English has been their school language for nearly a century).

But this is changing. Their families are larger and healthier than ever, and not all can work on the farm. Young men – and single young women too – go out to work. They nearly always find that English is the language of work, and young women, serving in stores and restaurants, do more of the talking. And it is the young women who are leading the linguistic changes. Silke van Ness explored the process of a grammatical change in the Amish dialect of Ohio: she found that the gender rules were disappearing, and they were disappearing from young women's speech first of all. For the older *Mir warre in mei Aunt ihre Garde* 'We were in my aunt's garden' the young women now say *Mir warre in mei Aunt sei Garde. Ihre*, which once marked a feminine possessor, has been replaced by *sei* to cover both genders.[38] Both versions, of course, include the English loanword *Aunt*; these days, Pennsylvania German contains a great many English words and phrases. And meanwhile a still more far-reaching change – the final shift, from Pennsylvania German to English as family language – is not inconceivable for some Amish.[39] Perhaps this change, too, will be led by the young women.

Maybe it is truer now than it would have been in the past to say that men are the last speakers of a disappearing language, and that they use it at work in traditional trades.[40] This trend is ominous as regards the continued use of all the local dialects of Europe – because fewer and fewer young men take up traditional work and learn it by working with their fathers. And meanwhile those languages' strong-hold in the family has fallen. Television is now an honoured member of every family: it provides scenes of prosperous daily life that everyone wants to emulate, and television does not speak a local dialect.

LANGUAGE AND COMMUNITY

Majority and minority attitudes

From the extended case study in Chapter 2, the growth of Latin and the disappearance of the ancient languages of Europe, we gained a much-needed perspective. Since that whole history is known from beginning to end, we can see how language shift happens in large empires from the first spread of the new language to the last words of the old. But we cannot learn from that particular example what minority language speakers were thinking as they made the shift in their own families from one language to another, or what majority language speakers were thinking as they encountered minority speakers. If we are to understand the rapidity of language change in the contemporary world, we need to know this too. We must look at more recent episodes of language shift, and some of them will be much nearer home: in fact we can begin with language shift in Britain. To set the scene, here is an outline of the linguistic situation in 731, as described by the first English historian: 'At the present time there are in Britain, in harmony with the Five Books of the Divine Law, five of the languages of the nations . . . the Angles, the British, the Scots, the Picts and the Latins. Through contemplation of the scriptures, Latin has become the common property of all the others.'[1]

This succinct statement by Bede needs a little enlargement. The Anglo-Saxon occupation of the British lowlands had been neither rapid nor complete. The Germanic settlers (Bede calls them 'Angles', taking a northern point of view: Angles held Northumbria) faltered in their westward movement as they reached the high hills. The Celtic language that was already spoken in the west remained (Bede calls it 'British').

Although he does not say so it was probably already divisible into three dialects, Cornish of the southwest, Welsh of Wales, and an almost unrecorded northern relative of Welsh that was once spoken in Cumberland ('land of the *Cymry*'), Lancashire, Elmet and Strathclyde: this third dialect can be called Cumbrian. There were also two other Celtic languages spoken in Britain, both quite distinct from 'British'. The language of the Scottish Highlands at that time was Pictish, which like Cumbrian is almost unrecorded: some modern scholars believe it was a Celtic language, others think that it was here before any Celts, or indeed any speakers of Indo-European languages, came to Britain. The language of Ireland, Irish or Gaelic, was in Bede's time newly to be heard in western Scotland, as the speech of the rulers of Dalriada, whose heartland was Argyll (Bede calls them 'Scots').

Latin, the language of culture in Bede's time, retained this position for many centuries – it is not quite dead even now, as anyone will realize who counts the Latin mottoes to be found inscribed on public buildings and monuments. What became of the other four languages of the island?

Cornwall was an independent kingdom until conquered by Athelstan, king of Wessex, in 936. Even after that date it was initially regarded as a 'British province' rather than a part of Wessex. But Cornwall's autonomy soon melted away under English bishops and Norman earls. For many centuries the Cornish peninsula was a poor and isolated region, where local people made their living in local ways – by mining for tin, by fishing and sometimes by wrecking. It is probably because Cornwall was a backwater that the Cornish language survived so long: in fact the longest surviving work of Cornish literature is a cycle of religious plays of the fifteenth century, the *Ordinalia*. But by the end of the following century it was noted by travellers that almost all speakers of Cornish were bilingual. That observation seems quite definitely to signal the beginning of the end for Cornish. As we have seen, the title of the 'last speaker of Cornish' is sometimes given to Dorothy Jeffrey or 'Dolly Pentreath' of Mousehole, who died in 1777, and sometimes to John Davey of Zennor, who died in 1891. At any rate, by the end of the eighteenth century it had become difficult for travellers and local historians to find anyone who knew any Cornish at all.[2]

The story of Pictish and of Cumbrian is probably similar to that of Cornish, if we only knew it. In fact we know practically nothing of these languages or of their disappearance. Although the Scots had brought their Gaelic language to the west of Scotland, their own Scottish kingdom – when it emerged from incessant warfare between Northumbrians, English of the south, Cumbrians of Strathclyde, Scots, Picts and Vikings – had as its ruling language the English of Northumbria, the language that we now call Scots. So it was apparently to Scots English, rather than to Scottish Gaelic, that the Cumbrian language of Strathclyde and the mysterious Pictish of central and northeastern Scotland eventually gave way. In any case, the two invading languages survived and the two older-established languages disappeared. But Scottish Gaelic, with 80,000 living speakers, very few of them monolingual, is now on the defensive as English gains ground.

Welsh was the language of independent principalities until the English conquered the last of them, Gwynedd, in 1282. From that point onwards Wales was ruled in English, yet down to the mid-twentieth century there were many monolingual Welsh speakers. Even the towns of northern and central Wales were largely Welsh-speaking, and the rural population seldom if ever needed to travel beyond them.

But now there are very few monolingual Welsh speakers still living, and soon there will be none. Practically all the 500,000 people who speak Welsh also speak English.

And so Gaelic and Welsh, though still spoken by large numbers, have now reached the status of a regional minority language whose speakers are almost all bilingual. This is the position that was noted for Cornish about 1600. From there, Cornish sank to extinction in something over two centuries. Will the fate of Gaelic and Welsh be the same?

Attitudes in the surrounding majority culture or national culture are not crucial in themselves. As a general rule, before the twentieth century, people speaking majority languages – if they thought about the matter at all – thought that speakers of minority languages such as Welsh were simply unlucky, or backward, or (as we would say now) under-developed. Such people, they thought, were simply in need of encouragement to abandon their language and their old-fashioned ways as soon as possible. In other words, attitudes were, nearly always, unfavourable to minority languages but benign (or, at worst, patronizing) to their speakers.

Sometimes we have to guess what majority views were. Sometimes they are set out clearly for us to read. We have no doubt at all what Spanish missionaries, in sixteenth-century central America, thought of the Nahuatl (Aztec) language. The fact that we can now read classical Aztec poetry and rhetorical prose is due almost entirely to the work of these missionaries. They gathered and recorded oral texts and sponsored the making of hieroglyphic manuscripts. They did so because these languages, and the mythology and philosophy encoded in them, were the work of the Devil, and they were intelligent enough to realize that they and their colleagues would need to understand the Devil's works in Nahuatl in order to replace them with something better. The something better might be delivered in Nahuatl – which the missionaries were encouraged to learn – or it might, sooner or later, be accompanied by a spread of the knowledge of Spanish. Father Bernardino de Sahagún, the greatest of all these investigators, wrote as follows in his introduction to the *Cantares Mexicanos*, 'Mexican Songs'.

Costumbre muy antigua es de nuestro adversario el diablo buscar escondrijos para hacer sus negocios . . . Conforme a esto, este nuestro enemigo en esta tierra plantó un bosque o arcabuco, lleno de muy espesas breñas, para hacer sus negocios desde él y para esconderse en él, para no ser hallado, como hacen las bestias fieras y las muy ponzoñosas serpientes. Este bosque o arcabuco breñoso son los cantares que en esta tierra él urdió que se hiciesen y usasen en su servicio . . . los cuales llevan tanto artificio, que dicen lo que quieren y pregonan lo que él manda . . . sin poderse entender lo que en ellos se trata, más de aquellos que son naturales y aconstumbrados a este lenguaje, de manera que seguramente se canta todo lo que él quiere, sea guerra o paz, loor suyo o contumelia de Jesucristo, sin que de los demás se pueda entender.

It is a very ancient practice of our adversary the Devil to seek out hiding places where he can do his business . . . Accordingly this enemy of ours has planted in Mexico a forest or jungle full of dense thickets from which he can do business and where he can hide and not be found, just like a wild beast or venomous snake. These forests and jungles are the songs that by his

arrangement the people of this country compose and perform in his service
. . . which are so cleverly made that they can say whatever they like and preach
whatever he commands . . . and what is said in them can only be understood
by natives who are familiar with the language. Thus they can sing with
impunity everything that he desires, be it peace or war, praise of himself or
insult to Jesus Christ, and no one else can understand them.[3]

Such attitudes had good as well as bad effects on minority cultures,
and it is the effects that matter here.

Throughout his work on his twelve-volume manuscript encyclopae-
dia of Aztec culture, all in Nahuatl, Father Sahagún may have never
felt for a moment that there was anything of positive value in the texts
he was compiling. Certainly he never said that there was. Still, for
whatever reasons, he went on compiling them. His Nahuatl informants
sometimes had quite different views: still, they went on working with
him, and we benefit today from the result of their joint labours.

In just the same way, Francisco de Avila, in South America, sponsored the compilation of a manuscript of Quechua mythology and
history, the book of *Huarochiri*, compiled in 1598. He, too, had no
doubt that the material he recorded was the work of the Devil. He
ordered the record to be made because 'diabolical practices are best
combatted by those who are fully informed of them'. His Quechua
amanuensis (known only as 'Tomás') was bold enough to set out on
the first page of the manuscript a much better justification for the work
they did together.

Runa Yno ñiscap Machoncuna ñaupa pacha quillcacta yachanman carca,
chayca hinantin causascancunapas manam canancamapas chincaycuc canman, himanam Viracochapas sinchi cascanpas canancama ricurin, hinatacmi
canman. Chayhina captinpas canancama mana quillcasca captinpas caypim
churani cay huc yayayuc Guarocherí ñiscap Machoncunap causascanta, yma
ffeenioccha carcan, yma yñach canancamapas causan, chay chaycunacta . . .

If the Ancients of the people called Indians [*Yno*] had known writing, then all
the traditions of their former life, now doomed to fade away, would have
been preserved. They would have shared the fortune of the Spaniards [*Viraco-
cha*] whose traditions and past prowess are on record. Since it is not so, I shall

write down the traditions of the Ancients of the land called Huarochirí, into whom one father breathed life: their faith and their customs as they are remembered to this day . . .'[4]

In the nineteenth century similar attitudes came, if not for the first time then more explicitly than ever before, to be conjoined with nationalism and racism. Here is the thoughtful Matthew Arnold, poet and educator, on the Celtic minorities of Britain.

I must say I quite share the opinion of my brother Saxons as to the practical inconvenience of perpetuating the speaking of Welsh. It may cause a moment's distress to one's imagination when one hears that the last Cornwall peasant who spoke the old tongue of Cornwall is dead; but, no doubt, Cornwall is the better for adopting English, and for becoming more thoroughly one with the rest of the country. The fusion of all the inhabitants of these islands into one homogeneous, English-speaking whole, the breaking down of barriers between us, the swallowing up of separate provincial nationalities, is . . . a necessity of what is called modern civilisation . . . the change must come, and its accomplishment is a mere affair of time. The sooner the Welsh language disappears as an instrument of the practical, political, social life of Wales, the better; the better for England, the better for Wales itself. Traders and tourists do excellent service by pushing the English wedge farther and farther into the heart of the principality; Ministers of Education, by hammering it harder and harder into the elementary schools. . . . For all modern purposes, I repeat, let us all as soon as possible be one people; let the Welshman speak English, and, if he is an author, let him write English.

This, to us, reads harshly, even though Arnold went on to encourage the study of Welsh music and literature. To some of his contemporaries, such as the writer of a *Times* leader, his views seemed 'sentimental', not to say weak. *The Times*, claiming to speak for 'strong sense and sturdy morality', preferred to say that 'the Welsh language is the curse of Wales . . . it is monstrous folly to encourage them in a loving fondness for their old language . . . the intelligence and music of Europe have come mainly from Teutonic sources . . . The sooner all Welsh specialities disappear from the face of the earth the better.'[5]

The attitudes, even now, had little influence in themselves. The big difference between sixteenth-century Mexico and Peru, on the one hand, and nineteenth-century Britain on the other, was that nineteenth-century governments were far more interventionist: attitudes were translated into practical administrative measures.

Look back at the unexpectedly violent metaphor used by Arnold in the quotation just given. This one sentence of his, focusing on nineteenth-century Wales, could supply a keynote for many of the stories to be told in this book. 'Traders and tourists do excellent service by pushing the English wedge farther and farther into the heart of the principality; Ministers of Education, by hammering it harder and harder into the elementary schools.' The first half of this is laissez-faire politics in the relatively prosperous Britain of the late nineteenth century; at the same time it is a premonition of what is now true almost all over the world. If business people and tourists have the freedom to go and to take their money wherever they want, they can be relied on to spread their language, because they will make people want to learn it. The second half of Arnold's sentence is quite different: here social change is being effected by administrative action. His brutal expression is no more brutal than the reality, which entailed the beating and ritual humiliation by teachers of children who spoke Welsh in school precincts.

The attitudes expressed by Sahagún, Avila, Arnold and the writer of the *Times* leader had not the slightest effect in themselves on the survival of Nahuatl, Quechua and Welsh. Their survival depended not on words but on deeds. In the case of Welsh, it did not matter to Welsh adults or children what was written in a *Times* leader, or what Matthew Arnold thought about their language. But what the teachers did certainly had an effect (and the teachers could draw on the views of Arnold and others for moral support). Only the most stubborn and self-sufficient of pupils were likely to put up determined resistance to repeated moral and physical abuse of that kind. Welsh was being driven out of one of its former strongholds, its informal use within a community – in this case, between children. What mattered to each child, and what will always matter to the survival of minority languages, were two highly practical questions. What will be gained by speaking the majority language? What will be lost by continuing to speak the minority language?

A footnote to those who think that terms such as 'brutality' and 'abuse' are exaggerated here: I find them used by Michael Krauss for similar cases in North America. There the speaking of native languages in school precincts was punished down to the 1950s (as it was in Australia even in the 1970s). 'That generation widely underwent what today would be considered brutal child abuse.'[6]

Let us quickly survey the various environments in which people use language, looking specifically at the speakers of a language such as Cornish or Welsh which becomes a minority language after conquest or some similar political upheaval.

What language will people use at work? That will depend whether the work goes on as it always did, whether it is directed or influenced by speakers of the national language, whether local special skills are important in it. For these reasons, Welsh hillfarmers and Cornish tin-miners were not among the first to change their language at work. It will also depend on whether people need to travel to find work. This usually means travelling to a city, which may well be outside the minority language area, and will in any case be a linguistically mixed environment. Cities are places where people of different linguistic backgrounds need to find a lingua franca, a common language in which they can communicate with one another. Not in every case, but in many cases, the national language is likely to be the best choice for communication among speakers of any other languages. So Welsh speakers, when they move to Cardiff or London, have no choice but to use English at least some of the time, even if they stick to Welsh among family and friends.

What language will people use to trade? Markets are multilingual places. But speakers of the national language are unlikely to trouble to learn the local language to do their shopping, so minority speakers, if they want to do business effectively, have to become bilingual. And this applies not just to urban shopkeepers but to farming people if they go to city markets. Welsh is to be heard at shops and markets in Cardiff, the Welsh capital – but even those who come there occasionally, to buy or sell, from a rural community where Welsh is still commonly spoken, are likely to have to use their English more than their Welsh when they visit Cardiff.

What language will be used at home? What language will parents teach their children? At the outset this will not be a difficult question. Only one language will come naturally – the language that the parents themselves learnt when they were children. However, as time passes and the community is becoming bilingual, the choice is no longer so clear-cut. It will depend to some extent on cultural identity, and it is partly because of the great strength of Welsh culture and national feeling through the seven centuries following the English conquest that the language has been retained by so many people till now. More than on any of these things, it will depend on parents' ambitions for their children. Are they to have the opportunity to move to the capital, to look for well-paid work, to study in the national language? Those opportunities might give them a higher status and greater freedom of choice. If those perceptions exist, parents may make the decision that their children should learn the national language first. And that is the decision that many Welsh parents are taking now, in spite of the language's newly raised profile and in spite of all the moral encourage-ment and practical educational provision and government money that support the choice of Welsh.

That is the decision that Cornish speakers were making, *en masse*, in the fifteenth and sixteenth centuries; and the long-term result was that Dorothy Jeffrey and her Mousehole neighbours, around 1770, were probably the last people in Cornwall who regularly spoke the Cornish language together.

Eventually, the decision to adopt a new language leads to the aban-donment of the old language – but not immediately. How long it is before that second step takes place varies a good deal. There must always be one generation that is reasonably bilingual. This is the generation of the parents who decide, for the first time, that their children shall learn the new language at home. To take that decision, the parents must themselves be able to speak it, as well as the language they spoke when they were children. But these parents will still speak the old minority language between themselves, and they therefore have to take a second decision – whether to teach their children this minority language as well. If they do, the children in turn will be faced with the same decision when they themselves marry and have children.

Bilingualism: how long can it last?

The main purpose of this chapter is to look more closely at bilingualism, and particularly at how long it can last, and at what causes it to end. Linguistically this has always been a matter of 'life and death', in that the end of bilingualism typically marks the disappearance of an old language. In our linguistic future it is a matter of life and death more than ever. Why? Because recent authors who try to be positive about the future of languages have often relied on the possibility of what they call 'stable bilingualism'. You may use your national language, or English, for various purposes, but you and your children and your great-great-grandchildren will go on speaking your local language to one another. So your local language will continue to exist.

To most of those in the twentieth century whose first language was English, bilingualism was a fairly unusual condition; indeed for many it was an unattainable one. It is quite difficult to become bilingual unless you have lived, preferably when you were young, in a community in which two languages are habitually in use. Few such people had done so. Britain, the United States, Australia and New Zealand are fundamentally monolingual (for most of their inhabitants) even if South Africa and Canada are not.

For many other people of the twentieth century, the opposite was the case. They lived in multilingual communities, and they could not have been monolingual if they tried. C. J. Daswani, to be quoted more fully on p. 119, asserts with equal simplicity and truth that 'every Indian adult is a bi- or multilingual speaker', having a practical knowledge of at least two languages: and that's a thousand million people, a sixth of the population of the world. Indians who go to school learn three languages at least, and even those who escaped school all needed a knowledge of more than one language to get by. Indeed, those least likely to attend school regularly are most likely to need multilingual skills.

India is not unusual here. According to R. M. W. Dixon, speaking of Australia in recent times, 'many Aborigines are gifted linguists and many, although not all, were multilingual, having reasonable proficiency in the languages of two or three neighbouring groups'.[7]

To take a couple of African examples, a recent survey in Tanzania concluded that 'although all the ethnic languages . . . are assumed to have developed as single languages serving specific ethnic groups, there is presently no true monolingual community in the country'.[8] Nigerians are likely to know three languages and very likely more. All Kenyans learn three languages at school. For people who live in countries such as these (and many others could be named) the step to becoming bilingual is not a big one. It happens naturally, and it happens in childhood. Schooling helps, but, as already observed for India, those who don't go to school are just as likely to become multilingual. In Europe, many gypsies, never mind their indifferent school attendance record, are expert linguists.

The impulse to retain a traditional community language, if effective over a long period, will have more specific and identifiable origins than the linguistic tension within families, or the special aptitudes of individuals, that we have looked at so far. We shall look at two such cases – those of Romani, one of the gypsy languages, and Yiddish, one of the traditional languages of the Jews – because we need to know the answer to the following question: are the social conditions which led to very long-term bilingualism among gypsy and Jewish communities, and so led to the survival of these two languages, likely to arise frequently in the future? If not, we can expect no long-term bilingualism, and more rapid language loss.

Romani, language of the gypsies of Europe, is in origin an Indo-Aryan language, said by some linguists to be closer to Panjabi than to any other. This detail is disputed: Romani has interacted so extensively with the languages among which it has been spoken that the evidence is not very easy to pick out. The first Romani publication I ever encountered, the 1970s newspaper *Romano Drom* 'The Romani Way', bears sufficient evidence of this in its title: the names Roma, Romani had been bestowed on the language when its speakers spread out of the late Byzantine ('Roman') Empire towards western Europe. *Drom* is a typical Balkan word, traceable to classical Greek (*dromos* 'track', racetrack') but also found in Romanian (*drum* 'road'). Both words tell something of the history of Romani; neither goes back to the distant Indian origins of the language.

The gypsies, the speakers of Romani, actually reached the Byzantine

Empire at the beginning of the fourteenth century. In Constantinople a usually sober historian, whose eyes were otherwise always fixed on the court and the army, allowed himself on this occasion a glance at the fairground. The arrival of the gypsies, their acrobatic shows, their dance and music are described observantly and sympathetically by Nicephorus Gregoras. He mistakenly traces their origin to Egypt, as so many others have done (the English word *gypsy* originated as *Egyptian*), but, uniquely and accurately, Nicephorus is able to record their passage through Persia, Armenia and other Near Eastern regions on their way to Constantinople, observing that they continued westwards and reached Spain not very long afterwards.[9] They are first heard of in Paris a century later, in 1427. Again, the event is recorded in some detail. Contemporaries were clearly bemused by this unusual migrant community which held on to its own highly distinctive beliefs and customs. In Paris the report comes from an anonymous writer known only as the 'Bourgeois de Paris', whose even-handed narrative manages to make clear how it was that gypsies aroused both fascination and mistrust in some of those they encountered.

On the Sunday after mid-August, the 17th August of the said year 1427, there came to Paris twelve penitents (so they said), a duke, a count and twelve men on horseback, who said they were very good Christians and came from Lower Egypt . . . On the day of the Beheading of Saint John the Baptist the whole community arrived . . . Their children were truly more dexterous, both boys and girls, than anyone else. Most of them, nearly all of them, had both ears pierced, and in each ear a silver ring, or two in one ear: they said that was a mark of respectability in their country. The men were very black, with curly hair, the women the ugliest and blackest to be seen . . . In their company were sorceresses who looked at peoples' hands and told them what had happened or would happen to them. They started quarrels in many marriages by saying, 'Look to your wife, cuckold!' or to a wife, 'Your husband has done you wrong!' What was worse, as they talked to people, by means of magic or other art or with the devil's help or their own dexterity they emptied people's purses, and put the devil in their purses, so it was said. In truth, I went there to talk to them three or four times, and I never found I had lost a penny . . . but these are the things that people everywhere were saying.[10]

These descriptions set the pattern for eight centuries, down to the present day, during which Romani speakers have never lived as a territorial people but have continually travelled among speakers of other languages. That many gypsies have retained a distinct language and way of life for such an astonishing length of time is evidence of the remarkable cohesion of their society. They have faced more repression than most other ethnic groups, some active hatred and cruelty, and several episodes of genocide. In the last two hundred years there have been signs that even Romani may not last for ever. In some countries, including England and Spain, the language is very little heard. In others, for example Romania, gypsies have been forced to settle. In nearly every country their traditional way of life is becoming more difficult to follow with each passing year.

Romani (like Pennsylvania Dutch) survived over long periods, and has continued to survive thus far, because of its speakers' exclusiveness. Their religious beliefs and social customs entailed a series of ritual practices and a lifestyle which made it difficult for them to mix fully with the surrounding community. Intermarriage has been limited. Children in each generation have been instructed in the rituals and in the language that had become more and more identified with them.

When it is used in this way a minority language may, little by little, become a secret language – one that outsiders are not expected ever to learn, one in which members of a distinct community conduct their private business with no fear of being understood by anyone else.

As a second example, take Yiddish. Its funeral rites have been long prepared, yet it has so far failed to die.

The roots of Yiddish can be traced to the Rhineland in the early Middle Ages (say the tenth century AD), where several towns and cities had Jewish trading communities with origins in Spain, southern France and northern Italy. From the Rhineland Jews gradually expanded eastwards across German-speaking territories. Whatever languages they had spoken on their arrival in Germany, German (the German of the tenth century) soon became their lingua franca.

There was mistrust and animosity between Jews and Christians,[11] but neither could manage without the other. Since Jews' community and religious ties were strong, they generally clustered in a single district in each town where they settled; since they kept in close touch with Jews elsewhere, and had religious rules limiting their interaction with non-Jewish neighbours, their German speech gradually became distinct from that of the surrounding population. And naturally it incorporated Hebrew and Aramaic and southern European words for concepts of Jewish religious practice and everyday life.

From the high Middle Ages until early modern times German speakers, both Christians and Jews, were spreading eastwards from Germany and Austria across eastern Europe, and eventually the numbers of both who were settled in cities, towns and villages surrounded by speakers of other languages became, collectively, very large indeed. Both tended to self-sufficiency in a community sense – in spite of the fact that both traded with their neighbours. Each group, the Christians and the Jews, looked towards their own co-religionists and to other speakers of their own language for cultural and moral support. The Christian Germans of this gradual migration were more locally based: they were farmers or miners or manufacturers. The Jewish Germans were traders, and had more need for long-distance contacts.

So it was that while the various dialects of the Christian German émigrés differed on the basis of their local origins, and continued to differentiate from that point, the speech of the Jewish Germans gradually became an identifiably separate language; therefore its usual modern name, Yiddish (in origin *Yidish* is simply the Yiddish equivalent of German *Jüdisch*), quite naturally identifies it as the 'Jewish language' as distinct from that of the Christians. Its difference came also from its special vocabulary and from the crucial point that when it was written down it was written in Hebrew script. In the past Jews quite generally used Hebrew script to write whatever language they were speaking, and this is the basis for identifying a number of other Jewish languages including Ladino (originally based on Spanish, now spoken in Istanbul and Morocco). There are specimens of Yiddish, or at any rate of German in Hebrew script, as early as the thirteenth century; many scholars for that reason date the separate existence of Yiddish as a language to the thirteenth century rather than earlier or later. By the sixteenth century, at any rate, it was being written and published. The first, ephemeral, periodical in Yiddish is dated as early as 1687. By the eighteenth century, Yiddish was the vehicle of a great literature.

By the early twentieth century the German and Yiddish diaspora numbered many millions. The Christian Germans were to some extent concentrated in German-speaking districts, including several large settlements in Transylvania and the relatively recent colony of German speakers on the middle Volga. There were a few areas, now in eastern Poland and Belarus, where Jews, too, had settled as farmers; but it is true of both religious groups, and particularly of the Jews, that they were almost randomly scattered across the map of eastern Europe and southern Russia. By now, however, a leap westwards had begun to complicate the picture. Both Christians and Jews in large numbers sought prosperity, along with freedom from oppressive governments and linguistic majorities, in the United States. Here too a proportion of the Christian German-speaking migrants became farmers, often clustering in large settlements such as that of the 'Pennsylvania Dutch', while nearly all the Jewish migrants settled in cities. Their numbers can be judged from the fact that in the 1920s the Yiddish press in the United States had a combined circulation of three-quarters of a million.

Yiddish was a language of a linguistically sophisticated people. Not all Jews were educated, but those Yiddish speakers who followed the traditional education all spoke at least four languages – Yiddish, their mother tongue or *mame-loshn*; Hebrew, the language of the scriptures and of religious ritual; Aramaic, the language of scholarship and the law; and, additionally, whatever language was spoken in the surrounding non-Jewish community, whether German, Polish, Russian, Hungarian or another. Many spoke more than one of these.

Already by the late eighteenth century the death of Yiddish was predicted by enlightened Jews. Indeed, it was looked forward to eagerly. It was the *zhargon* – yes, that was once almost a standard name for Yiddish – uncouth, ungrammatical and a marker of backwardness. 'Pure German', not this mixed language, was what intelligent Jews should be speaking. In Germany itself, where German was spoken all around, this did begin to happen: it is thought that by 1900 Yiddish was much less commonly spoken among Jews in Germany than it had been in 1800.

The late 1930s and early 1940s were – to focus on linguistic history – a catastrophic decade for German speech. In the racially inspired massacres of the early 1940s the Yiddish-speaking communities of eastern Europe and southern Russia almost ceased to exist: it has been estimated that 75 per cent of the Yiddish speakers in the world were killed in those events. As fortunes changed, in 1944 and after, the Christian German-speaking populations of the same regions were uprooted, the survivors generally fleeing to Germany. The Volga Germans were deported to Kazakhstan – whence many have finally made their way westwards; the Transylvania Germans have been gradually reduced in numbers by emigration under the pressure of Romanian nationalism and poverty. Under similar pressures, the Yiddish-speaking communities of Russia that were not reached by the German invasion in the early 1940s have since then gradually declined as their members have emigrated to Israel or elsewhere.

The dialects of the Christian Germans of eastern Europe are on their way to extinction, as the last survivors of the refugee generation are themselves approaching death. Their children naturally took to using the German that they heard spoken around them. The knowledge embedded in these dialects is – some of it – on record, in the big German dialect dictionaries and in a series of nostalgic and folkloric books and journals.

The fate of Yiddish is more complex. In Israel the language has always met with strong disapproval. 'The richness of Yiddish words – their emotional loadings, their innuendos, their diminutives, their endlessly nuanced connotations of collective experience – has been admired, envied and regretted by modern Hebraists faced by the comparative artificiality of Israeli Hebrew,' writes Joshua Fishman. Yet it is discouraged, not only by those who maintain the old view that it is a zhargon – with all the inferiority that that word implies – and by those who link language with politics and disapprove of its historical origin as a form of German, but also by those who see Yiddish as an ephemeral 'daughter of the earth', while Hebrew is the true and eternal 'daughter of heaven'. Thus in Israel, following the general pattern of migrant languages, Yiddish survives only one or two generations in each new immigrant family. By contrast, in the United States, Argentina and several other large centres of recent Jewish migration, Yiddish survives. It is especially favoured by orthodox Jews, who regard it as their proper everyday language: in this view the use of modern Hebrew in everyday life, as happens in Israel, is irreligious. But the orthodox Jews form a relatively small proportion of the total Jewish community of the United States. Thus Yiddish must be considered threatened, as are all the languages of migrants to the United States. Survival in this environment will be a new and harder test of the linguistic cohesion of Yiddish speakers.

If Yiddish disappears, at some time in the future, from everyday speech, it is one of those languages destined to live on in the borrowings of others. A whole school of writers have happily catalogued the Yiddish loans to be found in American English. There is Yiddish in German. There is Yiddish in modern Hebrew, too, as Fishman asserts with a plethora of references:

Even today . . . when all that Yiddish asks or can hope for in Israel is a fairly minimal symbolic nod, its echoes continue to reverberate in more poetic form in conjunction with memories of cadences lost, of songs and expressions borrowed but not acknowledged, of sensitivities denied, of laughter stifled and spontaneity yet to return.[12]

It is worth noting that L. L. Zamenhof (1859–1917), who had the idea of a universal second language – and devised Esperanto to fill that role – was a speaker and writer of Yiddish.[13] He therefore knew what people could achieve with an international language. He was able to judge in precisely what way a truly international language would have to differ from Yiddish if it were to succeed. He had been able to observe at first hand two crucial facts about Yiddish. It was useful and was actually used internationally for communication, with a range extending from southern Russia across Europe to North and South America – but knowledge and use of Yiddish was totally restricted to one ethnic and religious group. Non-Jewish speakers of other European languages would have found Yiddish easy to learn, much easier still if it had not been written in a strange script (in Hebrew script, that is), but the cultural context ensured that they did not want to learn it and in any case would not have found teachers. Both from outside and from inside, Yiddish was seen as the language of a closed community. Since outsiders never learnt it, it served this community in the handy role of a secret language. The same could be said of Romani.

Yiddish and Romani have unusual histories. However, to become the secret language of an exclusive group can happen to any language that is in the process of being superseded, and it does happen to many of them. The patois of central and southern France, unintelligible to Parisians, are handy for their speakers when they wish to be understood only by friends and neighbours. A linguist reported asking an informant to begin speaking patois to him. 'Why? Are too many ears listening to us?' she asked – as if this would have been her usual reason for switching to patois. Chuvash and Mari, minority languages of central Russia, have had the same type of use as almost-secret languages.

Bilingualism: limiting cases

With the help of the perspective supplied by Yiddish and Romani we can now look beyond, at certain cases in which bilingualism has a declining role: what may once have been a traditional local language is confined to limited use, as a secret or ritual language. Typically, it is no longer a complete language. Typically (like Gaulish, Etruscan and Lydian, last seen in restricted ritual uses in Roman times) it is on its way out.

Secret languages are particularly useful to those who live on the fringes of a majority way of life – and that applies to many minority groups. If the gypsies of Europe had not had a language of their own, a language very seldom learnt by any outsiders, perhaps they would have found it useful to invent one? In fact precisely this has happened with some other groups of 'travellers'. Irish tinkers – in Ireland, England, Scotland and the United States – traditionally confer in a private language known as Shelta, whose grammar is English but whose words are largely Irish, modified by reversal, rearrangement, substitution and addition of sounds, for example *dara* 'bread' reversed and modified from Irish *aran; lakeen* 'girl', from Irish *cailín* (the same word known in Irish English *colleen*). Its words come also from many other sources: *finif* 'five-pound note' from Yiddish *finf* 'five'; *macsti* 'cat' from Romani, which had borrowed the word from Serbo-Croat *macka*. Shelta was a truly secret language: although it is, at the least, some centuries old it was completely unknown and unsuspected even by those who were familiar with gypsies and travellers, until the

American writer C. G. Leland happened to hear it spoken, near Bath, in 1876.

English has borrowed from Shelta, just as it has borrowed from most other languages with which it has come into contact. *Phoney*, an example already mentioned, came from Irish *fáinne*, which means 'ring'. The word was transmitted, probably by way of Shelta, to the Romani spoken in England, in which *foni* still means 'ring'. Jewellery is not always as valuable as it seems, hence the change of meaning to English *phoney*. *Gammy* (in *gammy leg* 'bad leg') comes from Irish (*cam* 'crooked') by way of Shelta; so does *monicker* 'written name', and this demonstrates how Shelta words are modified from their Irish originals. The Shelta form is *monik*, which is taken from Irish *ainm*, pronounced *anyem*, by deleting the first syllable, reversing the second and adding a meaningless suffix *-k*. *Roger* 'copulate' and *lush* 'alcoholic' also come from Shelta, but they cannot be traced to Irish and their ultimate origin is unknown. *Buffers*, in Shelta, are the non-travellers, to whom this language is better not revealed.[14]

English thieves and vagrants have had a private language of their own, known as cant, recorded from time to time ever since the sixteenth century and continually replenished with new words as the old ones passed into general currency. Cant has borrowed words from Shelta, from Romani, from Dutch and from many other sources. Many modern English words that are only used colloquially, such as *booze*, *cop*, *dope*, *doss*, *doxy*, *gob*, *grub* 'food', *kip*, and even some that are now standard English such as *cosh*, *queer*, arrived in English by way of cant. Cant also builds on the resources of English – in the use of rhyming slang, for example. A comparable current French *argot* draws on Arabic, on Romani, and (rhyming slang being unknown in French) on the Parisian system of rearranged words called *Verlan*. This supplies, for example, *meuf* and *neuchié* both meaning 'woman' (rearranged from *femme* 'woman' and *chienne* 'bitch') as well as *teushi* 'hashish' (rearranged from English *shit*).

But thieves' cant is a limited language – its vocabulary is and always was largely confined to the necessities of food, drink and shelter, and to the successes and failures of life outside the law. Cant, *argot*, the other thieves' jargons of Europe, and practically all other secret languages of the world, are alike in this crucial point: they are incomplete, relying on another language for grammar and for many common words. Such languages could never serve alone as anyone's mother tongue.

Some English gypsies who no longer speak Romani still use an English-Romani jargon when working: they know it as Posh 'n' posh ('Half and half': linguists sometimes call it Angloromani). Nowadays it is not a mother tongue learnt in infancy; it is generally used among men, and boys learn it when they begin to work with their fathers. Thus the language of a whole community shades into the secret language or trade jargon of a single occupation. Caló, spoken in Spain, is a mixture of Romani and Spanish comparable to Posh 'n' posh. There are other languages, derived from Romani or its cognates, spoken now or not long ago in Iran, Armenia, Greece, Norway and the Basque country. And there are plenty of other examples: the so-called Loshlekoydesh spoken by the Jewish cattle merchants of Alsace; the special Greek of the Sarakatsani of Macedonia; Rodiya, secret language of the untouchables in Ceylon; Abdal, secret language of musicians and tinkers in Turkey and central Asia; Adurgari, secret language of nomads in Afghanistan; Béarlagair na Saer, the 'language of the stonemasons', used at least until recently by craftsmen in Munster and consisting largely of invented or modified Irish words in a language with Irish-like grammar.[15]

A language of Swahili medicine men was reported in the 1960s. There has been a special ceremonial language, Zar, used in curing spirit possession in Ethiopia. Tin-miners of Malaya traditionally used a secret language in their work, a special form of Malay with different vocabulary, doing so – it was said – to avoid offending the spirits that guard the valuable ore. The men called Tirilones, a community of Mexican origin settled in El Paso, Texas, use a special language called Caló ('gypsy language'). Women do not speak it. It is not truly connected with Romani: Caló of El Paso is originally based on Spanish, but contains many words quite unfamiliar to speakers of Mexican Spanish, and many more words that are used in new and unfamiliar senses. Like cant and other English forms of slang, Caló adopts new words so frequently that it is continually difficult for outsiders.

A most unusual mixed language, Nihali, is spoken by a community of about 5,000 people living largely by raiding and theft on the borderlands of Maharashtra and Madhya Pradesh in India. The words of

Nihali are taken mainly from nearby Indo-Aryan and Dravidian languages – but other words are borrowed from Korku, the neighbouring hill language (belonging to the Munda group of Austroasiatic languages) in which many Nihali speakers are bilingual. So Nihali can be linked with three totally different language families – and yet it seems to have a basis different from all three of them, which means that technically it is a linguistic isolate. Perhaps not surprisingly, it serves its speakers very effectively as a secret language. Outsiders are discouraged from learning it.

Some secret languages, like Shelta and cant and *argot* and Germania, the thieves' language of Spain, are built up 'artificially', mainly out of the resources of an everyday language. Others, like Posh 'n' posh, are definitely the remains of an earlier complete language. In some of these latter cases, nothing else will now be found of the ancestral language. This is its last gasp. One of the most fascinating cases is that of Damin, a secret language spoken by the Lardil people on Mornington Island off the northern coast of Australia. Damin has a range of sounds that are simply not used in their everyday Lardil – or in any other Australian language for that matter. These sounds include click consonants, which are otherwise known nowhere else in the world except in the Khoisan languages of southern Africa, and in Xhosa and Zulu under Khoisan influence.[16]

Among the most interesting of the semi-secret languages of work is Callahuaya, spoken by about two thousand itinerant healers in Bolivia. It is sometimes wrongly said to be the 'secret language of the Incas'. In fact the private, family language of the Inca ruling family was Chimú, quite different from Callahuaya; Chimú is fully recorded, though it is now extinct. As to Callahuaya, its structure is largely identical with that of Quechua, its speakers' everyday language; but its vocabulary (said by one enthusiastic linguist to amount to 12,000 words, an unusually large number for a secret language) comes partly from the now-extinct Peruvian language Puquina. Long ago, even before the Incas, Puquina was a language of empire in Peru. There is no doubt that the tradition of specialist healers in the central Andes goes back a great many years: fifteen hundred years, some say.

The language is said by some investigators to be almost forgotten now. Joseph Bastien, an anthropologist who recently worked with the

Callahuaya, was unable to encourage any of his informants to speak it. He suggests several reasons for its apparent disappearance. Herbalists have moved to cities, where they are still in demand, but they now rarely travel in groups, so there is less opportunity to converse with colleagues, says Bastien. Some Callahuayas, he adds, do not want to be set off as a distinct ethnic group, preferring to be counted as Spanish-speaking Bolivians: the secrecy of the past has not helped them to establish the current respectability of their profession, which is under attack from Western-style doctors and pharmacists. There could be still another reason: secret languages are meant to be secret, and that means not giving them away to anthropologists who might publish them in books. However, some appear to have had better luck. Louis Girault, who worked for twelve years among the Callahuaya herbalists, was far more successful than Bastien in eliciting Callahuaya names for medicinal plants – but Girault, too, confirms that the language is falling out of use. The Callahuaya with whom he worked had taken a more or less conscious decision, a generation ago, to cease practising their traditional healing.

Among the major medicinal plants whose uses the Callahuaya-speaking herbalists may well have been the first to highlight are Peruvian pepper (Quechua *mulli*; Spanish *molle, arbol de la vida*) and, now of world importance, coca (Quechua *kuka*; Spanish *coca*), analgesic and stimulant, source of cocaine. Medicinally the most important to date has been Peruvian bark or 'fever tree' (Callahuaya *jillis kkallis*; Quechua *kina, kkallisaya*; Spanish *cascarilla*) whose bark – with that of related species – is the source of quinine, indispensable in the fight against malaria. There has been doubt whether this drug was known in pre-Columbian times, but a report as early as 1654 by Bernabé Cobo confirms that it was already in local use at that time. All in all, medicine would have been considerably poorer without the knowledge that has been transmitted from Callahuaya. There is still more that remains unrecorded and is on the way to being lost.[17]

In most of the cases where we know bilingualism to have lasted an unusually long time, we know that religious or ritual beliefs have been there in the background, keeping the minority community distinct. If each generation in turn grows up in the confidence that this community's beliefs and practices are necessary and desirable, and are in some definite way better than those of the majority, there is a good chance that the difference will continue. If the rituals are accompanied by, and expressed in, a special language, the language will continue too.

The limiting case is that in which the language is eventually no longer used *except* in ritual. This is actually very common. Latin, New Testament Greek, Old Church Slavonic, Ethiopic (Ge'ez) were all used daily in Christian ritual until late in the twentieth century, when there was a rapid change of fashion in many Christian churches. In spite of that change of fashion, in some circumstances they are all still used today. Until about the same period, the seventeenth-century English phraseology of the Book of Common Prayer (1662), itself heavily influenced by the Authorized (1611) translation of the Bible, which was in turn influenced by the Hebrew and Greek vocabulary and sentence structure of the original texts of the Bible, constituted a special language that was in daily ritual use among many English-speaking Christians. In fact this Biblical English was so sanctified by use that the *Book of Mormon*, additional holy book of a breakaway religion, first published as late as 1830, is written in a pastiche of Biblical English (though with tell-tale variations showing that it was no longer a language of everyday use).[18] The 'Revised Version', a reworking of the Authorized translation published in 1881–5, is in a similar pastiche of Biblical English.

Parallel examples are to be found in Asia of languages which were in everyday use long ago, whose only use or chief use now is to be repeated in religious ritual. One of the most famous is the Vedic language of the *Rgveda*, a great collection of religious lyrics in the oldest known form of the Sanskrit language. The textual form of these songs became a matter of such crucial importance in Hindu ritual that they were preserved with (so it appears) absolute accuracy in oral transmission for many centuries before being written down. For this reason their dating is uncertain, but it can hardly be much later than 1000 BC and may be considerably earlier. Three later collections, partly overlapping with the *Rgveda*, are in essentially the same language, which was evidently already sanctified: they include the *Samaveda*, the magical *Atharvaveda* and the ritual *Yajurveda*. Sanskrit in its later, classical form is also enshrined in many texts, both religious and secular, including the esoteric Tantric poems. Pali, a later offshoot of Sanskrit, originating in a spoken language of northern India of perhaps 200 BC or later, is the language in which the dialogues of the Buddha were codified and recorded in writing. Thus it became the classical language of the scriptures of southern Buddhism. Buddhism eventually disappeared from India, and Pali now is familiar not in India but in Sri Lanka and southeast Asia, among people most of whose mother tongues are quite unrelated to Pali. In Iran the scriptures of the *Avesta* are written in several distinct varieties of the Iranian language group. The oldest of them are in a language otherwise unrecorded, now called Avestan, probably of 500 BC; the latest are in the medieval language Pehlevi. Hindus listen to the recitation of Vedic poems and study Sanskrit commentaries on them. Southern Buddhists learn Pali, or at least learn to listen to it and to hear the dialogues translated; some also use Pali for international communication, as Latin has been used in the Catholic Church. Zoroastrians recite Avestan hymns, though in nearly every case they do so without learning the language. There are now very few of them in Iran; most adherents of this ancient religion are Indians, who understand the venerable texts that they are reciting through the medium of Gujarati translations. Vedic, classical Sanskrit, Pali and Avestan are all four of them two thousand years old or more, and have survived in use through all that time, among speakers of quite different mother tongues, thanks to bilingualism. In each case, probably, this bilingualism has gradually become more limited in its functions: nowadays relatively few believers, and in the case of the *Avesta* scarcely any, have full understanding of the texts they hear and recite.

There is still another group of examples, this time from communities whose traditional culture is mainly or entirely oral. In some of these, too, religious observances (especially the initiation of children into the adult world) are carried out in a different language, one that is otherwise unknown: a sacred and secret language whose memory, in the typical case, is preserved by priests to be transmitted in turn to each new cohort of initiates. To name four of them: La'bi and To exist only as initiation languages used among Gbaya, Mbum and other neighbouring peoples of northeastern Cameroon. Isikhwetha is an otherwise unknown language traditionally used among adolescent initiates of the Xhosa in South Africa. Bao-Goama is an initiation language among the Mõõre of inland West Africa. These and other secret languages – difficult to research as they are, carrying information of historical interest as they certainly do – are under immediate threat of disappearance. In more and more such communities, adolescents are no longer interested in undergoing traditional initiation.

Kpesi is said to have been the aboriginal language of the now Gã-speaking country of southern Ghana: its only existence nowadays is in in the songs performed at Kple religious festivals. It is said that Lisu priests, in southern Yunnan, had a secret religious language, and (so one anthropologist reported) a hieroglyphic script in which sacred texts were recorded. And among speakers of Kadazan, the major linguistic minority of Sabah (northeastern Borneo), priestesses called *bobohizan* communicate with the dead using what is known as the 'ancient Kadazan' language, with a vocabulary wholly distinct from that of the everyday language. It is a lifelong profession for which girls are traditionally selected at the age of about ten, after competitive testing on their ability to memorize the ritual chants in this otherwise unknown language. The anthropologist T. R. Williams adds drily that although rituals must be recommenced from the beginning whenever a wrong word is spoken, he could not discover that this had ever happened. The priestesses, he reports,

use a personal, or familiar, spirit as a medium in contacting supernatural forces and beings . . . A familiar spirit is acquired for life. It can be invoked only through use of the *kambaranun* root in performance of a specific ritual act. When possessed by her familiar spirit and speaking in its voice, [she] is known as 'one who speaks with the voices of the wind, sun, rain and stars.' The familiar spirit is believed to ascend and descend the long stock of the *kambaranun* root to the lower and upper halves of the universe in her search for disease givers or souls of the dead responsible for crises. The root is especially cultivated by female ritual specialists and is brought to life through a brief ritual, then hung to dry in house eaves. Before the root can be used in major ritual it must be 'given the power' through a lengthy formal ceremony. In this act several female ritual specialists participate in recitation of verse and magical acts.[19]

A comparison with these examples gives us a bit more insight into why it was, under the Roman Empire, that Gaulish, Etruscan and Lydian were all three last heard of in magical and religious ceremonial. Once a language has fallen into such limited use, it may no longer matter whether anyone, at least any human being, still understands it. That is exactly the case with Hawaiian, as we shall see later: except in one small community, its use is confined to ceremonies performed for tourists, who do not understand it.

Even in such examples as these, where the retention of an old language is particularly well motivated because of its necessity in ritual, it is not retained for ever. Jewish communities (to return to that example) have followed rituals and customs of an essentially similar kind for nearly two thousand years, and some of them were already ancient even then: and yet Yiddish, the oldest of the Jews' everyday languages now, has a history of no more than nine hundred years. The language spoken by the Jews at the time of their diaspora, in the first and second centuries AD, was Aramaic. This was retained by them as a spoken language for many centuries but it has long since lost that role. However, Aramaic survives in use as a Jewish language of liturgy and scholarship, a language that many learn; while Hebrew, language of the scriptures, continues to be heard daily in religious worship.

In the nineteenth century adventurous European scholars found Syriac Bibles and religious books in use in Iraq and also in south India. The Christian communities in Iraq still spoke a form of Syriac, though the language of their books, dating to the early centuries AD, was no longer clear to them. The St Thomas Christians of south India spoke Malayalam and could no longer read their Syriac books at all. In both these cases, since the books were still revered by believers who were no longer able to understand them, it seems likely that bilingualism of the kind described for Romani, Latin, Vedic, Pali and Avestan had lasted a long time in those communities – but had eventually disappeared.

Bilingualism: how quickly will it disappear?

So much for the languages that lasted. What of the languages that are quickly forgotten?

Let us take first the case of a minority community that migrates to another country or region not as conquerors but simply with the aim of settling there. There are plenty of examples of this in Britain and western Europe in the twentieth century, most of the migrants originating in former colonies in Africa and Asia. There are also many examples from the United States and elsewhere in the Americas, most of the nineteenth and twentieth century migrants having originated in various European countries. We can now add another example – the 'barbarians', mostly speaking a Germanic language, who took service in the Roman armies in the third and fourth centuries AD.

In modern times, such communities have quite generally been observed to make a complete change of language within three generations. The migrants themselves, assuming they are adults when they move and are not skilled linguists, may never learn to speak the new language with full fluency. Typically, even thirty or forty years in a new country will not be enough to eradicate a strong 'foreign accent' and to get the speech patterns right. Their children will therefore necessarily be brought up to speak the old language, at home, but will also learn the new language from their parents' use of it, from neighbours' children and at school, with the result that they will eventually be fully bilingual. Typically, many will marry outside the migrant community. When they in turn have children, those children will grow up speaking the new language. Already a world away from the life that their grandparents led, they will generally not be taught the old language. No one will see any reason why they should learn it, unless they themselves feel some close sympathy with their older relatives (as a few will) and make the effort to understand them.

That is the general rule, but cases vary. Things will go even faster if the original migrants married into the new community. In that case the children of that first generation are likely to be brought up monolingual or at the most semi-bilingual, able to understand partially the language of the parent who is a migrant but not to speak it, since there will have been no reason ever to do so.

It will be interesting to see in the future whether the timescale of change may be adjusted in the opposite direction – whether change may be slowed down – as a function simply of the relative sizes of linguistic communities. If the question interests you, now is the time to research it. The Spanish speakers from Mexico and further south, now settling in the United States in huge numbers, may possibly be slower to abandon their Spanish than would have been the case if their numbers were smaller. My initial hypothesis, ready to be shot down by real evidence, is that size hardly ever matters. It is a matter of the coherence and exclusiveness of the linguistic community. The question is simply whether successive generations, who will successively decide this question for themselves, see good reasons to stay apart from the mainstream. We return to the Spanish speakers of the United States in Chapter 4, when exploring the purposes of the Official English pressure group.

Even with strong religious reasons to maintain their identity, and even when there is little overt pressure from the majority to conform, minority groups may shift to the new language just as quickly. This has been observed in the case of the Armenians of Austria. They are a long-established minority in Vienna, and have been widespread in other cities of the old Austrian Empire. Their first appearance in Austria has been traced to the raising of the Turkish siege of Vienna in 1688, after which Armenian merchants, already widely settled in Turkish cities, began to shift westwards in search of new markets. Suceava, now at the northeastern tip of Romania, was an Armenian centre (close to the Yiddish metropolis of Chernovtsy) which fell to Austria in the late eighteenth century and from which Armenians continued to spread across the Empire. They were soon to be recognized as a religious minority, and retain this official status in the modern Austrian republic: there are officially about 2,500 members of the Armenian minority in Vienna.

The community there has continued to receive new influxes of migrants and refugees up to the present day. They worship at the Armenian church and maintain community links, but there is no long-term tradition of Armenian speech. It seems that new arrivals typically speak only Armenian, or Armenian and another Near Eastern language. Their children speak Armenian and German, in most cases as competent bilinguals. Those of the third generation speak German alone.[20]

It might be argued that the change was less rapid in the past. We could argue from the notable Armenian publishing activities of the Mekhitarist community in Vienna that there was a long-standing and stable community of Armenian speakers there in the nineteenth century. But such evidence alone does not prove it; some Armenian printing was aimed at Armenian readers and scholars worldwide, some at the first and second generations of migrants – at the numerous people, then as now, who arrived speaking no German and whose grandchildren would speak no Armenian.

Multilingual policies and their results

Can government policies make a difference to the long term continuation of bilingualism – and in that way promote the survival of minority languages? It's a crucial issue: these days a lot of money is being spent on multilingualism, and it would be useful to know whether it's well spent. A few examples from different modern contexts will help us decide.

We shall see in Chapter 4 that education is extremely effective and powerful in advancing use of the majority language as against those of minorities. Irish evidence suggests that it is to be a one-way process. Education policy, in itself, cannot reverse the trend and increase the use of a minority language.

In Ireland the achievement of autonomy (the 'Irish Free State') in 1922 led to immediate action in support of education in Irish. This was the historic national language, but its use had been in decline for three centuries, since the defeat of the native Irish aristocracy in 1601 and the subsequent rapid spread of English colonial settlements. Thus from the seventeenth century onwards the administration of Ireland was conducted in English exclusively – and this naturally conferred high status on English and low status on Irish. To speak English became the only route to self-improvement. In accordance with the usual nineteenth-century trend the national school system, introduced in 1830, used English as the medium of teaching, with the expressed aim of turning the 'lower classes' of Ireland into English speakers. By 1911, according to the census of that year, only 17 per cent of the population (just over half a million people) spoke Irish, but probably most of these had learnt it as a mother tongue and spoke it fluently.[21]

The Irish Government in 1922 made it compulsory for teachers to learn Irish, and ruled that all schools where teachers were already competent in Irish must offer at least an hour of teaching of Irish each day. Additional measures gradually came into effect to increase the number of schools in which Irish was the main language of education. The most noticeable point is that the training and recruitment of teachers heavily favoured those who were Irish-speaking. Residential preparatory high schools, admitting only students who were native or fluent speakers of Irish, were established specifically to feed the teacher-training colleges; then, in the training colleges for primary school teachers, Irish became the medium of instruction soon after 1930 and remained so until about 1960. The result was that between 1930 and 1960 about a third of new teachers were native or fluent speakers of Irish. This was as much as three times the proportion of Irish speakers in the general population: it was a very significant form of linguistic discrimination.

In a separate area of policy, districts were identified in the west of Ireland where Irish was still currently used as the everyday language for most purposes. These districts, collectively called the Gaeltacht, were to be bolstered economically and culturally. Civil servants who worked there must already be, or must become, Irish-speaking.

Well, some things have changed. The profile of Irish has effectively been raised. It is accepted as a national language, in principle equal with English or even higher in status than English. Irish loanwords are heard not only in the English of Ireland but also (*taoiseach* 'prime minister', *Dáil* 'Parliament', *garda* 'police') in international English. Irish, and the distinctive Irish script, can be seen on signboards and signposts throughout the country. A million people know some Irish (they include all teachers and many other government employees), and that is more than twice as many as claimed to speak the language in 1922.

But overall the results have fallen far short of those that were at first intended. Policy-makers originally hoped that by the 1930s, or the 1940s at the latest, the majority of all education in Ireland would be conducted in Irish. That never happened. They hoped the proportion of native Irish speakers in the population would increase: it declined from perhaps 15 per cent in 1922 to an estimated 3 per cent in 1981. They hoped that the Gaeltacht would maintain its linguistic homogeneity. It has not. Economic development has, quite predictably, eventually diluted it, because managers and business people, arriving from elsewhere in the country, speak only English, and this means that English becomes the language of the workplace. They hoped that the Gaeltacht would not shrink, but probably only a third of the districts classified as Gaeltacht in 1922 would meet the same criteria today. Even in that small area, with a population of perhaps 20,000 Irish speakers, it is said that the majority of parents are now bringing up their children to speak English, not Irish, as mother tongue. In spite of government-assisted development, people in the Gaeltacht are in a backwater. Many of them are aware of it, and they want something different for their children.

Ireland, from 1922, has been an example of a kind of linguistic policy that is gradually spreading in the modern world, a policy in which more than one language is privileged. It is one possible answer to the questions that arise in nearly every country in the modern world. In what language are official and government matters to be dealt with? What is to happen when a citizen speaks a different language?

More than a century earlier the language question had for the first time been explicitly faced and resolved in Switzerland. For centuries this had been a loose federation of cantons, each proudly autonomous, the majority German-speaking but with some French and fewer Italian. Switzerland briefly toyed with centralization at the time of the French Revolution, but this Helvetian Republic (1798–1803) had differed constitutionally from its French model in one significant way. France set itself up as a monolingual state; in Switzerland, all three languages were assured of constitutional equality. The modern Swiss Federation, established in 1848, marked a final return to cantonal autonomy and retained the feature of national linguistic equality. In the 1980 census 74 per cent of citizens were German-speaking, 20 per cent French-speaking, 4 per cent Italian-speaking. The federal government and courts operate in all the three languages; the cantons decide their own language policies, and in most of them children must be educated in the single local language.[22]

Switzerland has had its linguistic problems. For a long time, French-speaking civil servants were unable to have their children locally educated in French, because the federal capital, Bern, is in a German-speaking canton. A continuing problem, though it rouses no conflict, is the decline of the fourth local language in Switzerland, Romansch, which has about 40,000 speakers, 1 per cent of the Swiss population. It is spoken in the high valleys of Graubünden. Although in 1938 it was given the status of 'national language' (which meant that it was recognized for certain purposes but was not an 'official language' of the Federation) Romansch continues to fall in number of speakers. As migration of non-Romansch speakers into the valleys speeds up, and as more Romansch speakers work in the tourist industry or move to the cities, the decline is becoming terminal: very few children are now being brought up to speak Romansch. Thus Romansch has been unable to benefit fully even from the favourable Swiss linguistic environment. But the three-way balance among German, French and Italian does work for Switzerland, bolstered by the fact that all three official languages are more than just that: they are also languages of major cultures, languages which there are many reasons for wanting to know.

Let us take two cases where the balance between nation and language has been particularly hard to strike. Canada and Belgium are both of them fairly new countries. Canada originated as a British colony and reached the status of a practically independent democracy in 1867. Belgium, formerly a place of shifting frontiers and allegiances, became an independent kingdom, permanently separated from neighbouring states, in 1830. Both were set up under conditions in which one language initially ruled: in the British Empire this position was held by English, in Belgium the language of court and government was at first French. In neither case did this position hold permanently: both countries had well-established communities speaking a second language, and these communities insisted on equal treatment.

In Canada's case, the British had fought to rule the former French territory that we know as Quebec. Victorious in 1759, they found themselves rulers of a well-established settlement of French-speaking colonists and their descendants, occupying all the more temperate parts of Quebec and overlapping significantly into southern Ontario. There were also French speakers in smaller numbers to east and west of this solid block. Through the nineteenth century the French speakers of Canada, relatively disadvantaged because they did not speak the language of government, shared equally with other Canadians the larger disadvantage of being ruled from across the Atlantic. When Canada gained independence (more or less) in 1867, an attempt was made at linguistic evenhandedness: English was protected in Quebec, French in the other provinces, and Canada's national diglossia was built into the constitution. For all that, the unfavourable position of the French speakers – a minority nationally and in Ontario; a large majority in Quebec – gradually stood out more starkly. Communities of French speakers in all the rest of Canada met with clear disadvantages, and were tending to shift to English; Montreal, the big city of Quebec, was a focus for English-speaking migrants from elsewhere in Canada and from abroad, and this immigration was continually nibbling away the French-speaking majority even in Quebec. The result was unending linguistic agitation on the part of French-speaking Canadians. In constitutional terms, they have largely won the day. Nationally they have reinforced their equality: the federal government and legal system are punctiliously bilingual, and all official documents are in both languages. New Brunswick and Ontario, both of which have long-established French communities bordering on Quebec, make generous provision for French: New Brunswick is officially bilingual. Meanwhile in Quebec, which retains a high majority of French-speaking voters and is thus guaranteed a provincial government sympathetic to French, the priority of French over English has been gradually asserted. A major landmark in this process was the 'Charter of the French Language', enacted in 1977, whose effect was to make French the language of work. Those looking for a new job, or for promotion, had to be able to speak French. An even more visible landmark was the legislation banning English from public signs in Quebec – a clear assertion that English-speakers in Canada were 'not equal'.

If you draw up the balance sheet, French is perhaps officially more favoured than English in Canada. A backlash against this perceived imbalance has led some other provinces to refuse all but the minimum linguistic rights to their own French communities. And somehow the proportion of French speakers in Canada continues to decline: people from Quebec will turn to English if they move away from the province, while new immigrants to Canada, whatever their original mother tongue, nearly all opt for English.

Belgium has had longer than Canada to work out its linguistic conflicts, and they are still bitter enough. When the country was established, French was the natural international language of governments, courts and high culture throughout Europe. Since in addition it was the native speech of nearly half the population of Belgium, it no doubt appeared to early decision-makers the country's obvious choice as national language. Admittedly there were very few bilinguals (the actual proportions were 42 per cent speaking only French, 50 per cent speaking only Dutch, 7 per cent bilingual, and 1 per cent near the eastern border speaking Low German). Thus fewer than half the population spoke the national language. But many of the bilinguals formed the upper class of the Dutch-speaking north, and they were a high proportion of the northerners who qualified to vote: being themselves lucky enough to participate in French education and culture, they had for themselves no reason to object to the choice of French as the only official language.

It was not so easy. The Dutch-speaking community – initially its middle-class element – became aware, fairly early, that it was being marginalized. It was possible to observe Dutch-speaking government in action across the country's northern border. But in Belgium you had to speak French to get anywhere. Brussels, the national capital, though originally Dutch-speaking and in a Dutch-speaking region, was rapidly becoming Frenchified, as employment opportunities went to French-speaking newcomers from the south.

So the initial authoritarian decision, to make French the official language, rapidly led to a swell of protest. As a first response, each village and town was given the local choice to have Dutch or French as its official language. In retrospect this was a bad solution, because at a higher level the languages were not truly equal: French opened more doors. An imaginary line across the country from west to east, passing just south of Brussels, dividing towns and villages that were Dutch-speaking from those that were French-speaking, was henceforth to have crucial political significance. As Brussels grew, official French spread from one outlying town to the next by local majority decision. Those elsewhere who wanted their children to do well were best advised to adopt French; those who saw no reason to change found that French was spreading across the local map. The protests continued, and in spite of various compromises they still continue. Much more slowly – because Brussels and the bureaucracy were preponderantly French-speaking, and had a vested interest in preventing change – moves began towards language equality in Brussels. There were also moves towards equality nationally, with the acceptance of Dutch as a language of debate in the Belgian Parliament (this did not happen until 1886) and with the text of laws being promulgated in both languages (from 1898).

Brussels is now officially a bilingual city, but Belgians in general are not bilingual in French and Dutch. Dutch is not the second language for most French-speakers, and French (in spite of its international significance) is not the second language of choice for most Dutch speakers.

The long-term legacy of the initial bad decision (advocates of 'official English' in the United States need to ponder this) has been nearly two centuries of polarization. Political disputes still flare up whenever one language community appears to encroach on the other. And the solutions that are found still tend towards monolingualism rather than bilingualism. For example, the university at Louvain (in Dutch-speaking territory) split into two universities, Dutch-speaking and French-speaking – an issue that brought down the government in 1968. Later, when the French-speaking university planned to expand, it was given no choice but to migrate to a site in French-speaking territory, a long way from Louvain but nostalgically christened Louvain-la-Neuve 'New Louvain'. In the 1990s the new solution was still basically monolingual: it featured a federal Belgium with regional parliaments, but it had to be a three-way split, the French-speakers, the Dutch-speakers and the people of Brussels, because Brussels simply cannot be other than bilingual even if many of its inhabitants insist on speaking just one language.

In another twist of compromise, the kind of thing that those who study language in politics become accustomed to, the language of the north was not originally labelled Dutch (which is what it was and is) but Flemish. Why not Dutch? Because Dutch was the language of another country, and using that name might give a foothold for a possible separatist movement. As a tit for tat, many insisted on labelling the speech of the south not French (which is what it was and is) but Walloon. After all, French, however much it was an international language, was the speech of another country too.

But in practice education authorities and successive governments have nothing to do with Walloon dialects, or with local Flemish dialects either. They use more-or-less Parisian French, with very few Belgian variations; they use Dutch, very much as spoken in the Netherlands, with a light Belgian colouring. Belgian French speakers are taught at school to speak Parisian French, or as near as the teacher can manage; even when they leave school they read manuals telling them which everyday words must be avoided because they are not Parisian. Recently the fiction of Flemish has been given up too: officially the language of northern Belgium is now called 'Dutch' (the native term is *Nederlands*) just like that of the Netherlands. In parallel with the speakers of Walloon or Belgian French, nowadays the speakers of Flemish or Belgian Dutch can read manuals teaching them to speak and write Dutch just like people in The Hague. All's fair: and the language struggle continues, as each successive prime minister has to choose a linguistically balanced cabinet, and as this or that village lying near the linguistic border votes for a mayor who speaks the wrong language (as at Voeren in 1983) or votes by a narrow majority to attach itself to the other language community. Since 1947, no one in Belgium has dared to take a linguistic census.[23]

In the last fifty years, as minority peoples have begun to feel their own power or have combined to support one another, the old nationalistic attitudes have been widely questioned. More and more countries have become pluralist in their linguistic politics. In some cases this has meant that an ancient language, with an ancient literary culture, has at last received equal status in education, or locally perhaps even higher status than the national language: that is the case of Irish. In some cases a sort of 'linguistic correctness' has led to the elevation to official status of a language or dialect that had seldom been seen in such terms before: an example is Aragonese, which now in its own region of northern Spain is taught in schools as a first language and has textbooks and dictionaries to match. As to Wales, you can now pursue university study and even write a Ph.D. in Welsh, and Welsh takes priority over English in public events at the University of Wales.

It took a sustained campaign of civil disobedience before the British Government, in the 1960s, grudgingly accepted its responsibility to deal with Welsh-speaking citizens in Welsh. Now, not only in Wales but in many minority-language regions across Europe, you will see bilingual signposts and bilingual government publications and forms; you will encounter radio and television broadcasting in minority languages; you will find public institutions whose official names are in a minority language and whose official activities give special status to minority languages. Canada, where English–French bilingualism has not by any means been universally welcomed, now accords special linguistic and administrative status to its Eskimo and Amerind peoples. In Newspeak these communities are called the First Nations.

Many of the new countries that came into existence as European colonialism retreated have proved to be hotbeds of monolingual ideology. In some of these, you had better learn to speak the national language because speaking it is part of the proof of your political loyalty, which everybody is expected to show. Nationalism is a new ideology for these countries, but all the more fervently believed. Malaysia is one example: we shall see more of this, and of some other cases of linguistic nationalism, in Chapter 4. Others, rather like the Soviet Union, have emerged as resolutely multilingual states – at least on paper. In South Africa there are eleven official languages. Guinea has eight national languages (in addition to French), and has imposed a linguistic rule comparable with one that applies in Ireland: you must qualify in one of these eight languages to become a civil servant. Ghana at one time had nine. Zambia has seven. Nigeria, Niger and several other former British and French colonies of west and central Africa are similarly multilingual at the regional level, with 'national languages' numbering from three to ten while English or French serve as supra-regional 'official languages'.

India is the greatest example among the multilingual states that emerged from colonialism. Here English and (contentiously) Hindi have national status; there are 16 state languages among the 25 states (several states have Hindi as their official language; English is the official language of one state, Nagaland) and there are in addition 101 tribal languages, which have some local status. The real total, though, is the astonishing number of 1,652 mother tongues recorded in the Indian census. According to C. J. Daswani, every Indian adult is at least bilingual. 'Even an illiterate rural Indian is able to manipulate several dialects or languages', while every schoolchild will study at least three languages, two of which will be Hindi and English.[24]

The European Union, not at first very interested in such matters, now gives a good deal of financial and moral support to the minority languages cause: Celtic speakers are leading lights in its Office of Minority Languages. The EU recognizes about fifty minority languages, and this means the ones that are historically established in a particular EU region: what are called in Britain 'community languages', those of recent immigrant groups, are counted separately. In the EU, too – as with Belgium in the nineteenth century and the Soviet Union in the twentieth – ideology causes a problem, for nationalism is still corrosive in Europe and the fact that languages spread across borders is a fact that terrifies nationalists. Just as Dutch once had to be called Flemish when it was spoken in Belgium – just as Romanian had to be called Moldavian when it was spoken in the Soviet Union – so the EU Office of Minority Languages has to call Albanian *Arbëresh* when it is spoken in Italy and *Arvanitika* when it is spoken in Greece. It is safer to pretend that these are two separate languages and that both are different from the language of the non-member state Albania. Why? Simply because of 'linguistic correctness': without this pretence, an Albanian minority could not expect to receive European funds under the auspices of any government of Greece.

In many countries multilingual policies have been in effect long enough for their long-term results to be evaluated. The Soviet Union, which was constitutionally multilingual throughout its existence, is the best case study. What will be the linguistic legacy of the USSR?

Imperial Russia promoted attachment to the emperor and to the Orthodox Church, but also promoted Russian as the linguistic vehicle for these. Publication in minority languages required approval from the censor – those who wished to start journals and newspapers needed approval from the emperor himself – and approval was often withheld. Higher education was in Russian (with German and French, both of them favoured international languages) and not in minority languages of the Empire. If the government communicated with its subjects, it did so in Russian.

Finland and Poland had been nation states before, and reasserted this status when the Empire fell. Estonia, Latvia and Lithuania did the same, with equal linguistic though less historical justification: reconquered during the Second World War, these three were the first to re-establish independence when the Soviet Union collapsed.

Essentially, the remainder of the Russian Empire grew into the Soviet Union. Within this vast and ethnically diverse state, the new government's nationalities policy was, conveniently, both respectable in terms of Marxist theory and extremely practical in the short run. Marx had argued for a political system that was essentially inter-nationalist. The minority peoples of the new Soviet Union had thus far been repressed, linguistically, culturally and politically, by the Imperial ethos, whose practical implementation meant that if any cultural expression at all was favoured it would be a Russian and an Orthodox Christian one. By encouraging minority self-expression (channelled through the creation of local Communist movements, unions and cultural groups) the central government really did enlist support among the 'nationalities' (as they were called) for itself and against the Whites and other counter-revolutionaries.

Thus the Communist revolution led to a total reversal of language policy. The Soviet Union established itself as a nationalistic yet decidedly multilingual state. Schools, teaching children in their local languages, spread rapidly. Alphabets were devised for previously unwritten languages, and these alphabets were mostly based not on the Cyrillic alphabet used for Russian, but on the internationally favoured Latin alphabet. Well over a hundred languages were accepted into the category of 'language of the Societ Union'. Publications were authorized, research was permitted and indeed encouraged, in practically all languages of the Soviet Union. Detailed ethno-graphic maps were published. One curious nationalist feature of the ideology was that the label 'language of the Soviet Union' could not be applied to the official language of any other nation state. German thus failed to qualify, though there were well over a million German speakers on the Volga and elsewhere. Romanian, language of Moldavia, was able to qualify only by being renamed 'Moldavian', and Persian, language of Tajikistan, by being renamed 'Tajik'. Azeri and Turkmen, though differing very little from Turkish, similarly gained separate identities. On the other hand, Aramaic and Yiddish were able to qualify because, though many of their speakers lived outside the Soviet Union, they were not the official languages of any other state.

Gradually, however, policies and practices were adjusted, and the adjustments nearly always favoured the advance of Russian: in these ways, at least, Soviet linguistic policy began to resemble rather more closely that of most other countries of the contemporary world. As early as the late 1920s, some minority languages with very small numbers of speakers, originally nodded into the category of 'language of the Soviet Union', ceased to be languages of education; and it was always necessary, if children from small minority peoples were to go on to secondary or higher education, for them to switch to Russian (or another major language) at some stage.

It was under Stalin (himself, as Joseph Djugashvili, a member of the Georgian minority) that the policy of 'Russification' gathered force. In 1938 Russian became a compulsory subject in every school, and all those languages that had previously used Latin alphabets were required to adopt a new Cyrillic alphabet. Shortly afterwards, in 1944, came the mass forced migrations and deportations whose result was to destroy whole linguistic communities as they were displaced (up to a quarter dying on the journey), mixed with others and forgotten for twenty years or more; most of them were permitted to return under Khrushchev's rule in 1956–8. There was now also massive encourage-ment for Russian internal emigration. The emphasis on Russian was to continue even when the more damaging of Stalin's policies were reversed: the number of languages used in education continued to decrease slowly, while in the Russian-language schools in non-Russian republics and regions it was often not possible to study the local language even as a subject. By the 1980s party (rather than national) policy was promoting Russian even more openly, channelling extra funds to the Russian-language schools. Ph.D. candidates found that doctoral dissertations could be written only in Russian.

In various fields of everyday life there were strong reasons for Russian to prevail. The great mass of the army consisted of conscripts from every nationality and with every mother tongue. But every army unit had to be ethnically mixed and no soldier was stationed in his home district. Within every unit the only common language would be Russian, and the language of orders and administration was also Russian: there was no other sensible choice in either case. Hence all conscripts needed a minimum of Russian, and would certainly stand up better to the social pressures of barracks life the more Russian they spoke. Clearly (though the Roman army was smaller and did not rely on conscription) both Roman and Russian armies were a powerful force for the further spreading of the majority language among each new generation of young men.

All this having been said, in the Soviet Union a certain linguistic balance was maintained. The numbers of speakers of many smaller languages certainly were in long-term decline (and just a few have ceased to be spoken), but those of the languages of the Soviet republics have in general increased. Individuals made their own statement as to their 'nationality' membership within the Soviet Union, and it is a telling fact that the children of mixed-language marriages (of which there were many) usually stated their nationality as Russian if they lived in the Russian republic – naturally enough – but usually claimed a non-Russian local nationality, rather than Russian, if they lived in one of the non-Russian republics. They could have chosen to call themselves Russian, and this outcome demonstrates that there was no great benefit to be gained by making that choice.

The statistics, as they were in 1990, need to be set out briefly. Of over a hundred linguistic groups, twenty-two (including of course Russian) could claim over a million members. Fifteen of these linguistic groups had a Soviet republic to their name, and together these fifteen comprised 90 per cent of the total population. Half of those whose mother tongue was not Russian claimed a second language in the census, and for nearly all of these the second language was Russian. It was felt by observers in the 1980s that while major nationalities were not in sharp decline, small ones definitely were. Some had already almost wholly 'become Russian': speakers (or former speakers) of those languages no longer claimed local but Russian nationality.

The residual force of Communist official multilingual policy meant that when *glasnost* came in the late 1980s, the nationalities were among the first to speak, asserting (with Marxist theory behind them) that the Russification policy must be ended. They were, however, no longer bound to Marx and Lenin, and were for the first time free also to assert nationalism, the seductive ideology of nineteenth-century Europe and of the twentieth-century world.

More significantly, bilingualism was seen not as benign but as a threat. Moves to increase Russian use and teaching roused violent opposition, and the quiet favouring of Russian was among the first casualties of the new atmosphere. National languages were made official in their states. As these became independent, the smaller 'republics' within Russia also began to move towards autonomy and even independence: Chechnya moved a little too far in that direction. The results in the 1990s have included war – in Azerbaijan, in Georgia, in Chechnya and in other more obscure locations.

In individual newly independent states, where Russian had previously been the only official language, the local language now became a competitor. In many cases, as in Estonia, Russian was demoted: although only 65 per cent of inhabitants are linguistically Estonian, and 28 per cent are linguistically Russian, people have to be able to speak Estonian to exert citizen rights. Similar problems have arisen or may well arise elsewhere. Internal migration of Russians, who in Soviet times went to work (in services or newly developed industries) in the various non-Russian republics, was a powerful destabilizing factor in the 1990s. In Estonia they remain, a very large minority, peaceful as yet, but disaffected and mistrusted. Similarly, only 54 per cent of the inhabitants of Latvia are linguistically Latvian, and a huge 33 per cent are Russian; 74 per cent of the inhabitants of Ukraine are linguistically Ukrainian (and 21 per cent are linguistically Russian). In central Asia, where there are additional large minority populations within the borders of several new states, only 39 per cent of the inhabitants of Kazakhstan are linguistically Kazakh, and thanks to massive Soviet resettlement and industrial development an almost equal number, 38 per cent, are Russian. In Kyrgyzstan, 48 per cent are linguistically Kyrgyz and 26 per cent are Russian. In Tuva and some other states where there is serious political instability or persecution the Russian speakers have fled back to Russia in considerable numbers.[25]

These days there is no shortage of observers anxious to show, with the benefit of hindsight, that the whole Communist experiment was bound to end in tears. Soviet language policy is not exempt from these reflections. The question is posed thus by David Marshall: 'Did the USSR's failure in language policy serve as a cause of increased ethnic and nationality tensions?'[26] Failure is a big word: looking at the United States and Australia and the expected disappearance of all their remaining indigenous minority languages, and then back at the Soviet Union, I wonder what outcome would have persuaded Marshall that that country's language policy had succeeded? Still, he raises an important question. Some of the language communities of the old Soviet Union had already shown signs of a desire for national autonomy before the October Revolution, but most of them had not. Whatever their aspirations at that time, the Soviet Union tended (with glaring exceptions already mentioned) to treat them all alike. Well, from 1991 onwards many more of them have either claimed independence or asserted greater autonomy, and in some cases they have done so violently. It would not be fair to say that Soviet policy had stifled separatist aspirations among minority-language communities without adding the corollary that Soviet policy tended to create these aspirations where they had not existed before. It would also be true to say, however, that language planning takes a long time, and that sixty years – two generations – was not long enough for the policy to attain its aims. 'Russification' was a part of it – not in the early 1920s, but certainly by the mid-1930s. By the time of the collapse of the USSR, those aware of the status of the languages of the various Soviet republics knew that the role of Russian was tending to increase, but these languages had certainly not yet been marginalized by Russian. It probably would have happened, but as yet it had not. Even Estonian speakers, though facing a very large Russian-language minority community, were in a position to assert, and to maintain successfully, that theirs was to be the single natural official language of their newly independent state.

We have already seen the results of Ireland's language policy: the rise in status of Irish, and at the same time the unstoppable rise in the proportion of Irish citizens whose first language is English. What about elsewhere?

For some decades now, practically all children whose mother tongue is Welsh have been bilingual in English by the time they leave school. Although there is a Welsh television channel, younger Welsh speakers would admit that most of their entertainment and most of their information comes to them in English. The census figures for Welsh speakers have risen slightly, but it is hard not to feel that the real daily use of the language goes on declining.

While the large minorities of the Soviet Union remained relatively autonomous in linguistic terms, members of the smaller groups in a federated republic such as Russia – perhaps individually numbering a few hundred or a few thousand – had to use Russian if they were to leave home. Army service was only one such occasion; prosperity, and sometimes survival, demanded that they move. Hence Russian, their second language at school, soon became more crucial for many than their minority native language.

Thus the first language of education hardly seems to matter, except that schooling in the mother tongue gives children a quicker start. Education must in due course offer them proficiency in the national language. Once they have that, then, in normal conditions in most modern states, they will find themselves using it more and more, with the result that use of the mother tongue will continue on its downward path. The policy of minority-language education might have been designed by dyed-in-the-wool nationalists who were simply more far-sighted, or more Machiavellian, than Matthew Arnold and his nineteenth century 'brother Saxons'.

This chapter has explored why it is that some minority languages persist while others are quickly lost. It depends on many things, including the cohesion of individual communities and the need they have to interact with others. We were better able to investigate the question because we had already seen the circumstances in which, sometimes quickly, sometimes slowly, the local languages of the Roman Empire had given way before Latin and Greek.

What we have not yet looked at in any detail is the effect that governments can have, should they decide not to promote multilingualism but to try to impose the use of a single language in their territories.

4
LANGUAGE AND NATION

The enemies of language

After a survey of the linguistic policies of the old Soviet Union, and their somewhat messy aftermath in the Soviet Union's 1990s successor states, David Marshall (in the paper cited at the end of Chapter 3) makes a concluding plea which has wider relevance. It is necessary, he writes, 'for each nation to find a concept of identity whereby all its ethnolinguistic minorities as well as its majority can participate as equals, and . . . the time left to find such a solution is more foreshortened with each passing day'.

Over the past two centuries, most national governments have not been looking for such a concept: many of them have been resolutely pursuing an opposite policy, and many still are.

To give one example, until about a generation ago United States policy was firmly fixed on eradicating non-European cultures and non-English speech from its territory as rapidly as that could be achieved. Even now, although federal policy has been officially reversed, the change has not been given full effect – and the Official English movement is having considerable success in nullifying any such changes at the state level. But the United States has not been out of step with events in the rest of the world. In this chapter we need to explore the spread and flourishing of what Arnold Toynbee once called 'the evil spirit of linguistic nationalism', and the United States will serve as one major example. The exploration is essential if we are to grasp the seriousness of the threat to our linguistic future.

First we must define it. It cannot be compressed into *one* proposition – it isn't a neat enough idea for that. A neat statement of it, in the form of *two* propositions, has been given by Geoffrey Nunberg: 'A group speaking the same language is known as a nation, and a nation ought to constitute a state.'[1] But to explain its full effect on modern politics I think we ought to say explicitly in what way a modern state differs from the political arrangements of other times and places, and for that reason a third proposition really has to be added. Linguistic nationalism, let us therefore say, consists of the following *three* propositions tied very closely together: 1. A 'nation' of people can be defined by the language that those people speak; 2. A nation ought to be a political unit with an independent government; 3. Such a government ought to rule within non-overlapping boundaries that can be visualized on a map. In the normal course of things, as we know, such boundaries are represented by physical barriers to free movement.

The defining of a so-called 'nation' by its language is, in itself, an old and widespread idea. Ancient Greeks considered that the speaking of Greek, and no other single factor, defined them as Greeks; however, no one supposed that Greeks, so defined, should form a single political unit, and in fact they have never done so. Among the Romans, another conceptual step was taken: that the people forming a political unit should all be speakers of the same language. There was an opinion, stated by several Roman emperors, that Roman citizenship should only be granted to those who could speak Latin (whether or not it was their first language) and could therefore participate fully in Roman politics. That kind of view flourished at a time when the citizenship was a far from universal privilege and had nothing to do with the right of residence. In fact, for a long time the great majority of those who lived under Roman government did not have citizen status. However, when this finally changed, and the emperor Caracalla made all free inhabitants of the Empire *ipso facto* citizens, no linguistic qualification was demanded. Roman lawyers, for their part, agreed that legal documents were effective only if drawn up in Latin (in some cases Greek was acceptable as an alternative). But no one ever put the argument that all inhabitants of the Empire should speak a single language: much more effective in spreading Latin was the fact that army service and civilian prosperity were in practice facilitated by a knowledge of Latin.

Medieval states, generally much smaller than the Roman Empire, tended to be multilingual. In many of them the language or languages of every day were not the languages used in education and in official documents; in early medieval England, for example, English was the majority language but Norman French was spoken and written by an elite and Latin was the usual language of official documents and scholarly writing. In medieval times there was, as a rule, no feeling that a nation should have just one language.

It is in modern history that the three ideas comprising linguistic nationalism, set out a few paragraphs above, first begin to come together as an ideology. A French enactment of 1539 (see below) and a gnomic statement made in 1683 by a German philosopher, 'History shows that language and nation flourish together',[2] have both been seen as early landmarks. A landmark of linguistic chauvinism, if taken seriously, would be Voltaire's cutting remark made in 1750, 'L'allemand est pour les soldats et pour les chevaux', 'German is for soldiers and for horses'! In truth, in preference to any of these dates, it makes most sense to see the French Revolution as a turning point – not only in French thinking but also in German. The Napoleonic occupation of Germany certainly stirred nationalist thinking in Germany, and it was at this point that J. G. Fichte set out more fully than had been done before a link between language and nation: 'Those who speak the same language are linked together by Nature – quite aside from any human intervention in the matter – through a host of invisible ties . . . They are an indivisible, natural unit. Wherever a distinct language exists, a distinct nation exists also.' Fichte lacked any real interest in the actual number of languages in the world: he was speaking of Europe, and of his native Germany in particular. He believed, as Klopstock and other thinkers had already believed, that a language was a nation's soul. He spoke of the 'immeasurable influence' of language on the 'whole human development of a nation'. He believed, moreover, that the less a language had undergone foreign mixture, the purer its influence on its speakers. English was a mixed language, an amalgam of Anglo-Saxon and Norman French (not to mention Latin and other loans in huge numbers). German showed far less of this kind of mixture – though not as little as Fichte thought – so it was more authentic than English, and more authentic than practically all other languages that came to Fichte's mind. It worked up new words from its own resources: so

German, according to Fichte, was a 'living language'. English, French and its other neighbours were 'dead languages'.[3]

You may see why this is nonsense. In case you don't, I'll tell you. German does none of these things. German does nothing at all – German is not an entity and has no independent existence. It is not alive or dead. It is the speakers of German who can make new compound words (like *Vogelausstopfgeschäftsinhaberswitwe* 'taxidermist's widow'[4] and *Orangensaftkonzentrat* 'concentrated orange juice'[5]) – and they can also borrow words (like *Computer*) from other languages. The speakers of English cannot usually make compound words, but they can make new noun collocations (like *dog food* and *Seville orange juice*) and they can also borrow words (like *pasta*) from other languages. Fichte by this very piece of nonsense threw doubt on his own contention that German was 'a language that is shaped to express the truth'. He also let himself down by his choice of title, *Reden an die deutsche Nation*, 'Addresses to the German Nation'. *Nation* was a Latin loanword.

But Fichte believed what he said, and many Germans and others went on believing it for a long time. In the first half of the twentieth century German psychologists spent a lot of time attempting to demonstrate that people who spoke German and another language had degenerate souls and were less intelligent (and more likely to be left-handed) than people who spoke German alone.[6] A respected textbook of the history of English, *Growth and Structure of the English Language*, first published by Otto Jespersen in 1906, revised and reprinted in Britain and the United States until at least 1960, reflects some similar views. Jespersen asks, 'Is the Latin element on the whole beneficial to the English tongue or would it have been better if the free adoption of words from the classical languages had been kept within much narrower limits?' In his reply to his own question (it is a much longer and more nuanced reply than there is room to quote in full here) Jespersen betrays the view that native words are good words.

But this wealth of words has its seamy side too. The real psychological wealth is wealth of ideas, not of mere names ... The number of words at your disposal in a given language is ... not the only thing of importance; their quality, too, is to be considered, and especially the ease with which they can be associated with the ideas they are to symbolize and with other words. Now many of the Latin words [in English] are deficient in that respect, and this entails other drawbacks to speakers of English.[7]

'Seamy side?' 'Quality of words?' 'Real psychological wealth?' At best, this writer is choosing his words more carelessly than a scholar should. Maybe he would have done better to leave the Greek loanword *psychological* and the Latin loanword *quality* alone. That aside, the character that Jespersen gave to English at its best is trenchantly stated in his 'Preliminary Sketch': 'It seems to me positively and expressly *masculine*, it is the language of a grown-up man and has very little childish or feminine about it.' Does this mean English is unsuited to well over half its speakers? Possibly; because Jespersen also asserted that 'an English lady will nearly always write in a manner that in any other country would only be found in a man's hand'.[8] He is quoted again below on the 'effeminacy' of Hawaiian, a character that he ascribes to Italian and Spanish also, if I understand him correctly: but then, Jespersen was a man of the North, a Danish scholar who had become an English pundit.

Fairly or unfairly, the idea of linguistic nationalism is often associated with France, and there is no doubt that a very early implementation of a very similar idea may be traced to a French decree of 1539, the Ordinance of Villers-Cotterêts. It was promulgated just seven years after Brittany, once independent, was formally united with France. The Midi, where Provençal was spoken, had already been subject to France for two hundred and fifty years. The wording of this decree deserves a close look: it is not the first or the last French document of which it could be said that its creative ambiguity makes it a better example of political propaganda than of political philosophy. The central phrase of this famous ruling by the well-named King François I made it compulsory for all legal documents to be drawn up and all legal transactions to take place *en langaige maternelle françoyse*. If this phrase is translated into English, its ambiguity is destroyed. There is no doubt that its overt purpose was the beneficial one of ensuring that the King's subjects would no longer need to know Latin – previously ubiquitous in the French legal system – if they came to court or were otherwise involved with the law. But must these transactions take place 'in a mother tongue of France', that is, in any indigenous language of France, thus legitimizing the use of Breton and Provençal, not to mention Basque and Dutch? Or are they to be 'in the French mother tongue', the mother tongue of the King himself and of much of northern France? The decree can be understood either way; it depends on a neat balance of conflicting implications. *Françoyse* may allude to the whole territory of France, but in combination with *langaige* it may more naturally be applied to the one language called 'French'. *Maternelle* may allude to the mother tongue of any French subject, or less obviously to the mother tongue of the King as promulgator of the text. History shows that in the interpretation of the decree that was actually applied, the second alternative was chosen in both cases. Legal transactions in the south of France which had hitherto taken place in Provençal were henceforth not permitted to do so. For Provençal (and the other local languages of France) a whole sphere of activity was outlawed from this point onward.

The leaders of the French Revolution, after some initial indecision over language, soon settled for the policy of extending the use of French, in keeping with their more general policy of centralization. This decision having once been taken, it was followed through more vigorously than had ever been done by the Monarchy – partly from philosophical conviction, but also because the Revolution vastly extended the areas of direct interaction between the French government and the mass of the population. As for the philosophy, it is well expressed (again with a creative ambiguity which fine French style renders dangerously easy) in a political speech of January 1794 by the prominent revolutionary leader Bertrand Barère. It is worth quoting here at some length: we shall return to it later, when we explore why it is difficult to translate precisely from one language to another.

Nous avons observé . . . que l'idiome appelé bas-breton, l'idiome basque, les langues allemande et italienne ont perpétué le règne du fanatisme et de la superstition, assuré la domination des prêtres, des nobles et des praticiens, empêché la révolution de pénétrer dans neuf départements, et peuvent favoriser les ennemis de la France . . .

Le fédéralisme et la superstition parlent bas-breton; l'émigration et la haine de la république parlent allemand; la contre-révolution parle l'italien, et le fanatisme parle le basque. Cassons ces instruments de dommage et d'erreur . . .

Laissons la langue italienne consacrée aux délices de l'harmonie et aux expressions d'une poésie molle et corruptrice. Laissons la langue allemande, peu faite pour des peuples libres jusqu'à ce que le gouvernement féodal et militaire, dont elle est le plus digne organe, soit anéanti. Laissons la langue espagnole pour son inquisition et ses universités jusqu'à ce qu'elle exprime l'expulsion des Bourbon, qui ont détrôné les peuples, de toutes les Espagnes. Quant à la langue anglaise, qui fut grande et libre le jour qu'elle s'enrichit de ces mots, la majesté du peuple, elle n'est plus que l'idiome d'un gouvernement tyrannique et exécrable, de la banque et des lettres-de-change.

Nos ennemis avaient fait de la langue française la langue des cours; ils l'avaient avilie. C'est à nous d'en faire la langue des peuples . . . il n'appartient qu'à elle de devenir la langue universelle. Mais cette ambition est celle du génie de la liberté; il la remplira. Pour nous, nous devons à nos concitoyens, nous devons à l'affermissement de la République, de faire parler sur tout son territoire la langue dans laquelle est écrite la Déclaration des Droits de l'Homme.

We have noted that the dialect known as Low Breton, the Basque dialect, and the German and Italian languages have prolonged the reign of fanaticism and superstition, they have guaranteed the domination of the priests, nobles and lawyers, they have obstructed the advance of the revolution into nine large departments, and they are capable of favouring the enemies of France . . .

Federalism and superstition speak Low Breton. Emigration and hatred of the Republic speak German. Counter-revolution speaks Italian. Fanaticism speaks Basque. We must smash these tools of sabotage and delusion . . .

We must put aside Italian, dedicated as it is to the pleasures of music and to the phrasing of a soft and seductive poetry. We must put aside German, of no use to a free people until the feudal and military government of which it is the all-too-worthy vehicle is annihilated. We must leave Spanish to its Inquisition and its universities until Spanish speaks of the expulsion of the Bourbons, who have usurped the people's throne, from every Spanish land. As for English, a great and free language on the day when it mastered the words 'The Power of the People', English is now no more than the dialect of a tyrannous and despicable government, the dialect of banks and letters of credit.

Our enemies turned French into a court language, and thus they brought it low. It is for us to make it the language of peoples . . . It is the destiny of French, alone, to become the universal language. That ambition, however, we leave to the genius of the French language to fulfil, as indeed it will. For ourselves, we owe it to our fellow citizens, and we owe it to the strengthening of the Republic, to ensure that the language in which the Declaration of the Rights of Man is written will be spoken across the whole territory of the Republic.[9]

Once more we pause to observe how stylistic ambiguity – bad language, may we call it? – makes propaganda. You cannot translate *faire parler* neatly into English. 'To ensure that [it] will be spoken' is wordy, and 'ensure' is much weaker than *faire*. The phrase says in two words what it needs to say, much more cleanly than any longer expression could say it, and implies the use of whatever force may be necessary, even beyond *émigration* to genocide, to achieve the stated effect. This is not to imply that genocide was directly an instrument of language policy under the French Revolution. But the massacres and destruction at Provençal-speaking Toulon (accused of complicity with the English enemy) had taken place just a month before Barère made this speech, and the massacre at Toulon was not the only such incident which may be associated with the suppression of linguistic minorities.

Enough on the two words *faire parler*. Notice, now, the ringing condemnation by association of German, Italian, Basque and Breton. Breton is described elsewhere in the speech as 'a barbarous instrument of superstitious thought . . . too long maintained and too widely spoken in the five departments of the west'. (Rather unexpectedly, Basque is admitted to be 'une langue sonore et imagée', 'a sonorous and express-ive language', but then Barère himself came from the Basque country.) In its resolute pairing of languages with political states of mind – in its implicit assumption that nothing good or revolutionary can be said in these other languages, that they can never be other than *instruments de dommage et d'erreur* – this text marks the beginning of true linguistic racism, a way of thinking that would gradually develop in the nine-teenth century and come to fruition in the early twentieth.

Finally notice the shortage of references to Provençal (Occitan), though Barère did not quite ignore it completely, as has often been the case in French linguistic politics since that time. Elsewhere in this speech Provençal is assimilated to the *patois*, the local dialects of northern France. It is assumed, just as they are, to lack history, litera-ture and legitimacy.

In the same year in which Barère, using the words just quoted, ordered every commune in the nine departments to employ a teacher of French, the Abbé Gregoire published the result of a national linguistic survey of France undertaken by him in 1790. His title was 'Report on the need to annihilate the dialects and to make the use of the French language universal, and on the means for achieving this'.[10] Grégoire's survey was an informed estimate, not a full census, but its figures are reasonably convincing. He estimated that of the 26 million inhabitants of France about 11 million spoke French as their mother tongue, while another 3 million spoke it as a second language. Thus well over half the population spoke a *patois* – meaning either a Romance dialect, such as would be counted Occitan by modern linguists, or a dialect of a quite different language such as German, Dutch, Breton or Basque.

From the time of the Revolution onwards the work of annihilating the dialects has continued resolutely, with no diversions beyond those caused by German occupation during the two World Wars. French has been the only language of schools, the only language in which teaching may take place. Already in 1861 – two generations after Grégoire – although it was still the case that fewer than half of all citizens had French as their mother tongue, a linguistic census of the school population showed that only one-tenth spoke no French (and they will have been largely the youngest children). The direct effort put into education has been paralleled by another. Since 1875 practically all young Frenchmen have served as conscripts in the army, in which French is the natural common language and the language of command. Just as in the Roman Empire and the Soviet Union, soldiers serve outside their home districts and in units of mixed regional origin. This, alongside compulsory education in French, had by the mid-twentieth century completed the effect at which the Revolutionary planners had aimed.

To put the matter in the terms used in this book: by about 1950 all French citizens, from whatever region, were good enough at French to be able to choose to bring up their children in French: and the perceived disadvantages of speaking a strongly marked dialect or a different indigenous language were strong enough that nearly all were making that choice. Since then, little has changed. In 1951 it was for the first time permitted to teach French regional languages as subjects in French schools, as extras, with limited credit. In 1975 the subjects were allowed to become slightly more central to the curriculum, but few children choose to take them. The use of Occitan, Breton and Basque is now in steep and perhaps terminal decline. Only older people use these regional languages habitually. No children arrive at school speaking these languages alone. Many younger people and nearly all children have not learnt them thoroughly; the majority, even in their traditional heartlands, have not learnt them at all. Catalan and German, both spoken by large numbers in border regions, have as yet declined less sharply. Their speakers have at least the moral support and the cultural influence of those across the borders, in Spain and Germany, who speak the same language in a different linguistic environment – and they have Catalan and German television.[11]

Modern linguistic nationalism

Between the French Revolution and the present day the ideology of linguistic nationalism has spread across the world, and there has never been a moment during which it was not being forcibly expressed in one country or another. In fact the ambitions of politicians and political philosophers continue to grow. It is no longer the case that a language selected for promotion as 'national language' will always be the majority tongue of the nation concerned: many modern nations have no majority language, yet in some there has been a political will to impose a minority language on the whole population.

Once or twice a language has been chosen for a national role although it has hardly been spoken by anybody till the moment of nationhood: this is the case of Hebrew in Israel. To be accurate, some children began to grow up speaking Hebrew as a mother tongue around 1910 – after a lapse of at least 2,000 years during which practically no one had done so.[12] Hebrew has been far more successful as a national language than might have been expected; but then its protagonists were able to build on traditional Jewish education, as part of which students had always learned to read Biblical Hebrew, and they were abetted by large-scale immigration to Israel from so many different countries that no other single language was available to be given the role of national lingua franca. The use of Irish, before Irish independence, was scarcely more widespread than that of Hebrew, though it was the everyday language of some isolated districts. For a number of centuries it had been illegal to speak Irish in public – the legislation is actually still in effect in Northern Ireland, where there are no native Irish speakers – and English had finally become Ireland's everyday language. Since independence Irish, unlike Hebrew, has not spread significantly: its role remains ceremonial and symbolic, as we saw in Chapter 3. English has been too convenient.

In certain cases the choice has fallen on the language of a relatively large minority: Indonesian is an example, because Malay (its older standard form) was already many people's mother tongue and was already widely used as a lingua franca when Indonesia became independent. Sometimes the new national language is spoken by a small minority elite or as a second language, as is English in Kenya and many other former colonial territories. Sometimes it is the language of one large region. India, as it struggled towards independence, had no obvious national language spoken by a majority of the population. Rejecting English meant that, in Gandhi's words in 1917, 'Hindi alone can become the national language', and this prediction is slowly becoming reality, although India's multilingual policies leave strong roles to regional and local languages too. There was a 'national necessity' to learn Hindi in other Indian states, Gandhi added. We need to look more closely at some cases of modern linguistic nationalism. They can be found in every continent: the examples in this section are Indonesia, Malaysia, Ethiopia, and finally the United States and its possessions.

Malay has been a language of long-distance communication for centuries. In its two modern incarnations – as *bahasa Indonesia* 'language of Indonesia' and *bahasa Malaysia* 'language of Malaysia' – it has become the national symbol of two states, both jealous of their nationhood and to some extent jealous of one another. It is interesting to observe the sharp contrasts between the two.

The Dutch, who ruled what is now Indonesia for more than four centuries, themselves had a nationalistic view of language. Here, as in Surinam, their settled policy was that the number of 'natives' encouraged or even permitted to learn Dutch should be kept to a minimum. The aim was to maintain a caste distinction between rulers and ruled.

Ironically, the effect was to maintain and even to raise the status of Malay, because its speakers had to use Malay for *all* purposes (whereas, for example, local people who rose beyond a certain level, in administration or in education, in British colonies or dominions found that they had to use English to do so). The sphere of Malay could not be invaded by Dutch, since so few people spoke Dutch. The use of Malay in local administration was acknowledged when it became the second official language of the Dutch East Indies in 1865. Its role was even reinforced, in a further twist of irony, by its use in resistance to the Dutch. While Indian nationalists, such as Gandhi, used English, Indonesian nationalists used Malay – which they renamed *bahasa Indonesia* as early as 1928. The Japanese occupation again worked in favour of Malay. When the Japanese seized power in 1942 they banned the use of Dutch – but Japanese could not replace it immediately (simply because very few Indonesians spoke Japanese and very few Japanese spoke Indonesian) and so Malay was necessarily adopted as the local language of government. In independent Indonesia the position of Indonesian as sole national language has never been threatened. Local languages have many millions of speakers: in numerical terms Javanese in fact counts as a major world language, with 75 million mother-tongue speakers. But in practice it is of local importance only, like the rest. The role of Malay, and now of Indonesian, has always been as a lingua franca, permitting communication among peoples across this vast archipelago.

Nowadays Indonesian is taught in every school 'as a means of strengthening and maintaining awareness of nationhood and unity'. Local languages may be used as teaching media for the first three years while Indonesian is learnt, but Indonesian, and Indonesian literature, are the focus throughout. Adult literacy classes also teach Indonesian while they teach reading and writing. There is enormous population mobility – some of it in badly planned *transmigrasi* colonies – and Indonesian becomes the lingua franca wherever two or more local languages are thrust together. An estimate is that half a million people spoke Malay as a mother tongue in 1928, and that 17 million did so sixty years later; the number has grown even more rapidly since then.

In Malaysia the history has been very different. British rule brought very large Chinese and Indian minorities to the country: between these and the almost-outnumbered indigenous population English had more potential as a lingua franca than Malay had, and their speakers had been given somewhat more encouragement to learn English. For all that, Malay was named sole national language on independence in 1957. In 1967, in clear imitation of Indonesia, the language as used officially in Malaysia was renamed *bahasa Malaysia*. In both countries, it has in practice been the case that you will do better if you speak Malay. In Malaysia it has been the overt policy to make use of this linguistic division, with the intention of maintaining the slightly precarious majority influence of the indigenous Malay-speaking population. In Indonesia, the long-term policy is quite the opposite – to unify the whole vast population by turning everyone into Indonesian speakers as soon as possible. And it's working. Some of the smaller local languages are already being given up. Even Javanese, with its elaborate and almost unique vocabularies of respect, is under serious threat among the younger generation, who find Indonesian (in which anyone can talk to anyone else without calling on a whole new vocabulary) an attractively modern and egalitarian language.

Ethiopia has 97 indigenous languages. It has been ruled by one of the more brutal regimes of recent history, whose attention was focused well below such matters as the well-being of the Ethiopian population, with the result that the total number of languages in the country has fallen as a result of starvation and genocide as well as more gentle methods of language planning. Amharic has the title of Ethiopia's national language, and has been so successful in this role that the eight million who speak it as a mother tongue are outnumbered by more than twelve million who speak it as a second or third language.

The first written language of Ethiopia had been Ge'ez or Ethiopic, a language which had fairly recently been brought by migration from southern Arabia and – by the first century AD – was the mother tongue of the kingdom of Axum, whose territory extended some way southwards from its base in modern Eritrea. Written Ge'ez became fossilized, from the fourth century onwards, in the form it had assumed as the literary and ceremonial language of Ethiopian Christianity. In everyday speech, however, Ge'ez split into dialects just as Latin did. When Axum lost power to a dynasty from the province of Lasta in the twelfth century, the local language of this dynasty, Agew – a member of the Cushitic family, very different from Ge'ez – clearly came to be used to some extent as the everyday language of government; Ge'ez must have been relegated to its written and ceremonial role. A century later, a dynasty from the province of Showa came to prominence in its turn. In this province (where Addis Ababa now is) the southern dialect of Ge'ez was spoken. Since previous precedent had turned Ge'ez into a ceremonial and written language and the current dynasty's local language into the official spoken language, the local dialect of Showa was what now replaced Agew as the everyday language of government. It was called simply *Lisane Nigus* 'language of the King': it is the language known to us now as Amharic.

Men of Showa ruled Ethiopia until 1868. Through this period Ge'ez continued in use in the church and in literature: it was *Lisane Sihuf*, the 'language of scripture'. Amharic spread very gradually, with the boundaries of Ethiopia itself. It was a decentralized country, with subordinate regional 'kings', but Amharic was needed as the language of army and administration. In the late nineteenth century two rulers were powerful and imaginative enough to weld Ethiopia into a more unified state: Tewodros and Menelik. Amharic was consciously placed at the centre of this development. Menelik took personal interest in the school system, in which Amharic was taught (though English has emerged as the language of secondary schools and universities). He centralized government and administration, and centralized functions had to be carried out in a single language, which was of necessity Amharic. He founded a new capital, Addis Ababa, and its inhabitants, although only a fifth of them had Amharic as their mother tongue, had to use Amharic as their lingua franca: there was no other choice. In unconscious support of national policy, Christian missionaries from elsewhere, working with minority populations who speak many other languages, have found it practical to work in Amharic – so they spread familiarity with and literacy in Amharic.

It is as if Ethiopia had shared in the explicit linguistic nationalism expressed by English-, French- and German-speaking theorists and politicians. That came later. In earlier days, national policy grew in a simpler way, from the recording of facts such as that when King Tewodros was presented with a religious text in Ge'ez he said, 'Why bring me a book like this which no one understands? Give me a translation.'[13] To insist on Amharic in writing and in religion was almost unprecedented – and had a powerful effect. As influential was the fact that Tewodros' effective successor, Yohannes IV, although his mother tongue was Tigrinya, retained Amharic as language of government. Somehow, then, Amharic had crossed a watershed: from being 'language of the king' it had gained a new status, and not long afterwards a new title was being explicitly used – that of *Yemengist Quanqua* 'language of government'. Under Haile Selassie, a new constitution in 1955 asserted that Amharic was 'official language' of the then Empire of Ethiopia. In the 1960s it began to be described overtly as *Biherawi Quanqua* 'National Language'. In imitation of the renaming of Tagalog in the Philippines, there was even talk of changing its name to 'Ethiopian', *Ityopyawinya*.

In the twentieth century, therefore, in European nationalist fashion, Amharic is taught in all primary schools – in 1964 classroom teaching in minority languages was ended. An Ethiopian Language Academy, renamed National Language Academy, develops terminology so that it can fulfil every function of a national language. Amharic is the language of the army and the police force, the language of the press, the principal language of television. Year by year, mobility and mixed marriages mean that more and more people use Amharic as second language or as mother tongue. The large minority languages, Tigrinya and Oromo, are still in vigorous use. Some of the smaller ones are disappearing as Amharic spreads inexorably.[14]

The formerly Spanish island of Guam, whose indigenous language is Chamorro, was annexed by the United States in 1898. Under Spanish rule Chamorro had been a language of education in Guam, though Spanish was spoken by the local elite. Along with compulsory education, a previously unfamiliar language – English – was now imposed. In 1922 the speaking of Chamorro was forbidden in school precincts. Such actions are familiar from many countries, but this time it was accompanied by something more surprising. Chamorro dictionaries were collected and burnt – an odd, superstitious act reminiscent of medieval Europe. The thinking behind early United States language policy in Guam was set out, as coherently as it deserved, in the *Guam Recorder* for February 1925: 'This is American territory. It is American to have public schools where only English is taught. Americans have an obligation and such they have never shirked.' Richard R. Day, who quotes this passage, remarks on the unexpected fact that a nation of immigrants could be linguistically so single-minded. He concludes the story of Chamorro thus: 'Since the late 1960s and early 1970s, bilingual Chamorro parents have been teaching their children English at home.'[15] It is an interesting language, a very early offshoot from the Austronesian family and thus distantly related to the languages of the Philippines and Indonesia; it is unusual too in its long symbiosis with Spanish. We have much to learn from Chamorro. Now that it is no longer being taught to children as a mother tongue, we have not long left to learn it.

A link between language, race and morality was felt by many in the twentieth century. In Puerto Rico, another recently acquired United States colony, it was argued with what appears startling dishonesty that 'if the schools become American and the teachers and students were guided by the American spirit, then the island would be essentially American in sympathies, opinions, and attitudes towards government'.[16] These 'American . . . attitudes towards government' included, in the United States, the right to participate in the choice of government in national elections, something that Puerto Ricans were in fact not encouraged to want. In Nebraska in 1923 it was temporarily ruled illegal for primary school children to be taught in any language other than English (there have been strong communities of European immigrants in Nebraska). The Nebraska supreme court asserted that foreign-language education would 'inculcate . . . the ideas and sentiments alien to the best interests of this country'. 'Of course this all seems silly now,' adds Geoffrey Nunberg disingenuously:[17] he knows all too well the residual strength of sentiments such as these, however unrespectable it may be nowadays to put them into words. At that time, however, Nebraska was compelled to withdraw its linguistic legislation, which, the US Supreme Court decided, interfered with 'the calling of modern language teachers, with the opportunities of pupils to acquire knowledge, and with the power of parents to control the education of their own'. Not surprisingly, Guam and its Chamorro-speaking 'Americans' remained outside the provisions of this law, and – as we shall see later in this chapter – the power of Native American parents to control 'the education of their own' was being flouted by the military boarding schools. The United States has been among the most active promoters of linguistic nationalism, with a long-term policy aimed at the destruction of indigenous languages and cultures within its territory. It is interesting to see that the early promoters of this policy felt that they needed to draw on European practice to justify their own. We can gather that in the 1880s the nationalist and colonialist assumptions that underlay it were not yet as universally shared as they would be in the first half of the twentieth century. This is the Commissioner of Indian Affairs, J. D. Atkins, in a report to Congress in 1887:

All are familiar with the recent prohibitory order of the German Empire forbidding the teaching of the French language in either public or private schools in Alsace and Lorraine. Although the population is almost universally opposed to German rule, they are firmly held to German political allegiance by the military hand of the Iron Chancellor. If the Indians were in Germany or France or any other civilized country, they should be instructed in the language there used. As they are in an English-speaking country they must be taught the language which they must use in transacting business with the people of this country. No unity or community of feeling can be established among different peoples unless they are brought to speak the same language, and thus become imbued with like ideas of duty.[18]

One crucial step in this argument is to be seen in the shadowy background of the text, never stated explicitly. It is that the 'Indians' have somehow ceased to be the 'people of this country'. They have become, in the writer's thought, a subject race whose only future must be to transact business with the current occupants of what he characterizes as a monolingual 'English-speaking country'.

This latter characterization is, needless to say, false. Many languages were and are spoken in the United States, and English is not even defined in the Constitution as the country's official or national language. However, that may change. Many today hope to impose monolingualism, in the form of 'Official English', on an ideal United States of the future. The Official English movement has succeeded by popular vote in installing English as the official language of several individual states, and is still thriving. Its success is owed partly to fierce debates over the desirability and success of what is called in the United States 'bilingual education' and is thus also linked to a backlash against large-scale migration of Spanish speakers from Mexico and elsewhere in Latin America. Unfortunately, in the United States political aims focusing on a specific racial or linguistic group are not easy to state publicly. Making English the official language (and thus imposing it in education and in dealings with government) is a covert way to stop badly planned and badly implemented bilingual education for the children of Spanish-speaking immigrants, and so to improve their educational opportunities and hasten their assimilation into United States society.

The relative failure of bilingual education in its United States form, and the heated political debate surrounding it, are not relevant to us in this book. We know children can grow up bilingual and be all the better for it. We only need to note the outcome, one that can be stated confidently on the basis of historical examples already given. The grandchildren of Spanish-speaking migrants will certainly speak English fluently, while their great-grandchildren will, almost as certainly, speak no Spanish. 'Official English' legislation will have no effect on this.

The rhetoric that accompanies Official English campaigning is of interest, however. Programmes such as the following demonstrate that the woolly ideology of linguistic nationalism is as alive as ever.

Language is a fundamental bond through which a people is held together. This bonding gives us harmony and unity . . . All languages and cultures are precious in our history and are to be preserved and maintained. These are not, however, public responsibilities. They belong, as they have throughout our history, in homes, churches, private schools and ethnic celebrations.

Where linguistic unity has broken down, our energies and resources flow into tensions, hostilities, prejudices, and resentments. These develop and persist. Within a few years, if the breakdown persists, there will be no retreat. It becomes irrevocable, irreversible. Society as we know it can fall into noisy babel and then chaos.

Our common English language is critical for our unity and for our democratic functioning. Protecting it in the months and years ahead is a deep personal responsibility of all our citizens.[19]

Here, as in the French Revolution, 'bad language' contributes to weak thinking. 'All languages and cultures . . . are to be preserved and maintained,' the writer asserts, apparently for the sake of 'our history'; does he accept their maintenance as his private responsibility, or does he shift it to others who are imagined to be more interested in 'our history'? It is difficult to guess a historical basis for the generalizations in the second paragraph. There is no state in history in which 'linguistic unity [broke] down' and, as a result, 'society [fell] into noisy babel and then chaos': therefore, in asserting that this can happen, the writer is going beyond current knowledge. Finally, the 'protecting' of English (from an unstated threat) is made a 'personal responsibility', presumably similar to the 'private' responsibility to maintain 'all languages and cultures'; yet the statement is intended to support a proposition to make the protecting of English (and not of any other languages) a government responsibility.

The Official English movement is also important to the subject of this book for a more serious reason. Although its intended target is Spanish speakers, who are thought to be not learning English quickly enough, it is an unfortunate side-effect ('collateral damage', to adopt a recent cliché) that language use by Native Americans is at least equally affected. Their Amerindian languages have also been targeted by policy-makers pushing the adoption of English Only language policies in schools.[20]

Linguistic nationalism and the real world

France provided us with an excellent example of how linguistic nationalism confronts reality. The underlying philosophy may be, as already quoted in Geoffrey Nunberg's words, 'A group speaking the same language is known as a nation, and a nation ought to constitute a state.' But the practice is, 'a state that we have previously defined as a nation ought to be made to speak the same language'; and once people have been convinced of the morality of this approach – which is frighteningly easy – they are quite prepared to put it as bluntly as that, at least, if they are the ones who already speak the national language. We have quoted some of them above. Basque, Breton, Occitan and the other regional French languages, since they did not fit into the self-defined French nation, must be made to disappear. Guam was American, so its schools must speak English only and its Chamorro dictionaries had better be burnt.

Since there are 5,000 or so languages in the world, and fewer than 200 nation states, anyone can see that linguistic nationalism still has some way to go. Unluckily for world peace and for our linguistic future, many people, possibly even a majority of the people in the world who give any thought to questions of national politics, accept linguistic nationalism as the model for a future political reality.

And that means not the philosophical nationalism summarized by Geoffrey Nunberg, but the practical nationalism summarized by me, because no one believes that there should be 5,000 independent governments in the world, even if it were possible – which it is not – to define non-overlapping boundaries for all the languages or theoretical 'nations' involved. The linguistic nationalists of the nineteenth and early twentieth centuries, who succeeded in setting up in eastern Europe several new nations defined (more or less) by linguistic boundaries, never seriously thought that their ideas should be applied wholesale and world-wide. Most of them did not even consider the application of their ideas to the outlying regions of France or Britain or Yugoslavia. On the contrary, modern international law and international co-operation tend to base themselves on the assumption that existing boundaries will now stay just the way they are: attempts to alter them are generally frowned on, and often lead to armed intervention, with widespread international support, aimed at maintaining the status quo. The only kind of changes that have a hope of international approval are the weakening of boundaries (as is gradually happening within the European Union) or the strengthening of them (as happened in Yugoslavia). They can change colour on the map, but they mustn't move.

So, in the current political climate, any practical work aimed at making the world and linguistic nationalism fit together better has to focus on reducing the total number of languages from 5,000 to about 200 or fewer. In France, Britain, the United States and most other developed countries, for most of the nineteenth and most of the twentieth century, concerted efforts were being made to achieve precisely this. This is one major reason why our linguistic future is now so seriously threatened.

In those same countries there has at last, rather suddenly, been a big shift in political opinion. In the last few years it has become fashionable to favour minority cultures and minority languages. Does this mean that the rapid decline in the use of minority languages will soon be halted? To get a clear answer we need to look in some detail at the linguistic situation of North America (the United States and Canada), an area sufficiently large and diverse to provide plenty of examples of the results of official language policy. Our central questions in the next two sections will be the following: can the trend be reversed in time? Will any of the Amerindian or Native American languages still be spoken a hundred years from now?

First of all, the current state of things. Of about 210 indigenous languages that can still be heard in North America today, 57 are spoken only by a few very old people, 84 are spoken by grandparents and the very old, 35 are spoken by parents and older adults; out of these same 210 languages that leaves only only 34 which are still spoken by children and adults of all ages. The situation is more advanced in the United States, where 155 of these languages are spoken, than in Canada. This United States figure includes 55 of the languages spoken only by a few very old people and 70 of those spoken only by grandparents and the very old. Thirty indigenous languages of the United States are spoken by adults of all ages, and only 20 of them are still spoken by children as well as adults.[21] This devastating but realistic calculation was presented by Michael Krauss to a committee of the US Senate in 1992. The Senate was reviewing the results of more than a century of US determination to assimilate the Native American peoples, culturally and linguistically. It was considering – at last – whether the policy could and should be reversed.

Krauss knows as much as anyone living about the present state of these languages (his own work is with the languages of Alaska) and he adds that before European contact well over 300 languages were probably spoken in what are now the United States and Canada. Krauss would, I think, agree that this is a conservative figure. A study of any map of North American Indian languages will show large areas where nothing is now known because no early records were made. This is true particularly between the Appalachians and the Mississippi, in the southeast generally, and in northern Mexico. Ives Goddard, in his introduction to the authoritative *Languages* volume of the new *Handbook of North American Indians*, lists 120 languages that are on record as having become extinct. Bearing in mind the likely number of languages that ceased to be spoken without ever being named in any European source, Goddard takes the estimated total of languages spoken before European contact to above 400.[22]

The future predicted by Krauss is even more devastating than the statistics summarized above. By 2010 the languages of the first cohort – those spoken only by a few old people – will certainly all be lost. And the losses will continue inexorably. Unless something most unlikely and unexpected happens, by 2070 only 34 of the indigenous languages of North America will still be spoken, including only 20 in the United States. That means that, at the most, fewer than one-tenth of the languages spoken before European contact will still survive. They, in turn, will be threatened: they are likely to be spoken less and less, and they may by that time be more or less disused, even if some old people remember them.

Can it get worse? Yes, it can. Krauss (and Goddard, who has worked with Krauss's figures) calculated which languages to allot to which age cohort based on all the available information. In Goddard's words, this means that 'errors are likely to be on the side of optimism'. And so Cherokee was counted in the last cohort, that of languages spoken by children and adults of all ages, because (as Krauss explains) 'with such a complex and widespread language situation . . . children are likely still to be speaking Cherokee somewhere' – but, for all that, in most Cherokee families that is no longer true. Nearly all Cherokee children are now speaking English at home, not Cherokee, and the continued use of the language is gravely threatened. The situation is known to be just as gloomy for White Mountain Apache, though that language also is classed in the last cohort. Finally, Krauss adds, 'we must not lose track of the dynamics. Change is in almost every case unidirectional for the worse. For example, 15 years ago Central Yupik had 25 villages where children spoke the language, but now has 17.'[23] Even those languages that are still being spoken among children are spoken in fewer and fewer villages every year.

An ironic point was made in the first issue of *Iatiku*, the newsletter on endangered languages: 'The USA probably leads the world at the moment in academic interest and effort devoted to arresting language loss: however, it may be just there that the rate of language loss is currently at its highest.' Inuit and the numerous Amerindian languages native to Alaska, *Iatiku* continues, are disappearing far more rapidly than they are in northern Canada: if the comparison is broadened to include other Arctic countries – Scandinavia, northern Russia, Siberia and Greenland – it is still the case that Alaska is the graveyard of indigenous languages. Only two of Alaska's twenty surviving native languages are still spoken by children (St Lawrence Island Yupik and Central Yupik). Greenland, by contrast, can claim a real success in halting the decline, with 99 per cent of its indigenous population reported bilingual in Inuit and Danish.[24]

How did it come to this?

North American languages and European settlement

Humans began to settle in the Americas long after the Old World was populated. The first settlers, it is generally thought, crossed from Siberia to Alaska perhaps fifteen to twenty thousand years ago – there are plenty of claims that archaeologists have found the remains of humans or their settlements dating from much earlier than this, but all the claims are controversial. From twenty thousand years ago onwards, several migrations probably happened. The last of them that can be traced linguistically and archaeologically was the one that brought the speakers of Eskimo-Aleut languages to Alaska, Canada and Greenland. These languages – both Inuit and Aleut – are spoken to this day on both sides of the Bering Strait. Some time before that, it is generally imagined, the Na-Dené languages (the Athabaskan group plus a couple of isolated languages in California) arrived: similarities have been seen, by some particularly enthusiastic 'lumpers', between Na-Dené on the one hand and Sino-Tibetan and certain Caucasian languages on the other. Earlier still, in one migration or many, in monolingual or multilingual groups, came the speakers of the language or languages ancestral to all the other Amerindian or Native American languages known today, and these gradually spread eastwards and southwards through the vast American land mass.

A map showing where North American Indian languages are spoken in 2002 consists mainly of white space, relieved by scattered dots. The dots mark Indian reservations – and nursing homes.

One looks back with relief to the satisfying patchwork of indigenous languages as they existed before European colonization.[25] The pattern is anything but uniform. First, consider the number of languages. Along the western coast, from the almost-Arctic frontier between Alaska and British Columbia all the way to northwestern Mexico and Baja California, language boundaries crowded close together. A journey through these coastal regions would lead the traveller through dozens of language communities, each wholly distinct from the next. What caused this astonishing linguistic diversity? Can it have been an effect of the mountainous terrain, reducing communication between communities? This is one of the explanations usually given for the linguistic diversity of the Caucasus region and of the southern Himalayas. Well, it's true that in British Columbia, Washington state, Oregon and California the terrain may have contributed to the overall picture: these, after all, are the mountains and valleys of the western Rocky Mountains. But that simply cannot be the full story; after all, along the eastern seaboard, from northeastern Maine to Carolina, the languages (so far as the map of them can still be reconstructed) were almost as crowded, and we might well get the same impression of the southern coast, all the way round to northeastern Mexico, if full records of the languages of Georgia and of the Gulf coast had ever been made. There must be more to it.

Now consider the number of language families – that is, the number of groups of languages that cannot be shown to be related to one another. Here again the west coast gives an impression of stunning variety, with nearly twenty distinct families represented on the map, and they are laid out in a very complex geographical pattern. Its complexity is almost matched by that seen along the Gulf coast from northeastern Mexico to Florida. Even though we know so little about the languages that must have been spoken along this coast, we know enough to be sure of this.

Inland, however, it's different. Half a dozen very widespread families divide among themselves the vast reaches of the Great Basin, the eastern Rockies, the prairies and the Canadian forests. One of those families, Algonquian, occupied the whole east coast from Nova Scotia to North Carolina, with a series of languages (most of them, of course, long forgotten now) each differing slightly from its neighbours in what was probably a very extensive dialect continuum. Within reach of the St Lawrence estuary and the Great Lakes, Europeans might have encountered two language families, Algonquian and Iroquoian. West, north and south of that belt of territory, they met Algonquian alone.

Why does the density of language variation itself vary? Why were languages crowded together along the coasts, but spread more spaciously inland? The answer is to be found in the way humans use their environment. The Great Plains were territory for pastoralists, who ranged widely here as they have done in central Asia. In fact their nomadic lifestyle was adopted for a while by Europeans too, but not for long: the huge herds of cattle and the long annual migrations soon conflicted with the land rights established by sedentary farmers. Meanwhile the coastal lands offered more varied resources, sufficient to be exploited all year round without any seasonal migrations. It was the lack of need for migration in those coastal lands, the relative ease with which a community could settle and remain where it was, which gradually brought a greater density of dialect variation and eventually of language boundaries.

The patterning of language families, by contrast, has to be explained at least partly by migration – by population movements at some time in the past. The west coast, from British Columbia to Baja California, shows the combined linguistic result of very ancient settlement, the passage of many peoples, the existence of many different ecological niches and the richness of resources that settled communities were able to develop. The resulting linguistic variation is richer than that of the Caucasus and the Himalaya.

As regards wider expansion by individual language families, one example will have to be enough. The spread of the early speakers of

Iroquoian languages is traceable though the researches of Marianne Mithun, who has worked on the names of animals and plants in the modern languages and their reconstruction at earlier stages. If a name is known in some of the modern languages, and can be reconstructed in proto-Iroquoian (which was perhaps spoken about four thousand years ago), then something under that name has been familiar to speakers of the languages in question through all that time. With that knowledge, it should be possible to locate within a certain range the places where these peoples have lived. To summarize some of her findings, the proto-Iroquoians lived among wildcats (Cherokee *kvhe*, Oneida *kvleks*), wolves (Cherokee *wahya*, Oneida *okwaho*), deer (Cherokee *ahwi*, Susquehannock *haagw*), chipmunks (Cherokee *khi-yuka*, Laurentian *caiognen*, Oneida *tsihlyokwv'*), either raccoons or skunks (Cherokee *tilv* 'skunk'; Oneida *atilu* and Huron *tiron* 'raccoon'), bullfrogs (Cherokee *khanunu*, Seneca *kwanonoh*), turkeys (Cherokee *khvna*, Tuscarora *kvnv'*) and bobwhites (Cherokee *ukhkwehi*, Seneca *kohkawi'*). They knew of tree species that included red oak (Cherokee *kule* 'red oak acorn', Cayuga *koweh* 'red oak'), soft maple or American beech (Cherokee *khusi* 'American beech', Cayuga and Seneca *kohso'* 'soft maple') and wild plum (Cherokee *kwanunsdi'i*, Laurentian *honnesta*, Mohawk *ona 'uhste'*). They ate a tuber (Cherokee *nuna* 'potato', Oneida *ohnvnata'* 'potato') but it cannot really have been potato, since that was certainly introduced from South America by Europeans.[26] Cherokee always has to figure in these word families: Cherokee is the only member of the Southern Iroquoian group, so without evidence from Cherokee a word cannot be reconstructed firmly in proto-Iroquoian. This makes identifying the region where proto-Iroquoian was spoken very difficult in practice, because the speakers of Cherokee evidently migrated southwards into a different ecological region, retaining names only for species that range very widely across eastern North America. However, the region to north and south of Lake Ontario has been suggested.

'Our ancestors knew at least three other languages, as trading practices required that they be able to communicate with the Navajo, Hopi, Paiute, and other Yuman-speaking tribes. It is said among Hualapai elders, however, that we are to continue to speak the Huala-pai language,' writes a modern Hualapai, speaker of a small minority language of California.[27] Her succinct description of a multilingual society indicates a linguistic state of things that was widespread in many parts of North America at the moment of first European contact.

There has actually been a great deal of bilingualism in indigenous North America, although European observers don't always report it very clearly.[28] Here are some examples. Among the last speakers of languages of the southeastern states, the linguist Mary Haas noted that one from whose information Tunica had been described 'spoke not only Tunica and Biloxi but Choctaw as well; and the last speaker of Ofo was the wife of one of the Tunica Indians. The association between the Tunica and the Ofo is a very old one, since these two tribes along with the Koroa and some others were living along the Yazoo River in 1700.'[29] Again, there was clearly widespread bilingualism between the Hurons, speakers of a once-powerful Iroquoian language now extinct, and their neighbours the Algonquian-speaking peoples, in the area in eastern Canada and New England in which the two language families lay close together. Sometimes such bilingualism was the prelude to language disappearance: independently of European encroachment, it was always the case, in pre-contact North America as in modern New Guinea and elsewhere in the world, that languages may rise and fall. In several regions, perhaps in many, there were lingua francas used by several neighbouring tribes who had regular trade relations. In the Great Plains, additionally, there was the Plains Indian Sign Language, used equally by speakers of many languages. Incidentally, all of these forms of language contact, wherever they existed, helped the European newcomers in exploration and settlement – simply because they made it possible to get by with one language instead of two or several.

Without a lingua franca, long-distance exploration became very difficult for Europeans. The Spanish explorers of 1771–6 had with them a missionary who spoke Pima. Pimas who spoke Quechan, and Quechans who spoke Cocopa, completed a four-language chain of interpreting which was continuously necessary while the explorers were among the Cocopa. The adventurous Meriwether Lewis and William Clark, while among the Flathead in 1805, made themselves understood through a chain of five languages (English, French, Hidatsa, Shoshoni and Flathead) – and even this would not have been possible without two lucky chances: a French–Hidatsa married couple was present in the party, while their hosts were able to produce a Shoshoni boy who had been enslaved by them years ago but still remembered his childhood language.[30] Sometimes it appears to have been a deliberate practice for children of chiefs to be fostered by a neighbouring people who spoke a different language, as a method of training future diplomats or interpreters – and the existence of this custom helps to explain why chiefs were sometimes willing to have their children educated by Europeans.[31]

Several lingua francas and pidgins developed around the time of European contact, and certainly some of them arose simply because they were needed by Indians to make themselves understood by Europeans. Among these, Chinook Jargon had wide influence on neighbouring languages, lending its word *sapolil* 'bread' to Squamish, Songish, Haida, Yakima and Klamath; its word for money, *tala* borrowed from English *dollar*, was transmitted to Squamish, Songish, Haida, Haisla, Heiltsuk, Quileute, Klamath, Gitksan and Eyak.[32] However, the lingua francas used by Europeans were often ones that they already found in widespread use. Thus Southwestern Ojibwa, an Algonquian language of middle Canada, was a second language among tribes of the western Great Lakes region. Ottawa (whose name now belongs to the capital of Canada) was another language of the Algonquian family which grew up as a lingua franca between Lake Michigan and Lake Ontario. North of the Great Lakes, Cree performed this function, and by the end of the eighteenth century, with the extension of the fur trade, Cree had spread as a pidgin much further west across the Great Plains.

Along the Mississippi the language known as Illinois or Peoria is reported to have served as a lingua franca for three hundred miles downriver from the Illinois river confluence. This is not to say that everybody spoke it, but rather that each successive community along the great river could produce at least somebody who spoke it. Along the northern limits of the Amerindian language areas, across southern Alaska and northern Canada, many peoples spoke a pidgin Eskimo, used by them in trading with Eskimos. It was perhaps through this pidgin that the Montagnais word *pakaakwan* for 'hen' was borrowed into Inuit *pakaakkuani*: the hen was introduced by Europeans, so this certainly happened after initial European contact, but no European language was involved in the Montagnais–Inuit exchange.[33]

Far to the south, Creek was the common language of the Creek confederacy, leading at least one observer in Georgia to an interesting if mistaken conclusion: 'As for their language,' wrote James Oglethorpe in 1734, 'they have two kinds, one which is a vulgar dialect, different in each town, the other a general language common to the Creek Nations, the Chactaws and the Blew Mouths, which if thoroughly searched into would (I believe) be found to be the radical language of all America.'[34] 'Radical language' means the root language, the origin of all the rest. Oglethorpe surely had at the back of his mind, when he put forward this idea, a familiar European parallel: Latin could be called the 'radical language' of western Europe, being the origin of Spanish, French, Italian and others, and yet Latin itself was still in use unchanged as an international language among scholars and in the Roman Catholic Church. Noting that Creek, too, was an international language, he imagined its origin and relationships must be comparable to those of Latin. At all events it is because of the use of Creek here, and of another Algonquian lingua franca a little to the north, and of Mobilian Jargon on either side of the lower Mississippi, that the local native languages of Georgia, Carolina and Louisiana are so incompletely known.[35] Europeans did not need to learn them.

Mobilian Jargon, now just about extinct, was once a very important and widespread lingua franca of the southeast. It drew on several local languages, and soon included loanwords from European ones also, such as *wak* 'cow' from Spanish *vaca*. Curiously, soon after James Oglethorpe had made his deduction concerning Creek, and quite independently, the young French settler J. B. F. Dumont de Montigny made the same guess concerning Mobilian Jargon: 'The Indian learns various languages and, in particular, the mother language. In this country, great and vast as it is, filled with such different nations, there is indeed a mother language spoken everywhere alongside that of each nation, just as Latin is among us.'[36]

As the individual Indian languages of the region disappeared, Mobilian Jargon served as the lingua franca for some of the last surviving speakers of each one. But at a much earlier period Mobilian Jargon was probably instrumental in spreading names of European goods newly introduced to North America. For example, the goat has a similar name, meaning 'stinking deer', in Biloxi (*itaxuhi*), Tunica and Chickasaw. Sugar is called 'sweet salt' in Biloxi (*wakhchkuye*), Tunica and Choctaw.[37]

Europeans made their earliest significant contacts with the speakers of North American languages in the century that followed Columbus's voyage.[38] I say 'significant' because arrows but no words (at least, no words understood on both sides) passed between the Vikings who briefly settled in Vinland and their indigenous neighbours.

As far as North America is concerned, the earliest European linguistic notes were made on 'Laurentian', a long-forgotten language once spoken on the banks of the St Lawrence estuary. The notes were made in France, after the explorer Jacques Cartier and his crew had returned from the great river in 1534–5 with a couple of kidnapped Indians (who, incidentally, went back as interpreters with the next French voyage). It has been argued that Laurentian was not one language, but several – the captives were multilingual and gave their questioners a bit of everything – and it has been proposed more speculatively that the information was gathered and recorded by François Rabelais, author of *Pantagruel* and certainly a man who was fascinated by language. The long-lost Laurentian, whatever exactly it was, lives on in the linguistic record. It was the source of the word *canada* 'settlement', now a place-name covering half of North America.[39]

Still within the sixteenth century, a Jesuit missionary wrote a grammar of a language of Georgia, Guale, but his grammar is lost; a Frenchman made a wordlist, perhaps of the same language, in 1562, though his notes remained in manuscript for three hundred years before being rediscovered and published. A few other notes by Spanish explorers of the southeast can be found, including some words of an extinct language of southern Florida, Calusa. The names of some plants and birds in Carolina Algonquian were noted by Thomas Hariot, one of Walter Raleigh's settlers in North Carolina in 1585–6. A few Eskimo words were recorded on Martin Frobisher's 1576 exploration and in 1586.[40] All these and other languages that were sketchily noted down in the sixteenth century are now long since dead, with two exceptions and with one caveat.

The one caveat, a point to which we shall return in Chapter 6, is that lost languages may live on in a shadowy form if their words and rhetoric were borrowed into languages that are still in use. Powhatan, the Algonquian language of Virginia, known only from a couple of brief wordlists and last spoken some time in the eighteenth century, contributed more words to English than any other Algonquian language, and perhaps more than any other North American language.[41]

Now, here are the two true exceptions. First: Eskimo (Inuit), in its inhospitable landscape, has not yet been overwhelmed by European languages. Europeans have drawn lines around the Eskimo dialects, teaching different scripts and spellings, and applying names like Inuit, Inuktitut and Greenlandic within their own narrow political horizons, but for all their efforts they have not yet made the language die. Second: the Californian language Coast Miwok, of which Francis Drake noted a few words, is still known to one or two old people. Every other North American Indian language touched by Europeans in the sixteenth century has disappeared and Coast Miwok will soon go the way of the rest.

The generalization would hold if we continued the survey into the seventeenth and eighteenth centuries. The sooner a language was encountered by Europeans, the sooner it ceased to exist. It's a little less painful if one restricts the generalization to languages, as I've done here, but I'm afraid it would be equally true if I said 'cultures' or 'peoples'.

At first Europeans were more interested in trade and limited settlement than in large-scale conquest. But already by the early seventeenth century the colonies were spreading. They were taking up more and more former Indian territory, and they were transmitting epidemics, to devastating effect. Meanwhile in the south the Spanish missions, more active at this stage than English or French proselytizers, were already forcibly converting Indian communities to Christianity and enrolling them as slave labour. The seventeenth century was decisive for the disappearance or retreat of indigenous peoples along most of the eastern seaboard. By the early nineteenth century Indians of the east were either confined to small reservations or had been driven beyond the Appalachians; Spanish encroachments and slave-raiding in the south had meanwhile continued.

The vast remaining territories of the Midwest and the West were engulfed in a far shorter timescale: by the end of the nineteenth century Indian peoples had been overwhelmed across the entire continent. By then, almost all of those who survived were entirely subject to US or Canadian government authority; in the US, most were already seeing their children abducted to boarding schools to be refashioned as English-speaking Christians.

So the early advance of Europeans in North America had been slow enough, and knowledge of European languages followed slowly too. The French were on the St Lawrence estuary in the sixteenth century, and already by 1600 wanted to teach their Micmac and other contacts (and Christian converts) to speak French, but found few enthusiastic learners. For the English, too, bilingualism came rather slowly in many places: in early contacts it is fairly often reported that 'a chief's son' acts as interpreter, suggesting that others could not. By the mid-nineteenth century, however, there was widespread bilingualism – in English, in French and in the southwest in Spanish. Even in the early twentieth century, long after the end of Spanish-speaking rule in the southwestern United States, there was a good deal of bilingualism in Spanish among such peoples as the Keresan, Taos and Yaqui.

The second half of the nineteenth century was the beginning of the last act for the indigenous languages of North America. It was in this period that the US Government took control of the whole of its modern contiguous territory, all the way to the West Coast; in this period Europeans began to move through, and to settle in, the western lands that had till then continued to provide sustenance for indigenous pastoralists. Populations in this vast region began a steep decline. Jane Hill, focusing on the Great Basin, tabulates the reasons thus:

(1) famine caused by depletion of resources when large groups of humans and livestock moved through the most favorable environments, and where settlement also occurred there (particularly in Utah); the cutting of piñon pine for firewood and fence posts, and the grazing of stock on grasslands which produced seed crops, were particularly devastating [pine nuts, product of the piñon pine, had been an important food in many parts of the West]; (2) predation on Indians by settlers protecting livestock (with mortality particularly high among effective food-producing adult men) and occasional, more

general massacres; (3) epidemics, particularly of venereal disease where even survivors were likely to have seriously impaired fertility.

It is reasonably clear that the indigenous populations declined sharply, for these reasons, from 1850 to about 1873. That is the date when population figures in the Great Basin were first collected on one of J. W. Powell's expeditions. It is absolutely certain that a severe decline took place thereafter, more or less without respite, from 1873 to 1930. The same factors affected the West generally and California in particular,[42] though in California the depredations of mining prospectors and the lack of any treaty between Indian nations and the US government led to even higher death rates.

Well before 1900, indigenous peoples throughout North America were under the direct control of US and Canadian governments. In nearly all cases, it had become impossible for them to continue their traditional lifestyle: the resources on which they had relied were no longer theirs. Massacres, disease and famine had done their work. From this point onwards the story of the final decline of the indigenous languages of North America is a relatively peaceful one, a story of the interplay of government policies and ideologies with people's lives.

As the native lands of many western tribes disappeared, in the late nineteenth century, the boarding schools began. What was to become US Government policy had already been foreshadowed when, in 1868, a Federal commission whose remit was to promote peaceful relations with the Plains Indians made language an instrument of policy. 'In the difference of language to-day lies two-thirds of our trouble,' its report stated. 'Schools should be established, which children should be required to attend; their barbarous dialects should be blotted out and the English language substituted.'[43] This useful opinion was to be quoted with approval in the *Annual Report of the Commissioner of Indian Affairs* (1887), at which date it was already being put into effect. The Commissioner, J. D. Atkins, appended his own, much more nationalistic, reasoning to that of the commission of 1868. Since the Indians

are in an English-speaking country, they must be taught the language which they must use in transacting business with the people of this country . . . The instruction of the Indians in the vernacular is not only of no use to them, but is detrimental to the cause of their education and civilization, and no school will be permitted on the reservation in which the English language is not exclusively taught.[44]

It was from 1879 onwards that the boarding schools set up by the Bureau of Indian Affairs began their task of destroying indigenous cultures as rapidly and completely as possible, enforcing the removal of Indian children from their families, around the age of seven, to boarding schools, to remould them as English-speaking Christians. It was assumed institutionally that any Indian custom was objectionable, while the customs of whites were the ways of civilization. School-children were taught to despise every detail of their ancestral way of life, including philosophy, religion, language, songs and dress. Their traditional dress was in fact exchanged for military uniforms; their hair was cut in the current fashion. English names were arbitrarily assigned to them. And many reports and reminiscences tell how children were punished and humiliated, often by teachers or other school staff who were themselves Indians, for speaking their mother tongue anywhere, at any time, at school: 'The schools operated on a military system, and if we were caught speaking Navajo, the dormitory matrons, who were Navajo, gave us chores like scrubbing the floors.' Long afterwards the writer of this memoir became a bilingual Navajo teacher at the first American Indian bilingual school in the United States, established in 1966 at Rough Rock: she 'had to pick up where I stopped when I entered boarding school, because my language and culture had been taken away from me'. The boarding school system was still in operation as late as the 1950s.

'That generation', Michael Krauss believes, 'widely underwent what today would be considered brutal child abuse – physical and psycho-logical punishment for speaking a word of their language at school.' Krauss adds, with evident truth, that this conditioning, and the psycho-logical wounds it caused, fully explain why so many indigenous children who went through boarding schools did not want their own children to learn the native language. 'One does not simply get over these experiences.' Although some disagree on this point – John Reyhner argues that the boarding school experience reinforced Amer-indian culture as those who escaped the clutches of the school went 'back to the blanket' and readopted tribal customs – a sizeable number of Amerindian observers concur with Krauss: 'Language loss began with parents not teaching their children the language because they did not want them to have a hard time in school.' 'There can be no doubt that the trauma of boarding school played a large part, consciously and unconsciously, in the decision by individuals, by families and by communities to abandon their traditional language.'[45] The educational policy of the period was thus extremely well designed for its purpose.

The change of mind

There were signs of a change of mind as early as the 1930s, when the punishments and humiliations were officially condemned (but tacitly allowed to continue); meanwhile, a few bilingual programmes in schools were begun. But it was Rough Rock school, established in a remote Navajo-speaking district in 1966, that eventually set a new pattern. Around the same period, as another sign of the loss of old certainties, it was possible for a teacher to begin 'teaching the students [small children] in Hualapai even though the principal had forbidden it and said there was a state law against speaking the native language in school'. Since about 1970 it has actually been legal to teach these languages in school in the United States. In 1990, as a belated official reversal of the century-long policy of eradicating Native American cultures and Amerindian languages, the Native American Languages Act became law.

The Act proclaimed it as the policy of the United States to 'preserve, protect, and promote the rights and freedom of Native Americans to use, practice, and develop Native American languages'. It affirmed 'the right of Indian tribes and other Native American governing bodies to use the Native American languages as a medium of instruction in all schools funded by the Secretary of the Interior'. It asserted that 'the right of Native Americans to express themselves through the use of Native American languages shall not be restricted in any public proceeding, including publicly supported education programs'.[46] It was followed by a second Act in 1992, which authorized a programme of grants to support these aims and claims. Federal help had been available earlier through the National Science Foundation and the US Department of Education, but for the first time the 1992 Act made tribes directly eligible for federal funding to support language conservation and renewal.

However, off the record, the death sentence has not been repealed. James Crawford describes the administrative inaction that followed the 1990 Act:

Among other things it called upon all agencies of the federal government, including the Departments of Interior, Education, and Health and Human Services, to review their activities in consultation with tribes, traditional leaders, and educators to make sure they comply with the policy of conserving Native American languages. By the fall of 1991, the President was supposed to report back to Congress on what was being done and to recommend further changes in law and policy. But the Bush Administration simply ignored these requirements. There is no indication that any review or consultation has taken place. After some prodding by the Senate Select Committee on Indian Affairs, the White House referred the matter to the BIA [Bureau of Indian Affairs], whose only response has been to compile a list of bilingual education programs in its schools. So, while the federal government now has a strong policy statement on file, its real-world impact has thus far been limited.[47]

After 1992, again, Congress was slow to appropriate any real money for the grants that had been authorized and the other costs that the change of policy necessarily entailed. The first sign of cash was a meagre one million dollars, voted in autumn 1994. Experience shows that it can be hard to find suitable teachers for bilingual school programmes, and that money for indigenous language work can easily be cut off for long periods – even at Rough Rock school there was a long gap in funding for Navajo teaching. Unluckily, 'bilingual education' is a political issue that generates more heat than light. In the United States, whenever bilingual education for Spanish-speaking children is unpopular (as it very generally is, among both English-speaking voters and Spanish-speaking parents) education in indigenous languages goes begging. For an exactly comparable reason, the progress of indigenous language rights in Canada was interrupted when English-speaking public opinion turned against a French–English bilingual accord in 1992.

In any case, it is now too late. Teachers were powerful enough to kill the indigenous languages: they are not powerful enough to bring them back to life. In nearly all Amerindian communities children now come to school having learnt English at home, not the old traditional language of their family. 'Nearly all' means *all* the communities that formerly spoke any of the indigenous languages of North America, with the exception of *some* families in *some* communities where the 34 languages 'still spoken by children' (as set out earlier) are still to be heard. There is surely now no school in North America (excepting possibly Arctic Canada) in which every member of each new class of children speaks the local Amerindian language. So, where teaching of indigenous languages and cultures is done, it generally takes the form of foreign language teaching. We know from our own schooldays that foreign language teaching does not give children native command of the language that is being taught. And even where children are being taught the indigenous language at school, they no longer use it actively – precisely because it is no longer spoken to them regularly by their parents. 'It is tragic', wrote one observer, 'to witness parents speaking Hualapai to other adults and, in the next breath, turning to their children and speaking English.' 'Even though there's the teaching at school, [children] don't get the reinforcement from their parents ... Today when I meet with the kids in my village I have to speak English because they don't understand O'odham,' said a bilingual teacher of Papago (now called Tohono O'odham) at a conference on 'Poetics and Politics' at the University of Arizona. Even in this, perhaps the most isolated and self-sufficient of all US Native tribes and one of the more numerous, few if any children are now learning the language from their parents before they go to school.

What the change in policy has done, ironically, is to relieve parents of any doubts they may have had over failing to teach their traditional language to their children. There is now no need, they feel: the school will do it. For one last time I turn to Michael Krauss, on this occasion for a summary of the effects on Alaskan languages of the reversal of educational policy.

Most school programs have not reversed language loss. Possibly they have slowed it down; we cannot know how much worse the situation might have been had not these changes in schools taken place. It might seem ironic that several Alaska languages that still had children speakers in some small isolated villages in 1972 when the Alaska bilingual education legislation was passed are now no longer spoken by children. With the beginning of bilingual education, it appeared that the main threat to Native language maintenance was removed, that our legislative victory had come just in time to save them. In fact, during that very decade of the 1970s, Alaskan languages ceased to be spoken to the children – in Upper Kuskokwim Athabaskan at Nikolai and Telida; Tanaina Athabaskan at Lime Village; Kutchin Athabaskan at Venetie and Arctic Village; Inupiaq Eskimo at Ambler, Shungnak, Kobuk, and Wainwright; Aleut at Atka; and Alutiiq at Nanwalek. Just as we trained teachers and developed school materials and programs for these languages in these villages, the children began coming to school speaking only English.[48]

Among the Navajo, for example, the shift from Navajo to English among parents and young children has clearly accelerated recently although official policies are now so much more liberal. In 1969 over 90 per cent of young Navajo children joining school spoke Navajo. Now, as many as 80 per cent of new Navajo schoolchildren are monolingual English speakers, and the Navajo-speaking children are scattered in rural areas. Even among the rural families who send their children to Rough Rock school a shift towards English is under way and fewer children now come to school having learnt Navajo at home. Yet at a 1991 Senate hearing on the legislation that would become the Native American Languages Act 1992, a Navajo delegation testified eloquently about the spiritual importance of their language without ever referring to the fact that very few Navajo children are now taught the language. 'In the corridor afterward', Michael Krauss reports, 'I asked them if they disagreed that perhaps 80 percent of Navajo children now speak English rather than Navajo. They agreed the percentage might be that high,' but they had evidently chosen not to raise the issue at the hearing. Parents can see clear advantages in encouraging their children to speak English, the language of social and economic mobility. In fact parental worries are now on the other side. Many parents want *more* English for their children: as one educationalist from Arizona reports, 'Concern remains among many parents that time spent in Navajo activities will hinder English academic development.' 'Here a major American tragedy is taking place,' Krauss concludes, 'and people do not want to know or talk about it, it seems.'

Thus, according to James Crawford, 'every step toward modernization puts the indigenous tongue at a greater disadvantage. Gradually its sphere of usage contracts to home and hearth, religious rituals, and traditional ceremonies.'[49]

One reason why it is now too late to reverse the trend is that by comparison with a century ago, when the boarding school programme was under way, the community pressures on *everybody* in North America to speak English have vastly increased. The boarding schools did indeed damage the status of Indian languages within their own communities; recently, however, other influences have been more powerful. In the modern US economic environment people move to work and to study; they marry outside their local communities. Government services must be negotiated for or demanded in English. Jobs outside the reservation must be applied for in English and carried out in English. Even the most remote of reservations are bathed in English-language media: the television and the video cassette recorder are everywhere. These are the new pressures impelling Native Americans to assimilate to the society around them. People observe for themselves that English leads to greater prosperity. It is all too true, and even if they did not observe it for themselves television would tell them so.

In addition, the very long period of boarding school education took its toll. The fact that children were punished for speaking their mother tongue tended to devalue it in the children's own minds, meanwhile instilling a feeling in communities beyond the school that indigenous languages were something to be ashamed of. It was 'a time when speaking the language was discouraged or at least kept quiet'; a speaker at a recent conference observed that when hearing Spanish and Vietnamese spoken openly in her local supermarket she 'wondered why these groups were not ashamed of speaking their language in public, while Indians at one time had been'. 'In a way I *wanted* to forget the language,' said another. She and her husband spoke the same language, 'but we were speaking English all the time . . . My children all learned only the English language. When my mother lived with us, we spoke the language with each other, in the house; but not outside.' In this way, many Native Americans came to accept American society's judgement on their languages. The result now is a groundswell of opposition to bilingual education among Native Americans who vividly remember the pain they suffered in school. They hope to shield their children and grandchildren from the same experience – and confer on their children the economic advantages that fluent English will certainly bring. The final outcome is that although US policy has been officially reversed, and now recognizes indigenous languages as a national asset, parents are still abandoning these indigenous languages in favour of English.[50]

5

HOW TO BECOME A GLOBAL LANGUAGE

National education and national development

In the nineteenth and twentieth centuries we can observe the emergence of a new, positive set of reasons for ceasing to use a minority language. Are these reasons going to be enough to ensure that long-term bilingualism (as we have described for Romani, Yiddish and several other languages) is less likely to arise in the future?

Probably they are.

The first reason for this positive answer is a very simple one. In the last two centuries enlightened states in every part of the world have begun to take an interest in their people's education. Such activities used to depend largely on charitable action by individuals, or on priests and monks, but governments are now involved in them everywhere. It became an ambition that every child should have the opportunity to attend school and be taught to read and write, and in many countries that ambition has been fulfilled.

Few will argue that this development is bad and should be reversed. What matters for the subject of this book is that it has had and is having a strong effect on the language map of the world. What language will be used in education? Some language or other has to be chosen, and whoever does the choosing has enormous power to influence the future.

When education was a private concern – between children, their parents and anyone paid by their parents to teach them – the choice was the parents'. The aim of charities that supported schools was to improve knowledge among the poor, including minority groups, and that meant beginning to teach in the language that children already knew. The interests that were served by such schooling were not national ones. Especially if a religious body took a hand in teaching, children often additionally learnt a language of religion and high culture (Latin in medieval western Europe, classical Arabic in Muslim countries, Pali in southeast Asia), whether or not some attention was also given to improving their knowledge of their mother tongue.

But when eighteenth- and nineteenth-century states began to control and extend popular education, they found that they had acquired the power to prescribe what language should be used in education. Those that were consciously nation states, in the modern sense, showed a strong tendency to follow the French lead and to make a single choice, that of their 'national language'. Switzerland, as an early follower of the French Republican model, was very unusual in specifically legislating to make its three major languages equal (in education as in other matters) – but Switzerland in the 1790s, formerly a federation of almost-independent cantons and soon to revert to that status, was a very unusual country. Apart from this example, even the countries that were definitely not nation states, such as Russia and Austria, some of which had no officially or constitutionally defined 'national language', often took steps to favour their ruling languages as against the many regional minority languages spoken within their borders. In its final incarnation, between 1867 and 1918, the Austrian Empire actually divided itself under the new name of Austria-Hungary into two linguistically separate halves, whose ruling languages were German and Hungarian respectively, while still granting few or no rights to the large linguistic minorities to be found in both halves. In the autocracy that was Russia, the only favoured languages were those of the emperor (Russian) and the Orthodox Church (Church Slavonic). The censors often refused permission for the printing of doubtful material, and that might include schoolbooks in minority languages.

The new states that meanwhile emerged in the nineteenth and twentieth centuries, especially in eastern Europe, had resulted from political movements closely linked with a single culture and language. This was generally destined to be the 'national language' as soon as the state had been created. In nearly every case this process meant ignoring smaller minorities who lived within that state's boundaries and spoke a quite different language. All in all it was unlucky, from the point of view of linguistic diversity, that the spread of state education coincided with the heyday of nationalism and racism. Policy makers often believed, and were not afraid to say, that the local languages and cultures of their country were inferior to their own and should be encouraged to cease to exist. *Anéantir* 'annihilate' was the key word in the title of the Abbé Grégoire's 1790 report: annihilation, thus precisely stated, was the fate he and his political allies had in mind for the local languages of France. 'The sooner the Welsh language disappears . . . the better,' so Matthew Arnold argued in 1867.

By the mid-twentieth century, such views had had plenty of time to penetrate throughout school systems. State education in many developed countries had favoured the national language for several generations. Grandparents, parents and children had all been through school and had learnt by example that the only proper language for education was not their home language or dialect but the language spoken at the capital. In many cases, as in Wales and in the United States, children had been taught that inadvertently speaking a word of a local language or dialect would lead to punishment and humiliation.

Alongside the spread of state education, in modern states many more people than ever before have to deal directly with government agencies. Even if it is possible to get round the need for speaking the national language – to take along a bilingual friend, to find a civil servant who is bilingual – speakers of minority languages in these circumstances soon learn that they are at a disadvantage. Whether they want to 'work the system', or just to make the system work for them as it ought to do, they can achieve what they want to achieve much more effectively if they speak the same language as the government.

Even where a state officially favours multilingualism, practicalities may exert an opposing pressure. China recognizes some very small linguistic minorities, like the 12,000 speakers of Jinuo in Yunnan: but there are no textbooks in Jinuo, and no one to write them, even if there were a script to write them in, so education for Jinuo children is perforce in Chinese. In the Soviet Union, as we have seen, the initial enthusiastic acceptance of every indigenous language as a language of education soon had to be modified: for some very small languages there was not only no writing system but no potential teachers.

Education is not the only driving force. The modern economic world is a harsh environment for countries that prefer the designation 'developing' to that of 'underdeveloped'. Many governments have determined for economic reasons that their countries would be better off with fewer indigenous languages. Nigeria has perhaps 410 of them (but no two counts agree); Cross River State alone, with a population of three million and a relatively small land area, has 67 indigenous languages. National policy in Nigeria tends towards narrowing educational provision and other government finance, just as soon as it is practicable, to the Three Majors (the three national or 'federal' languages, Hausa, Yoruba and Igbo) and English. Since as long ago as 1977 it has been the rule that children should be taught in one of the Three Majors and not in their mother tongue unless it happens to be one of these three. In practice, some minority language speakers in Nigeria are themselves shifting in the same direction, or even directly towards English, though there is also widespread and vocal opposition – opposition which is easily characterized, not altogether falsely, as tending towards tribalism and thus towards dividing Nigeria.[1]

The national language of the Philippines is, of course, Filipino. This is a white lie: the national language is Tagalog, which has 11 million mother-tongue speakers in central Luzon, around the vastly swollen national capital, Manila. Filipino and its earlier form Pilipino are reincarnations of Tagalog, incorporating modest additions from the other major languages of the archipelago, and promulgated as national language. There are well over 200 indigenous languages in the Philippines: by contrast with the situation in Ethiopia, all (not counting English and a couple of Spanish creoles) are related. All belong to the Austronesian family, which means that their speakers find Filipino relatively easy to learn. And they are doing so in vast numbers. Apart from those who speak it as a mother tongue Filipino can claim another 5 million speakers (and probably many more) as a second or third language.

The old French colonies have inherited from their former rulers a strong preference for French and a respect for the power that education confers. The old English colonies have inherited a strong preference for English as a language for issuing instructions and getting things done. In the view of many of those in government – in English- and

French-speaking former colonies and in some other countries too – there may be even better reasons than universal understanding and national development for restricting education to the former colonial language, or to a national language which they happen to speak. A better reason still for doing this may be to maintain their own privileges as the current elite. 'If the language of the bureaucracy is English . . . bureaucrats can offer strong resistance against the promotion of an indigenous language as the official language of state business,'[2] and the same is true – in Africa for example – of other languages besides English. The children of the elite can learn French or English (or Swahili or Amharic) at home, can afford books and tuition, and will not drop out of school; less fortunate children, whose parents don't speak the national language and can't afford extra tuition, will be lost in a French- or English- or Swahili- or Amharic-speaking classroom, will get nowhere and will remain as downtrodden as their parents were. This, certainly, has been observed to be one of the results of the education policy of Congo (Kinshasa), where over 200 languages are spoken and where only 5 per cent of children who enter the mainly French-speaking primary schools get as far as the French-speaking secondary schools.

The Ivory Coast, to take another example, has a vigorous and single-minded policy of promoting French. The population, it is intended, will be unified internally and the state will be more able to compete internationally if French becomes everybody's language of communication. So all teaching, from the first day on which children arrive at school, is in French. There is a problem, however: there is not a sufficient supply of teachers who speak standard French. A survey in 1975 showed that 0.5 per cent of the population spoke Parisian French, and a further 5 per cent spoke what might be defined as Standard Ivory Coast French, a form native French speakers can understand without much difficulty. The remaining 29 per cent of the population who spoke French at all spoke a non-standard local variety of French which those from other countries cannot understand.

Unesco regularly reports on the need to promote local languages. Its words are taken very seriously. In 1975 Unesco and the OAU together 'recognized and affirmed the irreplaceable role of African languages in any development policy'; they recommended that African states should 'choose one or more national languages', and 'national languages' is indeed now the terminology used in many states: the 'official language', usually English or French, which gets you money and power, is distinguished from the 'national languages' that most people speak. The two international organizations recommended that states should 'gradually increase the use of African languages as vehicles of instruction, establishing departments of African linguistics, setting up specialized language institutions ... supporting literacy training in African languages and collecting oral literature'. And in the following year the African Ministers of Education said the same. Several states did some of these things, but a report in 1981 admitted that even if the political will were present, civil servants and media workers were not prepared to implement local language policies: they had the 'wrong attitudes' and were not trained for the task.[3] Unesco Project Horizon 2000 aimed to promote African languages through the last quarter of the twentieth century, with specific targets for the millennium year. Somehow the targets continued to recede, however. In 1997 'African governments attending a fifty-one-country conference on language policies in Harare have agreed to an action plan to encourage the use of indigenous languages,' it was reported. 'The Intergovernmental Conference on Language Policies in Africa, organised by Unesco and the Organization of African Unity, was designed to enhance the link between indigenous languages and economic development. Each country was asked to produce a clear language policy document, within which every language spoken in the country would find its place, before the year 2000.' A language atlas of Africa was also recommended – it sounded like a good idea.[4] In the real Africa, in national contexts, divorced from international conferences, language policies vary considerably. Some states are overtly chauvinistic on the language question; some pursue resolutely multilingual policies. Yet the long-term results appear almost the same. Success in each country means belonging to the elite; to belong to the elite you must speak the official and international language. As soon as they can, that is what even the most down-trodden of minority language speakers will aim at, for their children even more than for themselves.

Finally, national education has spread literacy, in most countries, to a level it had never reached before. At the same time, cheap paper and fast printing have provided this newly literate population with information and entertainment in the form of popular books and newspapers. Now printing does not by its nature necessarily give special support to national or majority languages, nor does it under-mine minorities: in fact even very small minorities can support a publishing trade. But in practice printing, like the other media, does reinforce the trend. What is published in minority languages will tend to be of local interest or at an elementary level. Those who are literate in a major language will find that they have far greater access to the world of information. For example, Welsh and Irish speakers who want to read a daily newspaper have no choice but to read it in English. No one publishes a daily newspaper in these languages, because all their speakers who want to read a newspaper can read English. The English-speaking market offers a far greater volume of sales, and that means bigger, more informative newspapers. Plenty of best-selling English novels are translated into French, German and Spanish; no one ever bothers to translate them into Welsh or Irish, because every-one who speaks those languages and might want to read the books can read them in English anyway.

It is just the same with Occitan or Provençal, the language of southern France. 'What is killing Occitan?' asked a French linguist in 1986, and this was his answer: 'First there are the modern media through which ideas are spread: the national and syndicated press, the radio, the cinema, and television. All of these penetrate the deepest recesses of the countryside, and all of them are vehicles of French, a French language that impresses itself on every consciousness.' There are plenty of other practical reasons, including the increase in indus-trialization and in the numbers of large businesses, where French is the language of the workplace: 'the unending invasion of a multitude of workers employed locally, but with no local roots; migrant workers; and now also agricultural businesses of industrial proportions, which are to be found even in the most inaccessible of places. And then there is the annual invasion of tourists.'[5]

The combined effect of such pressures is to reduce the spheres of daily life in which local languages are used. A sign of the threat to the continued use of Pennsylvania German is that publications on the language have for some time had a noticeably folklorish flavour. It is easier to find mildly amusing phrasebooks of Penn Dutch, aimed at satisfying the wish of tourists to buy cheap mementoes, than it is to find really useful grammars or dictionaries. I need only cite *Quaint Idioms and Expressions of the Pennsylvania Germans: A Delightful Bit of Entertainment.*[6] Newspaper columns in Pennsylvania German are sure to take a humorous line, or to publish undemanding, folksy poetry. Exactly the same could be said of booklets and newspaper columns in the Yorkshire dialect of English. In this way, not only curious outsiders but also those who use the language every day are steered towards a view of it as being limited and somewhat less than serious in its functions – the same view that is evidently held by the anonymous writer on Official English, quoted on p. 144, who placed 'all languages and cultures', excepting English, firmly in the milieu of 'homes, churches, private schools and ethnic celebrations'.

There is, unfortunately, truth in the stereotype. Access to the great majority languages really does give access to a vast cultural heritage. You can read all the books that matter, because if they were not originally written in these languages, and if anyone supposes that they matter, then they will be translated, won't they? You can watch all the films and television series that matter, and you won't even be distracted by the original language of production, because if those films really do matter, they're sure to be dubbed into English or French. And if you happen to be watching television somewhere where one of the other languages of the world is spoken, you will find that English films are subtitled, not dubbed, so that you can learn English while watching.

Finally, it seems, English is all you need. This particular trend, now rapidly gathering pace, has been a long time developing.

The rise of English

English originated as the language of the lowlands of Britain – before it was spoken here, it did not exist as a distinct language or dialect at all. The territory over which English (that is, Old English, otherwise known as Anglo-Saxon) was spoken was fixed, quite firmly, with the establishment of the seven kingdoms of Anglo-Saxon England between AD 450 and 700. Everywhere east of a meandering line that runs from the mouth of the Tamar to the Firth of Clyde, English-speaking kings ruled and English was in use. So it remained for some centuries: neither Norse nor Norman French was eventually adopted anywhere in England as a first language.

The first overseas spread of English speech was to Ireland, where English conquests began in the twelfth century though the whole country was not subjugated until the sixteenth. At various times there was significant migration of English-speaking settlers to Ireland. At the same time the range of English was very gradually being extended in Britain itself. In Cornwall and Scotland, in both of which English was the language of government by the eleventh century, it spread through the population very slowly; in Wales, where English conquests were essentially completed by the thirteenth century, Welsh is still spoken by half a million people at the beginning of the twenty-first. As we saw above, Irish survives only precariously as a mother tongue, and Cornish was last spoken as such more than a century ago. Scottish Gaelic has about 80,000 speakers in the Western Isles and the western Highlands: its future is scarcely less threatened that that of Irish.

Further afield, it was in the late sixteenth century that English began to be spoken in colonies in North America. Much more than was the case in Ireland, the language spread in North America because of migration. There were French speakers to the north and south and a few Spanish to the southwest, and those languages survive in some of their original locations to this day. There have also been numerous self-sufficient communities speaking several other European languages, notably Dutch and Low German. Dutch, of course, was briefly a language of colonial government in the Hudson Valley region. In practice, however, English soon came to serve without dispute as the lingua franca among all these populations. With even less doubt or dispute, English has been the language that all later immigrants to the United States and Canada have wanted to learn. Most came to share in the prosperity of these two countries, and one did that by speaking English. The United States has at times been fertile ground for linguistic nationalism or imperialism – we've seen evidence of this already, with the Indian boarding schools and now the Official English movement. Canada, too, can be linguistically touchy. But, in practice, looking at the matter statistically, the overwhelming of all other languages in the

United States by English has had very little to do with any such overt pressure (unluckily, the Amerindian languages, statistically insignificant, differ from the languages of immigrants in that when they disappear from North America they are gone for good). It simply turns out to be the fact that you manage better in the United States (and in most of Canada) when you speak English well.

There have been other countries, too, which English-speaking migrants were able to treat as virgin territory, paying rather little attention to those who lived there already: Australia, New Zealand, and parts of southern Rhodesia (Zimbabwe), South Africa, Kenya and Argentina. In the first two, as in the United States, English was the one obvious lingua franca and is the national language today. In the others the English speakers were never present in such numbers, yet English has retained a national role in all of them except Argentina.

Meanwhile, in the nineteenth century and the first half of the twentieth, English served a brief term (if I may use this expression) as the language of a world-encircling empire or two. For some or all of this period, English was the language of high-level administration in the countries now called India, Pakistan, Sri Lanka, Burma, Malaysia and Singapore, Papua New Guinea, the Philippines, Alaska, most of the Caribbean, some of West Africa from the Gambia to Nigeria, much of southeastern Africa from Zimbabwe to Kenya, part of Somalia, part of Yemen and numerous smaller territories and islands – because all these countries were ruled by Britain or in a couple of cases by the United States.

It's not surprising in any particular case that English still has nationwide official and educational functions in these countries – as it has, in nearly every one of them. Languages of government and culture are often introduced by conquest, and they do sometimes continue to be used even if the conquerors go away. But it is surprising and unprecedented that just one language should fulfil these functions in so many territories all around the world. This makes us take a second look. What is it about the history of English that has made it turn so rapidly into the world language?

The kind of explanation favoured by Otto Jespersen – that English has a masculine or manly, adult and energetic 'character' – is out of fashion now for the very best of reasons. It quite fails to deal with the fact that women as well as men speak English, and that men who speak Italian and Spanish (and even Hawaiian) manage to assert their masculinity quite as effectively as those who speak English. Anthropomorphic characterizations of language would really tell us nothing even if any two people could agree on them. There is no reason to think that Jespersen was a more sensitive observer than Barère, a hundred and fifty years before him, who had argued from linguistic characterization that French was destined to become the world language; or than Horace, two thousand years before, who had known that Latin would spread across the world. All three were backing winners, but no satisfactory explanation is to be found in the 'character' of their languages.

There is an interesting similarity between the spread of Latin and that of English. In both cases it is possible to name *three routes* by which the spread took place, and all were active at the same time.

Route one: colonization. In Italy, Spain, Gaul and other parts of the Roman world, Roman and 'Latin' citizens from a vastly swelling population were resettled in *coloniae*, excellently located to become centres of trade and prosperity. The German city of Köln (Cologne) is one: many others could be named, but it happens that the modern name of Köln is still a reminiscence of its Latin title, which in full was *Colonia Iulia Agrippinensis*, so named in honour of two eminent Roman lineages of its day. Was Latin the ancestral tongue of all the people so resettled? Far from it: there is not so much room in old Latium. But, whatever their attainments in Latin at the moment when they moved, there was no other language but Latin that all were likely either to know or to want to learn. So there could have been no other lingua franca for them but Latin once they were *in situ*.

In the same way, extensive colonization took place in several territories under English-speaking government: the United States, Canada, Australia and others named above. Was English the ancestral language of all those people? Far from it. Even England is not big enough for that: and even though many family names have changed in the direction of English, a search through a telephone book in the United States will show what a large proportion of US residents have non-English-speaking roots. But English was eventually the only possible lingua franca for all these migrants. Some – a larger proportion, probably, than would have been the case under the Roman Empire – initially established their own linguistically unified communities: some of the German and Scandinavian speakers in the United States, many speakers of Hindi and Bhojpuri in numerous British colonies, and many slaves in the southern United States and the Caribbean whose first lingua franca will have been an English creole rather than English *tout court*. These and their descendants, naturally, retained their own languages longer than they would otherwise have done, simply because they formed part of a settled language community. Even so, most of them have eventually needed English to talk to their fellow-citizens, and in nearly every case the long-term maintenance of their old community language, if it has survived thus far, is now in doubt.

Route two: government and what it brings. Latin spread across every province of the western Empire, even where colonies were few and far between. Why? You needed Latin to join the army, and to trade with the army or with individual soldiers. You needed Latin to trade with migrants or colonists, wherever else in the Empire they might come from. Latin was the official language of municipalities, and you needed Latin to become a councillor. You remember that Ausonius' father managed to achieve this status at Bazas and Bordeaux with less than perfect Latin – but the Latin of the next generation, the Latin written by Ausonius the poet himself, is not bad at all. Latin was the language of the law, of provincial governors' courts and of every public and official function that took place in Rome itself. If you had ambitions to join in any of this, or for your children to do so, Latin was needed.

So it was in the British Empire. In some British possessions, notably India, there was a powerful indigenous cultural tradition complete with education system; but even where this existed, and even more where it did not, it was true for practically everybody that the best route to self-advancement and prosperity lay through knowing English. To rise above a certain level in local administration, or to succeed commercially beyond the local horizon, or to achieve anything at all in the wider Empire, English was indispensable. Local schools and colleges, whether under missionary or government patronage, steered pupils towards English – the higher the level they reached, the more total was the English emphasis. Advanced study was entirely in English, and by the mid-twentieth century a significant number of Africans and Asians of the Empire were pursuing their studies in Britain.

Route three: long-distance trade, notably trade by sea. No one can say for certain what languages were most popular on the ships and in the harbour taverns of the Roman Empire, but here's an informed guess: Greek and Aramaic were in gradual decline; Latin was taking over. And here are the reasons for making that guess. By medieval times there was a Latin-like language spoken on these seaways, not quite Italian, not quite Catalan, something different, and something that was used not only by the Romance language speakers of the west but also by Arabic speakers of the east, by Jewish traders from all over and by English and others who came to trade or to go on pilgrimages. It was called *Lingua Franca* by Italians (and that is why we now use that name, without the initial capitals, for any shared language). English travellers called it that too, or sometimes translated the words literally and said *Frank Tongue*. No one knows when this language began to be used. But under the Roman Empire one can see such a persistent pattern of exchanges between Greek and Latin of words for foods and other trade goods, for travel and commerce, that one can suspect the existence of a progenitor of the Lingua Franca as far back as Roman times. Why did Greeks begin to use Latin-like names for peach (*rodakinon* from Latin *duracinum*), apricot (*brekokkion* from Latin *praecocium*), lettuce (*maroulion* from unrecorded Latin *amarulum*) and many others, when there had been perfectly good Greek names for these things already (*persikon, armeniakon, thridax*)? And why were these new names sometimes not the regular Latin ones (*persica* 'peach', *lactuca* 'lettuce'), but names of varieties or qualities ('clingstone', 'early-ripe', 'bitterish')?[7] The likely answer: they were tradesmen's jargon, one aspect of an unofficial Latin that was destined to develop into the medieval Lingua Franca.

At the time of the early explorations, the fifteenth and sixteenth centuries, the first language of the ocean seaways and harbours was Portuguese. Sometimes it was Portuguese in a fairly standard form; sometimes it was a pidgin Portuguese that drew on the resources of the old Lingua Franca. However, by the nineteenth century Portuguese was much less of a world language and except in a few isolated areas pidgin Portuguese was forgotten. Meanwhile English and its relative, pidgin English, had gradually spread as English trade had done. The English of the shipping lanes, it has been argued, provides a better clue to the origins of US English than does any particular local dialect in England.[8] Pidgin English (not a separate invention, rather a new use of pidgin Portuguese with English words) lies somewhere behind the English creoles of the Caribbean, not to mention the creoles of the slave plantations in the southern United States. And those creoles belong in the ancestry of modern Black English, whether we decide that Black English is currently tending to converge with other forms of US English or to diverge from them. Pidgin English is the immediate progenitor of Hawaiian Creole English, a significant language in that multilingual US state; of Tok Pisin, the national language of Papua New Guinea; of West African Pidgin English, used by millions in Nigeria; of Kamtok, used similarly in Cameroon; and others too. These languages are sufficiently distant from standard English that it takes a little time to learn them; yet they are also in a symbiosis with English. They are close enough to provide a good basis for their speakers to learn a more standard form of English if they need to. Many speakers, locally, can handle both pidgin and standard English.

Here's the conclusion. All three routes for the spread of English, operating at the same time, had reinforced one another, just as had happened with Latin long before. In 1936, as the sun was about to set on the British Empire, H. L. Mencken, in *The American Language*, estimated the number of speakers of English thus:

First let us list those to whom English is their native tongue. They run to about 112,000,000 in the continental United States, to 42,000,000 in the United Kingdom, to 6,000,000 in Canada, 6,000,000 in Australia, 3,000,000 in Ireland, 2,000,000 in South Africa, and probably 3,000,000 in the remaining British colonies and in the possessions of the United States. All these figures are very conservative, and they foot up to 174,000,000 . . . Altogether it is probable that English is now spoken as a second language by at least 20,000,000 people throughout the world.[9]

This is how the stage was set for the enormous expansion in the use of English that was still to follow in the remainder of the twentieth century.

When the Roman Empire ended, Latin more or less ceased to spread further as a language of everyday use. But that was not the end for Latin as a language. It continued in use for many centuries (even, in a few special circumstances, until today) as a language of international communication. It was a spoken language, learnt at school and used by educated people especially when they were talking to others whose mother tongue was different from their own. It was also a written language. As such it was used at first for literature of every kind; it continued to be used throughout medieval times, for a whole millennium after the fall of the western Empire, for the majority of texts that we would now describe as scientific or academic or aimed at an international or educated audience. Perhaps it is not surprising that Latin was used in this way in countries to which it had originally spread as a spoken language, which roughly means the countries where Romance languages are now spoken. It is slightly more surprising, at first sight, that Latin was also used in just the same way in many surrounding countries, all the way from Ireland in the west to Hungary in the east. Some of these, like Hungary and western Germany, had been part of the Empire; others, like Denmark and Poland, had been a long way from its borders. They all came to use Latin.

Unfortunately, we cannot do a statistical comparison. The number of books and other documents of all kinds in Latin that survive from the later period, after the Empire fell, is enormously greater than the number surviving from the period of the Empire. You can read all the Latin texts from the Empire, if you care to spend your life on it; but even the Abbé Migne, who printed hundreds of folio volumes of medieval Latin in his *Patrologia Latina* and was bold enough to call it a *cursus completus* 'complete survey', knew in his heart of hearts that he could never find or read or print all of it. However, the reason why there's more medieval than classical Latin relates to the chances of survival: the later a text was written, the less likely it has been to meet with censorship, vandalism, vermin, fire, flood and forgetfulness. So we cannot tell for sure whether more people were writing more Latin in medieval times than they were under the Empire. We may well think so, though.

The linguistic result of the break-up of the British Empire has been, so far as we can yet see, comparable with that of the western Roman Empire.

Here are the obvious similarities. English remains in use in all the countries to which it spread so thoroughly as to become a majority mother tongue – from the United States and Canada to Australia and New Zealand. That is not at all surprising. English remains in use in most of the countries of the Empire to which it did *not* spread as a majority mother tongue: that includes – to name only a selection – India, the Philippines (a United States possession, not a British one), Nigeria, South Africa (where there is a significant minority speaking it as a mother tongue), Ghana, Kenya, Puerto Rico (still under US rule). Even in countries such as Tanzania, Pakistan and Malaysia, which have been least enthusiastic about English politically, English is still a significant language of education and culture. And English is still spreading, as a second language, to countries which were never part of the Empire. We can observe its ever wider use in the Netherlands, in Denmark and in western Europe generally; we can observe its use in Thailand, in Ethiopia, in Mozambique.

There are, however, two significant differences between the break-up of the Roman Empire and that of the British Empire. One of these emerges from the lists in the preceding paragraph. Most of the countries in these lists had their boundaries drawn in the period of European colonialism, for almost random European reasons, and those boundaries have been fossilized in the current post-colonial period during which nationalism is popular and regional secession and wars of conquest are not. Therefore many countries inherit no internal unity, and certainly no linguistic unity. If they began with English, they cannot do without it now – it is the only language which all their linguistic minorities will learn. It isn't so in Papua New Guinea, Tanzania, Malaysia, the Philippines and Pakistan, which can claim Tok Pisin, Swahili, Malay (renamed Malaysian), Tagalog (renamed Filipino) and Urdu as national languages – the two renamings indicate the need, even in such countries as these, for the national language not to be identified with a single ethnic group. But it is most definitely so in Nigeria, where any attempt to promote Hausa (the national language with the largest number of speakers) would be a recipe for conflict; it is so in India, where the special status of Hindi is the cause of resentment in many regions while the special status of English is not a regionally divisive issue.

The second difference is that the scale of these events is so much larger. Latin as a language of Empire centred on the western Mediterranean, but British and US possessions stretched around the world. Colour them in on a map of time-zones: they are to be found in every one. Latin as an international language never reached far beyond western and central Europe, but it is becoming very difficult to find countries anywhere in the world in which English is not taught to schoolchildren as second or third language, and education is every year reaching a larger proportion of the children of the world. These are some reasons why English now seems to be spreading far faster and over a far wider geographical area than Latin ever did.

So when we compare the figures quoted above, as given by H. L. Mencken in 1936, and those now to be quoted from Braj B. Kachru, precisely fifty years later in 1986, we find the most astonishing contrast not in the number of mother-tongue speakers (it had nearly doubled – but that, after all, is to be set beside the world-wide increase in human population over the same period) but in the number of second-language speakers of English. This figure, estimated by Mencken at 20,000,000, had multiplied as many as twenty times in fifty years if Kachru was right:

The number of foreign-language and second-language users together adds up to 300 to 400 million ... Whatever the exact figures, this is a historically unprecedented phenomenon of language spread. When we add to this figure almost 300 million native speakers, we get 700 million users of English around the world ... The roles which linguistic visionaries foresaw for an artificial international language have slowly been assumed by English. As the statistics show, those who use English as their second or foreign ... language now outnumber the users of Australian (15.8 million), Canadian (25.4 million), British (56.4 million), American (238.9 million), and New Zealand (3.3 million) varieties.[10]

In 1936 Mencken had estimated that there was a total of 194 million users of English. In 1986 Kachru estimated 700 million. David Crystal, eleven years later in 1997, estimated 700 million 'fluent' users or as many as 1,800 million 'competent' users of English.[11] If he is anywhere near the truth, English is approaching the position in which it is spoken by twice as many people as any other language.

In the world we live in now, people travel – sometimes over long distances – to study or to find work. This is not in itself new, but it is happening on a much larger scale. In practically every part of the world, far more children than ever before are attending a college or university. Far more of them than ever before are moving to a distant region or to another country in order to do this. And while they are doing it they become aware of work opportunities far from home. Many will never return to their home communities, or will plan to do so only when they retire from work.

This, too, happened in the Roman Empire: it was surely one of the principal reasons why Latin and Greek spread so widely. In the modern world it is happening internationally. There is no simple reason why the trend should serve to promote the use of English more than any other language. Indeed, it is true that there are also more speakers who are turning to other languages (including Spanish, French, Russian and Arabic) as a result of the same trend. Additionally, and for the same reason, there is an increase in the use of all national languages as against regional and local ones.

But English starts from a higher base. It is a national language of far more countries than any other language is, and among those countries is India, one of the two largest countries in the world and perhaps the most multilingual one. Not only is the proportion of people greater for whom – given that they are to learn their national language – that language happens to be English; English is also more likely than any other language to be the most useful choice when people travel abroad, outside their own cultural region. It is not the only choice, of course; and it is certainly not the preferred choice for any reason of linguistic character, such as Otto Jespersen might have given. In a recent textbook of the history of English, Thomas Pyles and John Algeo demonstrate how much more prosaic – and more convincing – is the modern answer to the question 'Why English?': 'The extraordinary spread of English is not due to any inherent virtue, but rather to the fact that by historical chance it has become the most useful language for others to learn.'[12]

That 'historical chance' has been the subject of the first part of this chapter. Let's now glance at the extent of the modern usefulness of English.

Bertrand Barère, quoted on pp. 132–3, said that by the eighteenth century French had become the language of royal courts (rather to the displeasure of revolutionary thinkers). It remained so, and was therefore also the first language of diplomacy, until some time in the mid-twentieth century. But English is certainly the first language of diplomacy now. What marked the change? It is hard to say precisely, though the increasing influence internationally of the United States had something to do with it. There was something more than symbolism in one particular geolinguistic shift. Geneva (in the French-speaking part of Switzerland) was chosen as the permanent home of the League of Nations, whose aim was to regulate international affairs after the First World War. The United States was not a member. After the Second World War its replacement, the United Nations Organization, was domiciled in New York, and the United States was the wealthiest member. The League worked in both French and English. There were initially five, later six, official languages of the United Nations (in international organizations the multiplication of official languages is an expensive business: the EU, the largest translation client in the world, consumes one and a half million pages of translation a year). Well, in spite of those six official languages, at the UN English is now used far more than French or any of the others, especially in informal committees. Most other international organizations use English without question as their main language of work, even if they also have French and perhaps Spanish as official working languages. In ten years the proportion of documents produced by the OECD whose originals are in English has risen from 70 per cent to 85 per cent. English seems to prevail even where it is not the obvious language for participants to use. 'I was shocked', says David Laitin, 'to observe in an inter-Baltic political conference in 1991, where all participants [were able to speak] Russian fluently, that virtually all participants took it as a point of honor to speak in (often halting) English.'[13]

Those in the seventeenth and eighteenth centuries who bewailed the poverty of German and English – speaking both of their limited vocabulary and their insufficiently precise syntax – were making a mental comparison with Latin, which was still in its heyday as language of scholarship and science in western Europe, and was often first among the languages that one would learn at school. It would not be true to say that any single language supplanted Latin. English, French and German were all major languages of scholarship in the nineteenth and early twentieth centuries, German perhaps being the most favoured of the three. Its leading position is now a thing of the past. Nazi anti-intellectualism and anti-Semitism played a role here; so did the great expansion of US universities through the twentieth century; so did the increasing number of international scholars originating from former colonial countries (notably India), because most of these will have English as a second language. It is worth adding, incidentally, that already in 1971, 74 per cent of scientific journals and 83 per cent of other scholarly journals published in India were in English.[14] It's now noticeable, and is certainly noticed by French- and German-speaking scholars themselves, that at international conferences even in France and Germany, and even where a large proportion of the participants are French or German speakers, more and more sessions take place in English, because English is likely to be the only language that is common to practically everybody in the room. If English is the language of scholarship generally, still more is it the language of science, and still more of computer sciences.

For some time now English has been accepted as the international language of air traffic control. Naturally, passengers will be addressed in languages appropriate to the flight they are on – usually in English and in the official languages of their points of departure and arrival. Linguistic innovations that go beyond this are not usually welcomed: for example, in the mid-1980s there was an experiment in the use of the Three Majors, Yoruba, Igbo and Hausa, on Nigeria Airways, but it appears to have been abandoned soon afterwards, 'possibly because of lack of staff . . . possibly also that with the rise of air fares only a small elite can afford to travel by air',[15] more likely that most travellers knew some English, found the duplicated announcements tiresome and felt that English was appropriate to this modern mode of travel.

In ways like this, English is becoming the obvious international language to many other people than the political and scientific elite. Almost across the world, and not only in airports, where there are bilingual public signs, one of the two languages will be English. If newspapers and magazines are for sale, and if there are any international titles at all, some of them will be in English. Not only that, but some of the journals in the local language, whatever it is, will be versions of English-language originals, often with an English title, and with generous use of English loanwords in the text. Among the television channels available, almost everywhere in the world, will be at least one in English, and some of the others will be broadcasting English-language shows with dubbing or subtitles. All this in itself gains in significance as those who pay attention to press, radio and television begin to make up a large proportion of the population.

Why is it that after a century of publication the *Jewish Daily Forward*, the historic Yiddish daily newspaper of New York, has seen its readership melt away – in a much more rapid decline than that of the actual number of Yiddish speakers? The reason is that Yiddish speakers in New York are practically all bilingual in English. *The Forward* tells them about their own community, and succeeded in keeping its niche market for many years by doing exactly that; but if readers' eyes are focused on the world, and not on their traditional community, the niche market disappears. English newspapers such as the *New York Times* offer far more than the *Forward* can.

Why is it that although 75 per cent of the eleven million population of Zimbabwe speak Shona and 16 per cent speak the second national language, Ndebele, there is not a single daily newspaper in either of those two languages?[16] Why is it that although Web translation – of a sort – is available to convert Web pages with English text into numerous foreign languages before the surfer's eyes, very few Web surfers use the facility? The answer to these two questions is the same as the reason for the sudden decline of the Yiddish daily paper: it is that readers and surfers rather expect the up-to-date, exciting, international information that they are looking for in their newspapers or on Web sites to be in English. They may know scarcely enough English to handle it, but that, after all, is how people have always learnt new languages – by needing to know them, and by practising until they do. It's hard work, but it's work that human brains are designed for.

Why was it that the speakers at the Baltic conference, in the quotation by David Laitin above, preferred halting English to fluent Russian? The negative reason was that until that very year Russian was a language of imperialism in the Baltic. Speakers who represented Baltic states struggling to assert their independence clearly preferred to find a common language that had no such political overtones, and English was the only other choice.

English and French are the two major international languages of sub-Saharan Africa, used for practical purposes and for international communication by many independent African states. They are the two major international languages of Europe, each being the official language of a large European country and with official status elsewhere too; each being widely taught in European schools as second languages. In Africa, and in Europe too, we might think that these two international languages are on an equal footing. Somehow it isn't so. English is gradually emerging as the first working language of the Organization of African Unity; in just the same way, though Britain and Ireland were very late in joining the EU, English is gradually becoming the first working language of the EU.

In France there is a long tradition of pride in the French language – we have seen something of its effect on minority languages in France – and the apparently inexorable progress of English does not go unnoticed. As in Quebec, there are laws in France that restrict the use of English (or, more precisely, laws that impose the use of French) in certain public contexts. In the same way, politicians and observers in many other countries have seen the rise of English as a threat to their own cultures. In 1946 Mahatma Gandhi complained that 'people seem to be drunk with the wine of English and they speak English in their clubs, in their home and everywhere. They are denationalized.' After Indian independence in 1947 Gandhi reverted to the same theme, urging the gradual abandonment of English as an official language in India: 'My plea is for banishing English as a cultural usurper as we successfully banished the political rule of the English usurper.' Ironically, these pronouncements were made *in English*. India did in fact adopt a policy on the lines proposed by Gandhi, with the aim of replacing English by Hindi within fifteen years. Sixty years later, in spite of this policy, English still remains co-official language with Hindi. Since Hindi is itself one of the regional languages of India, the promotion of Hindi continues to arouse resentment in other regions: English is neutral, being equally foreign to all. Gandhi in fact had a different answer to that very problem. It seems strange now, but his own preference was for the promotion of Hindustani[17] – a linguistic variety lying somewhere between Hindi (a language of Hindus) and Urdu (a lingua franca of Muslims). As Urdu flourished when India was dominated by Muslims, so Hindustani had flourished under British rule. Gandhi could, of course, have regarded Hindustani as a cultural usurper just like English – but Hindustani did at least originate in the subcontinent, and in any case the practical demands of nationalism allowed him to overlook the point. However, with the split of India and Pakistan, Hindustani lost its *raison d'être* and is now forgotten.

It is surprising how easily English can be adopted as a compromise language – because it is so widely known. In the 1990s Nigeria was planning its new federal capital at Abuja, a site purposely chosen as being initially dominated by none of the Three Majors. In Lagos the dominant languages had been Yoruba (because Lagos stood firmly in Yoruba country) and Nigerian Pidgin English, with standard English very much a third. It was immediately realized, however, that the new Federal territory would have a different linguistic makeup. Hausa, Yoruba and English would all be in contention – Hausa because it is Nigeria's largest language group and had been the administrative language of the region where Abuja was being developed; Yoruba because of its established position among civil servants in Lagos; but English (standard English rather than Nigerian Pidgin) was in contention too. 'English is also the language of the new international community of embassies, firms and consultants which, living in a cultural no-man's-land, will reinforce its use;' while new educational institutions such as the University of Abuja would certainly raise its prestige and increase its use locally. It was also foreseen that in Nigeria's new State Houses of Assembly English would play a greater role than in the Second Republic: candidates would need an educational qualification (entailing some knowledge of English) before registering. Apart from any such requirement 'it can already be seen in the Borno State House of Assembly that less Kanuri and Hausa are used than before – because representatives belong to a generation that has benefitted from public, i.e. Western-type, education.'[18]

We have seen how Russian prospered, almost in spite of the multilingual good intentions written into Soviet law, as the common language of the Soviet Union. We have seen how English becomes more and more indispensable, whatever national linguistic planners might prefer, in

Nigeria and in India. And now Europe is gradually moving (even while the British are rowing the other way) towards becoming a single multilingual state. Is English about to become the lingua franca of Europe too? The answer is that in many contexts it already is; and, yes, its use is likely to spread rapidly, though there will be even more opposition than there was in India to any formal recognition of a special role for English.

Signs of this development are to be seen in some already-multilingual countries of Europe. Dutch speakers of the northern half of Belgium, well aware of course that not many foreign visitors are likely to have a knowledge of Dutch, are generally cool towards a stranger who speaks French, even though they themselves probably know French quite well. The reason is simple: to speak French in northern Belgium is to make a political statement. They are much more welcoming to a stranger who speaks English, a language which in the Belgian context is neutral. In northern Belgium English might well be regarded even as a friendly neutral, since it is well known that the world-wide French-speaking movement, la Francophonie, collectively regards English as the primary linguistic enemy. Meanwhile in Estonia, with its Estonian-speaking majority and very large Russian-speaking minority, until recently the obvious inter-group communication language was Russian, but very soon it is going be English. English will be the only language that both communities can speak, since Estonians no longer want to learn Russian and Russians never did want to learn Estonian. Although Estonian is now the sole national language, there are still no incentives and scarcely any facilities for Russians to learn it: the Russian-language schools have no qualified Estonian teachers or Estonian textbooks. What they can and do teach, as do the Estonian-language schools also, is English.

There's much more, however. Whenever in Europe a native meets a traveller, and it seems unlikely the native's language will serve, English is the first language that is tried. In hotels and on all forms of transport, English is the second language – and occasionally the first. When French schoolchildren travel to Germany on exchange, and German children to France, the aim is for each group to practise the language of the other – but in fact, with or without the participation of their teachers, a good deal of the communication actually takes place in English. When French sports reporters interview German, Italian, Spanish or East European athletes, on nearly every occasion the interview language is English.

Converging on English

A very large and ever-growing number of English loanwords is to be found in many languages of the world: in fact it would now be difficult to find languages that have none. Often English words first become familiar in a foreign language in exactly the context that has just been described – in multilingual conversation. Often, too, they will be introduced by the person responsible for introducing a new idea or a new product to those who speak some foreign language. Often it is not easy to say who first introduced a new English loanword, and if a satisfactory term already existed in the other language it may be hard to say why the loanword ever became accepted.

It is clear why English once borrowed *flirt* (French *la fleurette*) and *stop* (older French *estape*, modern *étape*) and *Vaudeville* and *ticket* (*étiquette*) from French. Just so, it is clear enough why French has borrowed *smoking* (English *smoking jacket*), *parking* (American English *parking lot*), *sport* (English *sports*) and *weekend* from English. These were concepts, complete with associations, that had become well known in the 'lending' language before they were adopted by speakers of the 'borrowing' language. But many loanwords strike the impartial observer as superfluous. Why did English borrow *premier* as well as *prime minister* (both from French *premier ministre*)? Why did French borrow *flirt* and *stop* and *ticket* back again from English?

Then there are the words whose connection with English is symbolic, not real. Why is the game of *clay pigeon shooting* called *ball-trap* in French? Why is a *lapel badge* called *un pin's*, complete with functionless but stylish apostrophe? In both cases, the real English term happens to be clumsy and somewhat obscure – neither *lapel* nor *clay pigeon* are concepts familiar to every apprentice French speaker of English – but why did the innovators in these cases introduce an English-sounding term into French rather than a French one?

Some loanwords become closely integrated into the grammar of their new language. Pennsylvania German borrowed American English *gown* 'lady's dress' in the form *gaund*; but it created its own natural plural form for the word, *gaynd*, which has nothing to do with English *gowns*. Yiddish did the same with American English *shop* 'workshop': the singular is *shap* (Yiddish short *a* being the nearest available vowel to American English short *o*), but the plural is, as is natural in Yiddish, *sheper*. In the same way, an English phrase may be reworked into the new language grammatically, though the result is still wholly English: so *conscientious objectors* became *objetores concientes* in the Spanish of Florida, and *he changed his mind* became *er hat getsheyndzht zayn maynd* in Yiddish. Both expressions are grammatical in their new language, but meaningless until learnt.[19] These are calques or loan-translations, like the English example *prime minister* given above: that expression, too, is meaningless until learnt, since the adjective *prime* is otherwise used mainly as a designation of high quality meat. There are plenty of other examples in English, incidentally: *hold your tongue* and *how do you do* and *hotfoot*, all three of which must have puzzled the first English speakers who heard them, are loan-translations from Old French; *bury the hatchet* comes of course from a North American Indian language, and was perhaps first used in English in a diplomatic address from the Continental Congress to the Six Confederate Nations in 1775.[20] The modern Indian greetings *suprabhat* and *subhratri* look like ordinary Hindi compound words (*su-* means 'good'), but you will not understand their origin until you realize that they are loan-translations based on the original English phrases *good morning* and *good evening*.[21]

Where else would you get new words for new concepts, if they don't come as loanwords? There have, in fact, been other solutions. Algonquian languages have been famous among American linguists for not being easily stuffed with loanwords from other languages. Many other Amerindian languages borrow heavily from English, Spanish and French as they used to borrow from one another; Algonquian languages do not. German and Russian are famous among European linguists for exactly the same trait. Where English and French writers and speakers would borrow technical terms from Latin and Greek, innovators using German and Russian would, instead, devise new compounds from the resources offered by these languages.

As was said on p. 130, this long-term tendency in German to name new concepts without using foreign loanwords was once said to highlight a special 'living' character inherent in the language. It isn't so. There are two real reasons. One is that German actually does permit speakers and writers to form new compounds freely, when users of French and English can't (Aulus Gellius, quoted on pp. 51–2, made the same point about Greek as compared with Latin). But this is not all. It has also been a matter of conscious linguistic nationalism. G. W. Leibniz led a movement to enrich the German vocabulary, both by renewing the use of old words that had fallen out of use, and by forming new compounds to replace foreign technical terms, because they were easier to understand for people who had had no classical education. His admirers went further: in dictionaries they marked off 'German words' from 'foreign words', a thing that German dictionaries still do.

Language planners have had another idea. One of the plans for Tagalog, in its reincarnation as Filipino, was that its vocabulary would be extended by borrowing words from other languages of the Philippines. This would help to make it even more of a national language. In the same way, language planners in Mali have tried to encourage the re-use of local dialect words as technical terms.

With Filipino it worked up to a point (the Philippine languages are in any case similar, so the new words did not seem wholly alien) but there are still far more loans from English than from the other languages of the Philippines, and the number of English loans is growing all the time. I cannot say how it is with the Algonquian languages, or the languages of Mali, in 2002. But I know that German and Russian have dismantled those imaginary barriers by which foreign words used to be, so to speak, excluded. Both of these languages now have many English loanwords for everything from fashion to software.

Among English loanwords in recent Hindi writing Braj B. Kachru finds examples such as *darling, budget, record, cup, tournament, walk-out, dealer, agent, flu*. More drastic is the borrowing of whole phrases, as in *monthly contract, script writer and announcer* (yes, even the English word *and* is borrowed into Hindi), *medical leave, radio news, serious work, take up*. To these examples Kachru adds the splendid phrase *operation theatre mem surgeon tatha anesthetist ki tim* 'the surgeon-anaesthetist team in the operating theatre' in which the five nouns are all English loanwords, chained together with Hindi grammatical particles.[22]

As the pressure of new concepts and the pressure of English become more insistent, new grammatical forms and usages are wanted, to imitate expressions that come naturally in English. Sometimes, local creativity is involved here. Modern Hebrew, for example, has developed portmanteau compounds, like *midrakhov* 'pedestrian street' from *midrakhah* 'pavement' and *rekhov* 'street', and *dakhpor* 'bulldozer' from *dakhof* 'push' and *khfor* 'dig': in classical Hebrew you couldn't do that, but some way had to be found for creating new and acceptably brief technical terms in the modern language.[23] More often, the influence of English, even on the structure of new compounds and new phrases, will be immediately evident. When Hindi writers wanted an equivalent for the English verbal phrases *give help*, *give permission* they found an easy answer in adding the English nouns to the Hindi verb *dena* 'give', *permission dena*, *help dena*; similarly, using the verb *lena* 'take', *holiday lena* 'take a holiday'. And then there is the example of the two-word compound *operation theatre* in the Hindi phrase quoted above. It is English, not Hindi, that puts two nouns together in this way, written separately, to make a compound. So the form represents one more way in which English grammar has been borrowed into Hindi. Hindi newspaper language, meanwhile, has picked up the non-traditional expressions *kaha jata hai* 'it is said', *suna gaya hai* 'it has been learnt' from English. Traditional Hindi would certainly have used the forms *kehte hai* or *suna hai*, but they are not used because they do not correspond to English expressions.[24] A new journalistic style has developed in newspapers in Indian regional languages, whose articles used to be largely translated from English – and hence written in an English-like style. Now that does not happen, because journalists are writing original material in all the local languages, but the style is more English-like than ever, and (since the conscious act of translation does not occur) articles include far larger numbers of English loanwords.

When you begin to look, you will be astonished by the proportion of words in many modern languages, both spoken and written, that are almost identical with English words. This includes everyday words like *banana* and *telephone*; technical words in sports, travel, food, fashion and marketing, like *football* and *chips*; technical words in science, medicine, manufacturing and employment, like *academy*, *physics* and *aspirin*. Not every language has exactly the same range of international words, but all languages that have a large vocabulary of modern and technical concepts have most of them.

Many of these words can be traced back to Latin, Greek and other languages from which someone in Europe (usually) first borrowed them, giving them a new or extended meaning. This means that it is not so helpful to describe them as English loanwords in other languages; more accurately they are international words, even if in a proportion of cases it was English from which the immediate loan was taken. It is easier to borrow from English (and French) than from most other languages, because the vocabularies of English and French have a noticeably hybrid structure. Nouns in these languages need have no special shape, which is why many Latin and Greek loanwords are to be found in them, only minimally remodelled.

Because of its international terminology and other loanwords modern Hebrew, now successfully revived and in everyday use in Israel, is very different from the ancient language (which is why some linguists insist on giving it a different name, Ivrit). How does it differ? It has borrowed not just words (for example, *Aqademiyah* 'Academy') but also terminations, *-ar* from Latin via German, *-acia* from Latin via Russian, *-ist* from Greek via German, *-nik* and *-chik* from Russian. Modern international (originally Latin) verbs with the prefix *re-*, meaning 'back' or 'repeated', find a corresponding form in Hebrew with the prefix *sh-* (so *hekhzir* 'he gave back' but *shikhzer* 'he reconstructed'): originally a derivative prefix in early Hebrew, this is now used in a new international way. In the same way, the international (originally Latin) noun prefixes *super-*, *sub-*, *pre-*, *post-* ('over, under, before, after') have corresponding forms in modern Hebrew, *'al-*, *tat-*, *qedam-*, *batar-*, although in classical Hebrew you simply couldn't do that.[25] And this is not the first time that Hebrew had undergone such heavy foreign influence. The written Hebrew of the period of the Roman Empire (this too revived from a point where it had almost ceased to be spoken) contains hundreds of new loanwords from Latin and Greek.

An equally fundamental change in Japanese, bestowing on this unique language a structure much more closely resembling that of

European languages, is ascribed to the enormous number of transla-tions from English and other languages (but especially English) that have appeared in Japanese in the last century:

Pre-modern Japanese texts did not usually consist of an array of complete sentences with subjects and predicates exhibiting a finite verb form at the end; rather, loose concatenations of clauses were much more common: phrases merged into each other connected by parts of speech that would have one grammatical function in the first and another in the second . . . Japanese was influenced consciously and artificially . . . by those intellectuals who devoted themselves to the difficult task of translating philosophical, scientific and literary books . . . As the modernization of Japan was so sudden and drastic, its linguistic repercussions are particularly obvious.[26]

Here, too, this was not happening for the first time: the older Japanese discourse structure had something to do with the structure of Sanskrit clauses in Buddhist texts. These, particularly in literal translations in other Asian languages, are often concatenated in just the way that is described here.

In many countries there are language or terminology councils whose main task is to invent new terminology, or to control others' inven-tions. For Swahili, for instance, there is the Institute of Kiswahili Research in Dar es Salaam. This has worked in the past on terminology in literary criticism, theatre, linguistics, chemistry, physics and biology and I am certain that it is now working on terminology for Windows and the World Wide Web. However, institutions of this kind are essentially national, not language-wide, in their function. This one does not serve, or even try to serve, all Swahili-speaking countries. Kenya, Uganda and the Congo may through this kind of work become more rather than less isolated from one another linguistically, each one separately being dependent on English for its new terminology, but not necessarily borrowing the same terms with the same meanings. In Nigeria the Nigerian National Language Centre (now defunct) had the job of devising terminology for the three national (or 'federal') languages, the Three Majors, in eight major fields of public adminis-tration. A similar activity takes place in Hindi. The Constitution of India provided in 1949:

It shall be the duty of the Union to promote the spread of the Hindi language, to develop it so that it may serve as a medium of expression for all the elements of the composite culture of India and to secure its enrichment by assimilating without interfering with its genius, the forms, style and expressions used in Hindustani and in the other languages of India . . . and by drawing . . . for its vocabulary, primarily on Sanskrit and secondarily on other languages.

The work here is done by the Commission for Scientific and Technical Terminology in New Delhi. State governments have done the same sort of thing for their own regional languages. The result is that although Hindi of India and Urdu of Pakistan may grow further apart, because the Commission has no links with Pakistan, Indian languages are growing more like one another (this is no new development: there has always been massive borrowing and calquing among them) and more like Sanskrit (which is also nothing new), but now they are also growing more like Hindi and more like English.

Borrowing from English, and borrowing of international words, are not in any way illegitimate procedures. They are part of the way that language has always changed to serve its function. The curious thing, though, is that now for the first time so many developments, in so many languages, are tending in the same direction. I hardly like to say this, and almost hope I will not be believed when I say it: there is a society, a regular series of congresses and a journal, *Neoterm*, dedicated to speeding and generalizing this process of assimilation throughout the world. Neoterm, if successful, will achieve something far more drastic and stultifying than Zamenhof, whose modest aim was to create a universal second language under the name Esperanto. Neoterm wants our first languages to grow closer and closer together until eventually there will only be one.

English or Englishes

I did not invent the plural *Englishes*. Once upon a time, not very long ago, the local dialects of English, in Britain and the United States, were a focus of enthusiastic research. They still are – but they have been overtaken in popularity among researchers and their sponsors by the national varieties of English written and spoken in all those newer countries in which English is an official language. At least three academic journals, with titles like *World Englishes*, are devoted exclusively to the subject, and that fact by itself indicates that there must be scholarly money in it.[27]

Each country where German is the standard language has its own standard: Austria, Switzerland, Luxembourg and even Liechtenstein. While East Germany was a separate country, there was a quite distinct East German standard. In Austria there has been a resurgence of regionalism, with more use of local dialects among young people and in politics: the development was already noted in the 1980s. But at the same time economic domination from Germany, and a flood of German tourists, keep on adding Germanisms to Austrian German, and that makes people's speech a little closer than before to the standard German of Germany. Switzerland, a highly devolved state, has local dialects which everybody uses, while at the same time people are quite able to speak standard German with a mild Swiss accent.[28]

In just the same way, each country where English is spoken has its own standard English – and since there are many more countries, that means many more standards. There has been a long-running debate about this among the TESLs (Teachers of English as a Second Language), a debate that has occasionally turned into a *fight*, using that word in the United States sense, which need not imply what the British call *fisticuffs*. How should TESLs regard these national standards of English? Are the ones spoken where English is a mother tongue more acceptable than others? Among them, is any one standard to be taught to students in preference to others? Take one example: there is at present plenty of discussion in India (as one of the countries where English is not a mother tongue) as to what kind of English ought to be taught in schools there – and indeed whether journalists and other writers ought to be persuaded to aim at the same standard. Should it be the standard of the best local speakers, if that concept can be satisfactorily defined? Whoever they are exactly, their usage will evidently show some differences in accent and vocabulary from, say, British and United States standards. Or should it be the British or United States standards themselves that are set up as target – and if so, which of the two?[29] Thus far it's a pointless question, of course.

Teachers can only effectively teach a language that they know: hence the great majority of teachers in India will be teaching an Indian standard of English – and in Malaysia a Malaysian standard, and so on – whatever the theorists say. Students learn from more than one teacher, and they learn English from many sources outside school, so in any case the English they learn to speak will not be that of any single teacher. No, the real issue for the TESL people, though it isn't often put in such bleak terms, is: where does the examiner put a red mark? Is British English (*I haven't got any*) acceptable to United States examiners? Is Indian English (*My son was graduated last Monday*) acceptable to British examiners? How do they decide?

Which leads us to our next important question. Are the various standards of English destined to split into daughter languages? Will what happened to Latin at the end of the Roman Empire now happen to English? Once the political unity of the western Roman Empire was at an end, once communication and population exchange among its former provinces had been interrupted, there was no sufficient influence ensuring that the forms of Latin spoken in each region would remain a single language. Eventually, therefore, in the natural process of linguistic change, they differentiated. By the time they began to be written down, in the ninth century and after, most linguists would say that they might already be defined as separate languages. Certainly Spanish, French, Italian and the others differ extensively now, and for many centuries they have not been mutually intelligible. Each, in its own region, is the modern incarnation of Latin.

Will that happen again? Will United States, Canadian, British, Irish, Indian, Malaysian, Australian, New Zealand, South African and the other African and world-wide standard varieties of English grow gradually apart, so that in a few centuries they could be defined as separate languages, each unintelligible to speakers of any of the others unless they have studied them in foreign language classes at school? As long ago as 1789, the great lexicographer Noah Webster predicted precisely this:

Several circumstances render a future separation of the American tongue from the English necessary and unavoidable. The vicinity of the European nations, with the uninterrupted communication in peace, and the changes of dominion in war, are gradually assimilating their respective languages [Barère disagreed!]. The English with others is suffering continual alterations. America, placed at a distance from those nations, will feel, in a much less degree, the influence of the assimilating causes; at the same time, numerous local causes, such as a new country, new associations of people, new combinations of ideas in arts and science, and some intercourse with tribes wholly unknown in Europe, will introduce new words into the American tongue. These causes will produce, in a course of time, a language in North America as different from the future language of England, as the modern Dutch, Danish and Swedish are from the German, or from one another.[30]

It was this prediction of Webster's, signally untrue as it has so far turned out to be, that justified H. L. Mencken in the choice of title for his book *The American Language*, first published in 1919.

To devise an answer to the question, let us look at some of the English words that are specific to various countries where English is used as a standard language. First of all, in Webster's support, we can cite the names for local plants and animals and other features of the natural world. So long as the local species and phenomena continue to exist, and so long as they continue to be of interest to English speakers locally, they must have names, and these names will mostly never be known to English speakers elsewhere. Henry Yule and Andrew Burnell, in their matchless dictionary of the special vocabulary of Asian English, *Hobson-Jobson*, published in 1886, list many words of this kind, and some of them still survive in everyday use in modern India: *hog-deer, flying-fox, musk-rat, barking-deer, amla* (a fruit sometimes called *emblic myrobalan*), *putchuk* (a Kashmiri aromatic known to the Romans as *costus*). Similar examples can be found in United States English. Several originating in Amerindian languages will be cited on pp. 231–3; for the present let's mention *jimsonweed* (named after Jamestown, Virginia), *bullfrog, razorback, applejack* and *goldenseal*. There are many in South African English: *morogo* 'wild greens', borrowed from Sotho, *tsessebe* 'kind of antelope', borrowed from Tswana, *marula* 'kind of fruit tree, source of edible berries and of oil', borrowed from Sotho, *mahem* 'the crested crane', borrowed from Xhosa *amahemu*, and *tegwaan* or *thekwane* or *hammerhead* or *hamerkop* 'the ominous bird *Scopus Umbretta*'. The English of

Queensland, in northeastern Australia, has five or six loanwords from Dyirbal, one of the few Australian languages that is still actively spoken and is perhaps still being learnt by children. These local English words include the bird name *chowchilla* and the names of four useful timber trees, one of which is the very hard wood *jitta*.[31] The English of Burma (unlikely to survive long as a separate variety) has one or two of its own local terms, including *marian* 'species of mango'. You would need to have been to Barbados to know that *merrywings* is a midge – this charming name, incidentally, is borrowed from French *maringouin* 'mosquito', from Spanish *maringuín*, and originally from *mberuim*, the name of a local mosquito in the Tupi or Lingua Geral of Brazil.

Where species or products have become known in several English-speaking regions, they may well have a different name in each region, often because English speakers learnt about them in different contexts from speakers of different languages. Here are some examples, both familiar and surprising. The food grain *Zea Mays* is called in the United States *corn* (originally *Indian corn*, because this was the cereal native to the 'Indies'); in South Africa it is *mealie* or *mielie* (a word borrowed from Afrikaans *mielie*, said to derive from Portuguese *milho* 'millet') while in Britain it is *maize*. The spice and colouring agent called *turmeric* in Britain is known in South Africa as *borrie* (a loan from Malay by way of Afrikaans) and among South African Indians as *arad*. The European spice known in Britain as *coriander* is called in Indian English *dhania* or *dhunia*. In the United States the fruit is *coriander*, the leaves *cilantro*, a word borrowed from Spanish. The Afghan spice known as *hing* in Indian English is *asafoetida* in Britain and the United States, *duiwelsdrek* in South African English, this last being a Dutch version of the term used among European pharmacists which means 'devil's dung'. *Jeera* in Indian English is *cumin* in British and American. Indian English *methi* is British English *fenugreek*. Indian English *sitaphul* is known elsewhere as *custard-apple*. Indian English *alu* is British English *potato* (and *spud*). The fruit *okra* (a loan from Akan of Ghana) is also known regionally as *gumbo* (a loan from Mbundu of Angola), *bhindi* (a loan from Marathi) and *ladies' fingers*. The *chickpea* is also *chana* (borrowed from Hindi) and *garbanzo bean* (borrowed from Spanish). Indian English *imli* is British English *tamarind*. Indian English *chenar* is world English *plane tree*. In South African English we have *tollie* (borrowed from Zulu *ithole* 'calf') for *bullock; tolofiya* or *itolofiya* (borrowed from Xhosa) for *prickly pear*. The drug cannabis has many regional names in English, including *hemp* (the older English name of the plant and the fibre it produces), *cannabis* (borrowed from Latin), *hashish* (borrowed from Arabic), *marijuana* (borrowed from Spanish), *pot, grass*, South African English *dagga* (originating in Khoe *daxa-b* and also used as the name of a local drug, see next paragraph), Indian English *bhang* 'cannabis leaves', Jamaican and Australian *ganja*. Even where the English names derive ultimately from a single foreign term, they may have different forms and connotations in different regions, like South African English *sosatie* versus British English *saté, satay* (three forms of one originally Malay word); and likewise United States English *kabob* for British English *kebab* (a Turkish word in origin); and South African English *kraal* for Jamaican English *crawl* and American English *corral* (three forms of one originally Portuguese word).

Such names may vary even within the English of a restricted region. On occasion they faithfully reflect older cultural and linguistic divisions now overlaid by English. Thus the fruit known elsewhere in the English-speaking world as *watermelon* is an ancient southern African crop known in South African English as *tsamma* (borrowed from Khoe) and also as *makataan* (borrowed from Tswana). The South African narcotic plant *Leonotis leonurus* is known in South African English as *dagga* (from the Khoe name) and also *insangu* (from the Zulu name). In eastern Australia you will probably call the small rat-kangaroos *bettong*, a loanword from Dharuk, the 'Sydney language'. Around Perth you will call them *boodie* and *woylie*: two species are distinguished, both now very rare, and the names come from the local language Nyungar. Inland you will call the boodie *tungoo*, a word that originally belonged to the Western Desert language. In eastern Australia you will find the rabbit-eared bandicoot is called *bilby*, from Dharuk; in Western Australia it is *dalgite*, from Nyungar; in South Australia *pinkie*, from the 'Adelaide language' Gaurna. In Queensland the local cabbage palm is called *piccabeen*; in New South Wales it is *bangalow*, a loanword from the Dharawal language once spoken on the coast just south of Sydney. *Kylie*, a loanword from Nyungar, is the term used in Western Australian English for the weapon that English speakers elsewhere call *boomerang*, a word borrowed from Dharuk. Even in a single small district, some individual species will be found to have many names: 'for example, *golden apple* in Barbados has regional variants such as *pomme, cythere, jew plum, golden plum, box, meeting-turn, pardner, sousou, syndicate*'.[32]

Examples of this kind will surely continue to exist. A few of the notions concerned might spread to the consciousness of English-speaking people generally: most of them never will, and English will continue to vary on a geographical basis simply for that reason.

When we take a different set of examples – words more directly connected with human life and culture – the long-term answer turns out to be different. They tend to spread. It's true that unless you have studied current affairs you probably do not know Indian English *ahimsa* 'non-violence' or *goonda* 'hired rowdy', or Singaporean English *kiasuism* 'the obsession with trying to get the best deal' or Malaysian English *adat* 'traditional Malay law', or South African English *indaba* 'problem, concern' – but, like *apartheid*, any of these words might quite easily reach the world press and become a part of world English. Unless you know Jamaica you do not know that *anancy* is a non-poisonous spider, *tumble-turd* a beetle and *Congo Peggy* a red ant (but you may well guess that *bottle-arse* is a fly). Unless you have lived in southeast Asia you probably do not know Malay English *kampong* 'enclosed village or farm'; yet you will certainly have seen it in its alternate British form *compound* without ever realizing that it was a Malay word.

Unless you have some knowledge of South Africa you probably do not know *biltong* 'dried meat', *bredie* 'kind of stew', *moerebeskuit* 'rusks', all borrowed from Afrikaans; or *amasi* or *maas* 'sour milk' or *gwaai* 'tobacco, cigarette', borrowed from Zulu; or *dagga* 'cement', borrowed from Shona; or *bobotie* 'a curried mince dish' or *sambal* 'relish', both of which probably reached South African English from Malay by way of Afrikaans. But you may learn *hanepoot* 'muscat blanc d'Alexandrie; wine made from this' from a wine label next year; and much more familiar to you already are South African English *kraal* 'enclosure' and *aardvark*, both borrowed from Afrikaans; *impala*, borrowed from Zulu, and *tsetse*, borrowed from Tswana *tsê tsê*;

sjambok 'whip', borrowed from Malay. You may have come across *kudu* 'kind of antelope', originating in Khoe.[33]

From southern Asia you may not know of the fruits called *bael* (a loanword from Hindi for the fruit sometimes called 'Bengal quince'), *bilimbi* (from Tamil), *jamun* 'jambolan' and *jamboo* 'rose-apple', or of some other native species, *bajra* 'species of millet', *barasingha* or 'swamp deer', *bharal* 'Himalayan blue sheep'. But you will know of *ghee* 'clarified butter' and of the *betel leaf*, and you might well have heard of the *bandicoot* (a borrowing from Telugu), though these were once words that were unknown to any but local residents. You might have read of the *deodar*, an Indian cedar, and of the *sal* tree under which the Buddha often taught.

There is an old fashion of making lists of differences between British and American English. If you set out to make such a list in 2002 you will be struck by the fact that it is hard to find differences which most of your readers are not perfectly familiar with already, whichever side of the Atlantic they live on. *Postman, railway, luggage, parcel, ill* (meaning 'suffering from a disease'), *blinds* (meaning 'window shade'), *shop* (meaning 'retail outlet')[34] are commoner in British English but pose no problem to Americans. *Condominium, apartment, eggplant, panties, pants* (meaning 'trousers'), *mad* (meaning 'angry'), *sick* (meaning 'suffering from a disease'), *gas* (meaning 'petroleum fuel') are more familiar in American than in British English, but no English speaker these days is likely to be puzzled by them.

Some of the false friends of British–American translation have disappeared. Everybody now is supposed to mean the same thing by *billion*. Some of those false friends remain, like *chips* and *corn*: the latter is usually 'wheat' in Britain, 'maize' in the United States, so you don't know what *Corn Flakes* are made of until you know where they were invented. New words and new usages have to start somewhere, and there will always be some that have not yet crossed the Atlantic – such as *maven* 'expert', a Yiddish loanword known at present only in US English, something like a *pundit* in fact, a Hindi loanword commoner in British than in US English – but most of these words and usages eventually do cross the Atlantic, in whichever direction, and become familiar on both sides. There remains somewhat more potential for misunderstanding between Indian English and the rest, and the reason is that the volume of communication between Indian English on the one hand and British and American English on the other is probably smaller: but it is growing. Even if Indian film and television programmes are not much seen in Britain or the United States, more and more Indians are influenced by the British and US media in their own use of English.

The conclusion to which our own evidence is leading us is that the need for debates about standards of English will gradually, after much fluctuation over two or three generations, disappear. Examiners, should such people still exist, will have one fewer problem on their minds. India and South Africa are influenced by the international media just as Britain and North America are. Meanwhile Hindi and the regional languages of India, and Afrikaans and the other official languages of South Africa, are themselves growing closer to English, and will in the future be less likely to influence the local English of India and South Africa in a different direction. Thus the local standard of English in these countries will gradually grow closer to British and United States English, as those two also will grow closer to one another. Scholars of the distant future, looking back on English of this period, will find it more and more difficult to identify regional differences, as do classical philologists when they look back at the regional Latin of the Roman Empire.

It is the media that make the big difference here. When Latin was splitting up, in early medieval Europe, the 'media' of the period were manuscript texts that not many people outside the monasteries ever had a chance to read. International communication was limited to a few traders, a few religious people, a few political emissaries and a variable number of migrants. All cross-cultural communication continued to take place in Latin, and the Church, which remained international, retained Latin as its working language, but these influences were simply not powerful enough to prevent Latin from splitting into dialects in everyday use, or to prevent those dialects, once they had formed, from continuing to grow apart. Nowadays, as we have said already, television is in practically every home, talking like one of the family, in fact the most honoured member of the family, the one to whom you cannot talk back. Neglected children – and there are many of them, at every social level – hear the television talking more than they hear people talking. Listening to speech in infancy is how you learn to speak. That's why people in Britain were seriously worried that children would learn to speak like the Teletubbies: they didn't, of course, because the Teletubbies were limited to one small slot in the schedule and because their language made no sense. That's why I as a parent disliked a programme aimed at older children called *Red Dwarf*: I probably need not have worried, for the same reason.

That, finally, is why British English, Australian English, US and Canadian English, in spite of their vast geographical separation, will not grow further apart. Television is the current common denominator, in every household, helping to teach our children to speak – and if the Internet develops in the direction of being a voice medium, it will have exactly the same effect. In so far as we learn from television we shall soon all be speaking in more or less the same way.

6

WHEN WE LOSE
A LANGUAGE

Language loss and culture loss

The spread of English is part of a connected world-wide series of linguistic shifts. While the use of English spreads all around us we are also seeing an increase in the use of national languages – and the rapid disappearance of hundreds, eventually thousands, of minority languages. We have looked at the effects of nationalism (Chapter 4); we have looked at the global destiny of English (Chapter 5); we must now focus on the loss of languages.

The question throughout this chapter is a perfectly simple one: what do we lose as each language is forgotten?

We begin with the example of Hawaiian, a challenging case because this was the language of an independent, self-sufficient and fairly isolated state until European intrusions multiplied in the early nineteenth century. In two centuries, Hawaiian has come to the point of disappearance. This development took place alongside the loss of Hawaiian political independence, the loss of culture, the loss of the natural environment, and – equally significant for our future – the loss of knowledge of what the local environment has to offer.

This unusual language marks the far northwest of the epic migrations of the speakers of Austronesian languages. Before the European expansion began – in the era of Columbus and Vasco da Gama – Austronesian languages had spread much further across the world than any other language family, from Madagascar to Easter Island and from Hawaii to New Zealand. After the initial voyages in which the islands were settled, Hawaiian evolved in relative isolation (as did Maori far to the south) because the vast distances across the northern Pacific precluded regular contact.

Although Captain Cook visited Hawaii in 1778 – and was killed there – the first meaningful contact with Europeans did not follow until after 1800, when Hawaii began to export its local species of sandalwood, *Santalum pyrularium* and *S. freycinetianum*. Foreign traders became aware of other natural riches; trade soon expanded and brought immigration with it. The usual common language of visitors and settlers was English. In speaking with Hawaiians, traders initially used Pidgin Hawaiian; it was not long, however, before they had seized the linguistic upper hand. It became the practice for Hawaiians who needed to trade to learn English. Meanwhile Christian missionaries had begun to work in Hawaii. At first they too used Hawaiian in schools and churches, but this was soon to change.

The last act in the history of Hawaiian begins in the 1850s. The missionaries were by now keenly aware of the collapse of Hawaiian society that they saw around them, a collapse to which they themselves had largely contributed, though traders, whalers and disease had all played their part. They began to press for English-language education. Some at that time were already sure that the whole culture was doomed to disappear. Others among the missionaries felt that English education would enable Hawaiians to resist the pressure and survive. King Kamehameha IV of Hawaii, in a keynote speech in 1855, put forward a similar view. His statement appropriately appears at the opening of this chapter on language disappearance and immediately following our exploration of the rise of English: 'It is of the highest importance, in my opinion, that education in the English language should become more general, for it is my firm conviction that unless my subjects become educated in this tongue, their hope of intellectual progress, and of meeting the foreigners on terms of equality, is a vain one.'[1]

In the twentieth century vast numbers of people, in many countries, have shifted from their traditional language towards another – and particularly towards English – and the reasons, though few people state them openly, are exactly those set out a hundred and fifty years ago by the King of Hawaii. The linguistic environment was changing in favour of English: he already sensed it.

From then on English was to be the preferred language of education in Hawaii, in spite of some dissent. Soon after 1870 English became the language of legislation. It did Hawaiians and their culture little good. Numerically they were soon overwhelmed by the importing of plantation labourers, and by the growing number of children of mixed parentage. The latter, even then, were not being educated in the local culture.

The monarchy was overthrown by a coalition of foreign business interests in 1893. Their first act was to raise English to the status of sole official language. Soon afterwards the United States annexed Hawaii – not many years after Britain, under similar pressure from business interests, annexed the kingdom of Burma.

On the twentieth century position I will quote Richard R. Day: 'Somewhere during the early twentieth century, bilingual Hawaiian parents began teaching their children English instead of Hawaiian. [By "English" Day in fact means Hawaiian Creole English, a language which has had no official status and very little social respect.] By the 1940s, at least, there was a generation of Hawaiians who did not speak Hawaiian as a first language, and perhaps not even as a second language.' In general they have not, as Kamehameha hoped, had the opportunity of 'meeting the foreigners on terms of equality', being generally found in jobs that are low paid and low in status.

Even now Hawaiian is not quite dead: on one small island, Ni'ihau, it is still said to be in everyday use. Apart from that it is the language of traditional ceremonies, regularly performed for tourists.[2] If we compare the fate of Hawaiian with that of one of the minor languages of the Roman Empire, we will find them to be very similar. Some of these, too, had quite possibly disappeared within about two hundred years of their speakers' first encounter with Rome. Some were still used in rituals that few of their hearers understood.

What do we lose when such a language at last dies? Hawaiian, although clearly a member of the Oceanic group of Austronesian languages, has some very special features of its own. In 1938 Otto Jespersen (quoted above, p. 131, on the 'masculinity' of English) wrote a dismissive characterization of Hawaiian: 'No single word ends in a consonant, and a group of two or more consonants is never found. Can anyone be in doubt that even if such a language sound pleasantly and be full of music and harmony the total impression is childlike and effeminate? You do not expect much vigour or energy in a people speaking such a language.'³ Jespersen had obviously failed to reflect sufficiently on the adventurous migration by which Hawaii was settled. Hawaiian has (he might have added) the smallest inventory of phonemes of any language in the world, a total of only eight consonants, ʻh k l m n p w, and only five vowels. Linguists are now more prepared than they were in the Jespersen era to face the challenge that any language of unusual structure offers to our understanding of language in general; but when Hawaiian goes, this challenge is no longer on offer. We lose it even earlier if the speakers of Hawaiian, now all bilingual, modify their Hawaiian to assimilate its structure to that of English. As we shall see later in this chapter, that is just what happens when a language is on the way to disappearing.

Hawaiian is interesting, too, for its adaptation to its special environment. The common Oceanic word for 'turmeric', *renga* in the parent language, occurs as *lena* in Hawaiian but – since turmeric did not grow there – means 'yellow'. In the same way, all the inherited Austronesian and Oceanic words for animals, fish and plants were adapted to new uses in the very different ecology in which the migrants to Hawaii found themselves. By the time Europeans began to disrupt their culture, Hawaiians had a remarkably deep knowledge of their environment. English has eventually borrowed a few words from Hawaiian – *hula, ukulele* – words for cultural things that other people could easily take over from their Hawaiian inventors. But there are not many of them. Some of the traditional Hawaiian knowledge of nature and its uses has been transferred into local forms of English: in Hawaiian English there are thus plenty more loanwords, *kukui* 'candlenut', *imu* 'earth oven', *poi* 'pounded taro', *haole* 'European settlers and their culture'. But that fact doesn't guarantee the survival of local knowledge, because local forms of English are meanwhile tending to assimilate to a global standard, and local traditional trades (including herbalism and medicine) are less likely, year by year, to be passed on to a new generation. The international traders who came for Hawaiian sandalwood, back in the early nineteenth century, and soon used it all up, will have eventually ensured that some of the other natural resources of Hawaii will be lost and forgotten along with the language that described them.⁴

Every language that disappears for good is likely to take a culture with it, as Hawaiian will do. Something survives, as surely as some aspects of the Hawaiian way of life survive among certain speakers of Hawaiian Creole English. But much is already lost, and more will have gone when there are no longer any speakers of Hawaiian as a mother tongue. Hawaiian was a language of politics, of a rich oral literature, and of many technical skills: some of all this is on record in English, but much is not. It is like this, or worse, every time. So it was with Gaulish and Punic, perhaps the last to disappear of those local languages of the Roman Empire. Punic had been the language of a unique political system, an adventurous trading empire, a fabled religion; it had been a language of historical and scientific literature and no doubt of poetry too. All is gone, except the little that Roman writers were interested in and the little that archaeologists can now reconstruct. Gaulish, the language of the Druids ('philosophers', as uncomprehending Greeks and Romans called them), had spread across a vast region of central Europe: it too was a language of political debate and the vehicle of a vast literature which was entrusted to memory and not written down. Nothing is left except a few inscriptions and a few fairly unsympathetic comments by classical writers. If two thousand five hundred languages are to be lost in the course of the twenty-first century, don't be in any doubt about what that means for us: in each of those two thousand five hundred cases a culture will be lost, even if *a few* of those cultures may have as high a world profile as Hawaiian had and may as a result be fairly well recorded before they go.

Let's focus for a moment on the local knowledge of the natural world which belongs to each culture and each language. Here is one piece of the knowledge jigsaw, of considerable importance in human health world-wide, the first indication of which came through a small, now threatened, minority language, North Frisian. There are just two thousand remaining speakers of the Ferring or North Frisian language on the islands of Föhr and Amrum off the north German coast; these islands are awash in summer with forty thousand German tourists, so, even in its own very local context, North Frisian is now a minority language. In fact, speakers have tended to regard it as a secret language; especially among older people there has been a strong feeling against printing and writing North Frisian, because that would enable outsiders to learn it, a development which was felt to be wholly unnecessary and undesirable.[5] Now in all modern European languages (writes Frederik Paulsen) the pituitary gland has a Latin or Greek name, implying that it was an anatomical feature of which those who had not studied scientific anatomy were simply unaware. In most larger animals it is only the size of a pea, and passes unnoticed by farmers and butchers of pigs, sheep and cattle. But in North Frisian it has a well-established popular name, namely *brajnkoop* or 'brain button'. Why? Because the North Frisians, during their centuries as whalers around Greenland, noticed this gland: in whales it is indeed much more noticeable, being as big as an orange. North Frisian even makes use of the word in an idiomatic expression which must have been first used in whaling times: *Hi wiar so areg, at ham a brajnkoop baarst* 'He was so angry that his pituitary burst'. The whalers, you see, had observed that a whale which was butchered after a long and hard fight with the harpooners showed evidence of haemorrhage in the *brajnkoop*. When the Canadian endocrinologist Selye thirty years ago published his stress theory and thus invented the psychological sense of the word stress, he confirmed by experimental research what the North Frisians had been saying for centuries – namely, that stress results in damage to the pituitary.[6]

Here are a few more examples of crucial medical knowledge that came to us by way of local traditional medicine. Paul Cox and Michael Balick, in an article in *Scientific American*, have listed some of the most important drugs that began to be used in medicine only because scientists took the trouble to start investigating plants that were used in traditional herbalism. Their examples include aspirin, from meadowsweet; codeine, from the opium poppy (they might have added opium itself, an indispensable analgesic for at least two millennia until less addictive substitutes became available); ipecac, from ipecacuanha; pilocarpine, which reduces pressure in the eye, from *Pilocarpus Jaborandi*; pseudoephedrine, a nasal decongestant, from *Ephedra sinica*; quinine, from 'Peruvian bark', *Cinchona Calisaya* and related species, a discovery by Callahuaya healers; reserpine, which lowers blood pressure, from Indian snakeroot; scopolamine, from a species of jimsonweed; theophylline, which opens the bronchial passages, from the tea plant; and vinblastine, which combats leukaemia, from rosy periwinkle. 'Plants exploited for their poisonous effects are also of interest: blowgun poisons such as curare have in the past been found to contain compounds able to serve as anesthetics.'[7] Some of these plant names have been mentioned already in this book because they represent knowledge derived from languages that are no longer spoken or likely to disappear soon. Another, by contrast, came from English long ago – but this too came in the form of local knowledge gathered by chance.

In 1785 William Withering, a British physician, reported that ingestion of dried leaves from the foxglove plant eased dropsy . . . Withering credited an unexpected source for his information. 'I was told,' he wrote, that this use of foxglove . . . 'had long been kept a secret by an old woman in Shropshire, who had sometimes made cures after the more regular practitioners had failed.' Digitalis has been helping cardiac patients ever since. Today two of its components – the glycosides digoxin and digitoxin – are prescribed to hundreds of thousands of people throughout the world every year. Indeed, these glycosides currently serve as the treatment of choice for rapid atrial fibrillation, a dangerous cardiac irregularity.[8]

Cox and Balick add that in the mid-1980s this would have been regarded as nothing more than a historical anecdote. By the mid-1990s the pendulum had swung back towards 'an appreciation that plants used in traditional medicine can serve as a source of novel therapeutic agents'.

Cross-cultural exchange between different systems of medicine and therapeutics has been going on for thousands of years. An early, closely datable record is in the manuscripts of the ancient Greek textbook of materia medica compiled in the first century AD by Dioscorides of Anazarba, who served with the Roman army. The manuscripts list the names of many medicinal plants in additional languages not known to Dioscorides himself, and one of these is Dacian, a language spoken in what is now Romania. This territory was conquered by Rome in AD 106; it was heavily garrisoned and extensively resettled and there is no evidence that the Dacian language continued to be spoken for many generations after the conquest. So why do these 'barbarian' language names appear in the Dioscorides manuscripts? It can only be because local Roman military physicians needed to get their medicinal herbs from Dacian suppliers – who were already, even before the conquest, famous for their skill with drugs and poisons.[9] According to a scene depicted on Trajan's Column, the defeated king Decebalus shared out a suicide draught among the last defenders of his mountain capital Sarmizegethusa.[10]

For the same reason that Dacian glosses were included, the early users of Dioscorides' manual also added plant names in Latin (of course), Gaulish, Etruscan, Iberian, Libyan and Egyptian. Exchanges of this kind naturally occur whenever a language – along with a conquering culture – is rapidly spreading through a region where other languages have been spoken previously. I could give a long list of the new drugs, from sarsaparilla to sassafras, about which explorers of the New World were eager to learn. Yet the transmission is somewhat chancy at the best of times. Balsam of Peru, still so useful in wound dressings and cough medicines, was discovered by Spanish soldiers not from a traditional healer but because they saw local warriors applying it to their own wounds and thought it worth trying. That was lucky: its only source is a very small geographical region in El Salvador (not in Peru) and it might easily have been completely forgotten. One of the names of the *cider gum* tree is given to it because Tasmanian aborigines used to tap the sap and allow it to ferment before drinking it. But it has been given several other names, even locally: 'in districts only a few miles apart the cider-gum . . . is identified as the swamp-gum, river-gum and white-gum',[11] so it is the merest chance that just one of the names that English settlers gave to this tree indicates that they had noticed a use for it.

The Jamaican toad *Bufo marinus* is called, unobservantly, *bullfrog*, and the Jamaican terrapin is a *land turtle* if its name is to be believed. There are only so many methods of naming the plants and animals in a new environment. If you use what was already a local word, that means that you learnt something – and it may be that it was something useful, such as food or medicinal uses – from the existing inhabitants. If you use a name that comes from your own previous homeland, that often means that you learnt little or nothing locally. If there had been a secure line of transmission, Jamaican English would contain more Carib and Taino names than it does and fewer African and European names like *bullfrog* and *land turtle*.[12]

Cox and Balick attribute the recently renewed interest in drug discoveries derived from local traditional medicine to the growing number of ethnobotanists, and they may well be right, but it also has something to do with the very rapid spread of national languages. What's disturbing – you now see – is that the current spread of languages and cultures, culminating in the international spread of English, risks being the last such movement. Local cultures are being abandoned for good. 'There is some urgency to this work,' write Cox and Balick; 'many healers are elderly and lack apprentices. As they die, much of their knowledge of local vegetation dies, too.'[13] Younger people are no longer interested in becoming apprentices to a traditional healer. If there is no ethnobotanist around, the knowledge very often disappears.

The human scale of language loss

Let's look more closely at what happens when languages disappear.

It may be a quick process or a very slow one. The quick process is either effected by a massacre, or else by an infectious disease introduced by invaders, an infection to which the indigenous population has no inherited resistance. Both processes are typical of our modern world. We spread deadly diseases because we now travel across great distances and because we impose ourselves suddenly on a population with which we have had no previous contact. We massacre whole language communities because we are now powerful enough to do so. In the whole of world history before the sixteenth century there is only one clear record of the extermination of a whole language and culture in a single massacre. This was in 1226, when Kublai Khan ordered the death of all inhabitants of a central Asian city under siege because his father Genghis Khan had been killed in the course of the siege. These were the speakers of Tangut or Xixia, a language which, almost from that moment, ceased to be spoken, though it is still on record in its enigmatic written literature. There are now several examples, in countries recently settled by Europeans, of languages that have ceased to be spoken as a direct result of massacres. R. M. W. Dixon and his co-authors provide some case histories from Australia.

One way of killing a language is to get rid of all the speakers. In a few places in Australia there were massacres of such severity that there were literally no speakers left to pass a language on to the next generation. There is known to have been a language called Yeeman spoken around Tarooma in south-east Queensland. That is all we know – its name. Not one word of the language was recorded before the entire tribe was wiped out in 1857.[14]

They report elsewhere that in the 1880s 'most members of the Warrgamay tribe were hunted and killed by the Queensland Native Police (Aborigines from a distant tribe who were given guns and told to shoot on sight)'. Although this massacre did not result in immediate total extermination of the Warrgamay, its eventual consequence was that by the time Dixon himself began to study the Warrgamay language in the 1970s it was no longer in everyday use. There were only three people who remembered a few scraps of it, all of them born before 1900.[15] Biyaygiri, once spoken near Cardwell in Queensland, had by that time completely disappeared from use, as Dixon explains in an earlier memoir:

Cardwell has just one long street, running parallel to a shady, sandy beach. A few hundred yards across the sea to the east is Missionary Bay, at the end of Hinchinbrook Island. A Reverend Mr Fuller had gone over there in 1870 to establish a mission for the Biyaygiri tribe. He stayed for five months, during which time not a single Aborigine came near him . . .

In retrospect, the Biyaygiri might have done well to seek his protection. In 1872, Sub-Inspector Robert Johnstone – who was convinced that there was only one way to 'teach the Aborigines a lesson' – led a party of police and troopers who beat a cordon across the island and cornered almost the whole tribe on a headland. Those who were not massacred on land were shot as they attempted to swim away. There are no Biyaygiri left today, and scarcely any records of the language.[16]

More typically, perhaps, massacres are combined with the enslavement of a small number of survivors, especially young women and children. This is equally effective in ending the use of an indigenous language. It may take longer. It may not: the invaders' aim will certainly have been to destroy a culture which they considered evil or dangerous, so surviving slaves are likely to be deprived of any opportunity to maintain their own culture. Sooner or later, every social context in which that language might be used will cease to exist, and the language will no longer be heard. 'Perhaps the greatest loss to the complete study of Australian languages', writes Dixon, 'was the total annihilation of the original languages of Tasmania. There were, in 1803, at least eight separate languages in Tasmania but only a few fragments were recorded before their speakers died or were killed.'

We can add – I am in no doubt that Dixon would agree – that much more was lost here, even linguistically, than an opportunity to complete the survey of Australian languages. It is usually said that all Australian languages are related, belonging to a single language family or phylum. That case is still arguable – it is not proved. As for the languages of Tasmania, it is simply unknown, and probably now it never will be known, whether these belonged to the Australian family or not. Not enough is recorded of them even to make a balanced judgement. What is known is that 'there appears to have been no contact between the people of Tasmania and those of the mainland since the Bass Strait was submerged at the end of the last Ice Age, about 12,000 years ago.' At any rate, Tasmanian languages showed no striking resemblances to Australian ones, and that is certainly just what we would expect if separate development over a period of at least twelve thousand years – and maybe much longer – separated the two groups. Tasmanian languages might have been as different from all other languages of the world, in some feature of phonetic or grammatical structure, as are (for example) the Khoisan languages of southern Africa.

We shall never know. 'By 1830' (I am quoting Dixon again) 'there were only 300 Tasmanians left out of a population estimated to have numbered about five thousand.' No competent linguist ever listened to a Tasmanian language: the few records that exist come from short wordlists compiled by local observers in the nineteenth century. 'Truganini, the last full-blood Tasmanian and pretty certainly the last person with command of a Tasmanian language, died in 1876.'[17] By that time all others had either been killed, died of disease, or, in the case of some young women, had been captured to serve as concubines and slaves. These last, each of them isolated from all the rest, had no

217

one to whom they could speak their language: their children (whose descendants still survive within the general Tasmanian population) were brought up to speak English. So it is that the last Tasmanian language, whichever it was, was most probably heard for the last time in 1876.

The enslavement of the surviving Tasmanians was in essence a private enterprise, though, as in the case of the California Indians between 1845 and 1870, the local administration gave practical support both to massacre and to enslavement. Elsewhere a form of slavery, instrumental in destroying languages and cultures, has been effected by direct government action. From the late nineteenth century until 1969 the government of the state of New South Wales took part-Aboriginal children (that is, the children resulting from rape and other temporary sexual relationships between white men and Aboriginal women) away from their families and trained them for domestic work and labouring.[18]

The term 'language shift' characterizes the other usual reason (as opposed to massacre and disease) for which languages cease to be spoken. It was certainly in the past the usual reason, and in spite of the increasing barbarism of the modern world it probably is so still.

As James Crawford insists, language shift ought not to be described in Darwinian terms, as if the language itself had somehow become unable to survive in a modern, changed environment.

Unlike natural species, languages have no genes and thus carry no mechanism for natural selection. Their prospects for survival are determined not by any intrinsic traits, or capacity for adaptation, but by social forces alone . . .

Conceiving language loss as a Darwinian process implies that some languages are fitter than others, that the 'developed' will survive and the 'primitive' will go the way of the dinosaurs . . . Some scholars of 'language death' have helped to perpetuate this misunderstanding by ignoring its social and historical causes. By focusing exclusively on 'structural-linguistic' factors, they imply 'that a language can "kill itself" by becoming so impoverished that its function as an adequate means of communication is called into question.' The research literature demonstrates precisely the opposite: such structural changes are the result, not the cause, of language decline.[19]

What is happening is really this. The speakers of a language find that their need to survive and prosper is better served by another language – so they learn that – and eventually find no residual use for their traditional language – so they cease to use it and do not teach it to their children. Between the first of these steps and the second, some people, perhaps in only one generation, perhaps in several, will be bilingual, and in Chapter 4 we explored this bilingualism and its timescale. If the bilingualism lasts for more than one generation, and the social conditions remain similar, speakers will gradually find themselves using their traditional local language in fewer and fewer circumstances. The traditional language, falling gradually out of use in this way, will gradually have a more limited vocabulary and grammar – because resources formerly used are no longer called for. The language does not 'kill itself', even though it is difficult to avoid metaphors from the life sciences like ecology, survival, extinction and genocide in this context. If anything, its own speakers might be said to cease to nourish their language. Some linguists have spoken of 'linguistic suicide' in such cases. 'Language death' is an expression that many have used.

For the moment let's accept this metaphorical term and explore how it might be defined. You can say that a language has 'died' when the last person who ever learnt anything significant of it dies. How much of a language is that? A few words? But then languages live on in their loanwords, and those few surviving words may simply be clouding the issue. Under this definition, one would probably say (discounting the Cornish loanwords that are still in use in the English of Cornwall) that Cornish 'died' when John Davey of Zennor died, in 1891. It is in this sense that we say that 'about half of the original languages of Australia are no longer spoken or even remembered, except in some cases through a couple of dozen words retained in the English spoken by descendants of the original tribe.'[20]

You can say that a language has 'died' when the last fluent speaker dies. That point also is not as easy to fix as you might think – not only because, once there is only one speaker, there is no one to speak fluently with, but also because by that stage in its obsolescence a language may be used in few contexts, and thus may well already have become less versatile in expression and less rich in vocabulary than a couple of generations earlier. Under this definition it might be true to say that Cornish died when the last of Dorothy Jeffrey's circle of Cornish-speaking friends died soon after 1777.

You can say that a language has 'died' when the last conversation has taken place in it – when no community exists in which conversation in that language can take place, and when any surviving speaker or speakers have no one to talk to. It is in this sense that Cornish died precisely in 1777, when Dorothy Jeffrey of Mousehole died, for she was the animator of the last conversations in Cornish. Under this definition, many Australian and North American languages still listed as 'living' have in fact died, since their last remaining speakers are isolated in retirement homes or hospitals or among families speaking only English, and never have the opportunity to use their unique linguistic knowledge.

The last definition is exemplified in a brief description of New Jersey Dutch in 1910. 'Up to thirty years ago', wrote J. Dyneley Prince, New Jersey Dutch 'was the common idiom of many rural districts in northern New Jersey, employed alike by Dutch, German, English and French settlers. It has . . . been driven from its former territory by the public schools, and now survives only in the memories of some two hundred old persons, nearly all of whom are over seventy years old.' There was a second variant of the language, Prince added: 'a small colony of old Negroes living on the mountain back of Suffern, N.Y. . . . still use their own dialect of Jersey Dutch, but they are very difficult of access, owing to their shyness of strangers.'[21] From Prince's wording here we can gather that Jersey Dutch, like so many of the Indian languages of California today, had in his time just recently ceased to be spoken currently in white communities – it survived 'only in the memories'. On the other hand the form of the language used by Negroes might still be heard, 'on the mountain back of Suffern', if one were lucky. Both forms of Jersey Dutch are now never heard at all – they are wholly lost.

The last definition – a language 'dies' when it is no longer used in conversation – is in some ways the most sensible one to use, and it corresponds to the terms used elsewhere in this book: we have not usually spoken of 'language death' but of languages ceasing to be used. If we take this definition, we will probably make a mental exception for the anthropologists and linguists who are often around at these final stages, encouraging one-way communication into their tape recorders, and sometimes being sufficiently skilled to take part in a real conversation themselves. Under this definition, very few of the languages of California are still 'alive' or in current use. Under this definition, Itelmen, a language of Kamchatka, is no longer alive (it is said that Itelmen 'lives only in memory'); although dozens of people can still speak it, and they are in considerable demand from linguists working on several projects simultaneously, no one uses it any more. Under this definition, many more than half of the languages of Australia are 'dead', and the work done recently on some of these languages by Luise Hercus, R. M. W. Dixon and others can really be described as linguistic archaeology. Dixon is one of the linguists who has done most to record disappearing languages, and has naturally experienced some of the poignant moments when it becomes clear that a language will never again be spoken.

In some cases the linguist comes too late. Warungu is listed as still spoken in recent reference books, with the following note: '2 speakers reported in 1981, northeast of Einasleigh, Queensland'. Dixon's information, here quoted from his 1984 memoir, is more precise and also more final: it came in conversation with his long term helper Chloe Grant, herself a fluent speaker of several Australian languages.

Chloe Grant . . . berated me for not having got Peter [Biran] and his sister Nora to converse in Warungu, which they knew as well as – or better than – Jirrbal. But we'd missed our chance there. The news filtered through that Peter had hit Nora over the head during a drunken argument that Christmas. She died quite soon afterwards, and Peter only survived her by a few months.[22]

There turned out to be another informant, Lizzie Simmons, who would give Dixon a few words of Warungu – the language of her late husband – in return for a good supply of beer. But what he really wanted from the quadrilingual Lizzie was Mbabaram, the language that she had learnt from her father. As to that, she would give him nothing: 'Lizzie Simmons grasped her stick a little tighter, and directed her beady eyes at mine. "No," she creaked. "Barbaram too hard. Too hard for me. Far too hard for you."'[23] Dixon wanted Mbabaram not only because, like so many other languages of southern Queensland, it was about to be lost for good, but also because existing notes suggested it was very different from all the rest. He found another informant: 'Finally [Albert Bennett] volunteered a word. "You know what we call 'dog'?" he asked. I waited anxiously. "We call it *dog*." My heart sank – he'd pronounced it just like the English word, except that the final *g* was forcefully released. I wrote it down anyway.'[24] For Dixon's breakthrough in linking Mbabaram with other Australian languages, and for the etymology of Mbabaram *dog* worked out by his colleague Ken Hale (which has nothing to do with the English word *dog*: the resemblance is pure coincidence), you will have to read Dixon's own narrative. He adds that 'the work on Mbabaram had just been completed in time. My 1972 Christmas card brought a letter from Doreen McGrath: '. . . Albert passed away in July. Very sudden . . .'[25]

During the same period of dogged fieldwork Dixon managed to rescue some information about a once-significant language, Kamilaroi, spoken in southern Queensland and across a large area of northern New South Wales.

I went to the police station and enquired if there might be anyone who remembered Kamilaroi, the original language of that region. They gave me a couple of names down at the Aboriginal settlement . . . Nobody actually used Kamilaroi any more, but I was able, by going back two or three times, to record almost a hundred words that had been remembered by Tom Binge at the settlement and Charlie White at the hospital . . . The phonetics of the words were clear, which could be a help in explicating some of the fuller materials on Kamilaroi taken down by missionaries in the last century. The following year . . . Peter Austin did more work around Moree and then in 1976 . . . Corinne Williams did an honours sub-thesis on the Yuwaaliyay dialect of Kamilaroi, at Walgett and Lightning Ridge. Peter and Corinne were able to rescue all that was left of this important language.[26]

It is clear that Kamilaroi, by this time, was never spoken: no one living had been a fluent speaker, and those who still knew something of the language were isolated from one another and had no one to speak to in it. In one of the more unexpected linguistic revivals of the twentieth century, Kamilaroi now lives in cyberspace, thanks to the efforts of Peter Austin and David Nathan: 'We would like to announce that a dictionary of Gamilaraay/Kamilaroi (northern NSW, Australia) has been put on the World Wide Web: it is the Web's first page-formatted, hypertext dictionary.'[27] In the same way several Amerindian languages that have fallen from use are the focus of revival movements. There has been talk of reviving Mohegan, whose last fluent speaker died in 1958, and Wampanoag, which ceased to be spoken well before living memory. The Californian language Ohlone has now only one speaker and is no longer in current use, yet some hope to revive it from this speaker's information and the field notes of J. P. Harrington.[28]

An additional focus of Dixon's work at this time was Yidiny, another language of southern Queensland. His grammar of Yidiny was published just as Yidiny finally disappeared from use, when the last active speaker, Dick Moses, 'died just about the day the book was published, the book into which he'd put so much of his knowledge and spirit, the heritage of his people'.

Without Moses's help it wouldn't have been a quarter as detailed or complete . . . Pompey was still there, sitting on a bench overlooking the sea, puffing on his pipe. We talked for a bit. He was getting old and slow, but still enjoyed life. We didn't mention Moses. But as Pompey spoke Yidiny, melodious sentences, long vowels strategically placed to engender a euphonious rhythm, it became hard to respond. This was Moses's language, and Tilly Fuller's, a mystical magic tongue. And I would never again hear it spoken, hear Yidiny stories, as they had pronounced them.[29]

Similar linguistic obituaries can be found wherever linguists have investigated disappearing languages. In 1908 John R. Swanton discovered the last speaker of Ofo living among the Tunica near Marksville, Louisiana, and learned, to his surprise, that that language was of Siouan affinity. He collected what he could of the language and prepared a dictionary.[30] The last speaker of Old Town Penobscot (the southern variety of Abenaki), Madeline Tower Shay, died in 1993; the words that she remembered helped the comparative linguist Frank Siebert to explore the early history and migrations of Algonquian peoples.[31] The last speaker with an extensive knowledge of Quinault (a language of Washington state) died on 27 April 1996; this was

Oliver Mason, grandson of Taholah, who once signed the treaty by which the Quinault successfully claimed much of their traditional territory. Their leader was charged with knowing tribal lineages, each person's duties and work, traditional fishing sites, stories and songs – in fact the whole of Quinault language and culture.[32]

I was on the Stockbridge-Munsee Reservation in Wisconsin [writes Barbara Boseker], when the last native speaker of Munsee, a 90-year-old tribal elder, died. The Munsee had been moved from Massachusetts in a previous century by the expansion of white settlement from east to west . . . Since [they] had no reservation, the Menominee of northern Wisconsin generously offered them a corner of their reservation, where the remaining Stockbridge-Munsee live today. It may be argued that when the last Munsee speaker died, the Munsee culture died with him.[33]

In September 1934 Morris Swadesh and Mary Haas made a brief survey trip through southern Louisiana, east Texas and eastern Oklahoma in an attempt to locate speakers of one or more of the various remnant groups of Indians that had been reported in the area in the late nineteenth century.

We did succeed [Haas reported] in finding one woman who remembered a few words of Biloxi. She was Mrs Emma Jackson . . . She told us she was born in 1847 and that would have made her 87 years old in 1934. At that time she had not spoken the language for 21 years. We succeeded in eliciting 54 words from her with great difficulty. What she was able to remember checks out with complete fidelity. It seems clear that she had once known the language quite well.[34]

The fortunate discovery of Emma Jackson allowed Mary Haas to write her paper 'The Last Words of Biloxi', at the same time using the new material Mrs Jackson had provided and comparing it with nineteenth-century reports which had been made less carefully. The new material 'checked out' – it corresponded to the old, and made sense of what had previously been obscure. By two of the definitions above, Biloxi was by now 'dead': there was no community of speakers, and the single remaining speaker was no longer fluent in the language, remembering only about fifty words of it, though 'she had once known the language quite well'.

Among the languages of the Caucasus, many of them spoken by very small numbers, some language disappearances may result from the current warfare and instability in the region. The North West Caucasian language Ubykh lost speakers as the result of a much earlier period of instability, that of the Russian conquest in the mid-nineteenth century. Most speakers of Ubykh migrated to Turkey; others, now forming a community that was too small for self-sufficiency, have merged into other neighbouring peoples. Those in Turkey retained their ethnic identity for several generations, but have eventually merged with the surrounding Turks. The linguist Ole Stig Andersen reports that Ubykh 'died at daybreak, October 8th 1992, when the Last Speaker, Tevfik Esenç, passed away. I happened to arrive in his village that very same day, without appointment, to interview this famous Last Speaker, only to learn that he had died just a couple of hours earlier. He was buried later the same day.'[35]

Ubykh has been known among linguists for a long time. Much less is known of Kanoe, a language isolate of South America, spoken in 1996 by a tiny indigenous group (four people) just discovered to be living in the rainforest in the Brazilian state of Rondonia and also by about six elderly people, none of whom was in contact with any of the others, in other parts of Brazil. At the time of the report the indigenous group was under threat of massacre from local landowners. Another group, speaking a previously unknown language of the Tupi family, was contacted at the same time: no work has yet been done on their language, and they are under equal threat of massacre.[36]

The unluckiest cases are those in which the first discovery of a language is followed so closely by its disappearance that no one has time to record it. Bruce Connell, while engaged in field work in Cameroon in 1995, 'found a language called Kasabe, which no westerner had studied before. It had just one speaker left, a man called Bogon. Connell had no time on that visit to find out much about the language, so he decided to return to Cameroon a year later. He arrived in mid-November, only to learn that Bogon had died on November 5.'[37]

If a language that is about to disappear from use is the only survivor of its linguistic family – if, that is, it has always been a 'linguistic isolate', or has recently become one since all its relatives have already ceased to be spoken – it has more differences from all other known languages than any of the rest, and it offers more knowledge of the whole potential range of human language. This was one reason to regret the disappearance of the Tasmanian languages, for example.

Another language group of equal importance has just ceased to be used in South Africa. This is the Southern San language family (once better known as Bushman), one of the three families in the geographical grouping of Khoisan languages of southern Africa. All three have been spoken by fairly small numbers of people, but while Nama, one of the Khoe languages, is a national language of Namibia and has tens of thousands of speakers, the others have no such official status and the Southern San languages are now no longer in use at all. No Khoe or San language has ever been taught in a South African school.

Elsie Valbooi of Rietfontein, according to Nigel Crawhall writing in 1998, was the only surviving speaker of /'Auni, which was the last Southern San language. She was then ninety-six years old: her family had been 'desperate to record her language and her life story' and had been hoping to find a linguist willing to help – though they had not been sufficiently desperate to want to learn her language themselves. Elsie also spoke some =Khomani, a closely related language, as did eight other old people: in 1998 a glossary and recordings of =Khomani were being made, just in time, before this language and /'Auni disappeared for good. Two Khoe languages, Gri and !Ora, have fairly recently ceased to be spoken but there were said to be still people living near Campbell who remembered some words of these two languages.[38] In the old South Africa speakers of Khoisan languages were labelled 'Bushmen' and 'Hottentots' and were usually forced to register as coloured (a convenient slot bureaucratically, though the term properly meant 'mixed-race'). 'We were told that we were coloured, that Nama was a useless language, that our traditions were nothing. Our history was hidden from us.' The largest such language community in South Africa is that of the Nama (the language of Namibia mentioned above) but while older people still speak the language fluently youngsters are almost embarrassed to use it. They never hear it at school or in the media. South African schools still tend to treat Khoisan language speakers as ignorant and backward.

At last, it is said, Nama in South Africa is being put to positive use once more: Richtersveld National Park uses Nama speakers, with their unrivalled knowledge of animal behaviour, tracking, plant identification and local ecology, as field guides. Those who do not live in the National Park are less fortunate. 'We used to dance all night. Young people cannot do that any more. The old people were so healthy in the past when we used our medicines,' according to a Nama speaker in Witbank. They still have their knowledge of local medicinal plants, but, driven off their lands, they have no access to the wild herbs that once kept them healthy. Now the =Khomani are pressing for the return of their own traditional lands in the Southern Kalahari and want to use their knowledge of the bush to promote tourism – but meanwhile they have lost their language, and their local knowledge is slipping away.[39]

The after-life of languages

In modern South Africa, Penny Silva confirms, all the Khoisan languages now survive 'mainly through those words which have been absorbed into other languages'. Their speakers may now be regarded as backward, but their local knowledge was once highly valued by early European settlers. So it is that Khoisan languages, particularly Nama and Khoe, provide many loanwords in the English of South Africa, especially in the area of useful and medicinal plants. Here are some examples: *gogga* 'insect' comes from Nama *xo xo*; *kudu* 'kind of antelope' from Nama *kudu-b*; *oribi* 'kind of antelope' from Nama *orab*; *buchu* or *boegoe* 'medicinal leaves, often infused in brandy: a so-called Old Dutch Medicine' from Khoe *buku*; *ganna* 'plant once used in soap-making' from Khoie *kanna*; *guarriboom* 'shrub whose fruit can be fermented for vinegar', from Khoe *gwarri*, also borrowed into Zulu *umgwali*; *karree* 'root which is powdered and fermented to make "honey beer"', from Khoe *karib*; *kukumakranka*, from Khoe, 'aromatic fruit used for scenting rooms and infused in brandy'; *tsamma* or *tsamma melon* 'watermelon', from Khoe *t'sama*; *dagga* 'the drug *Leonotis leonurus*; now also used for cannabis', from Khoe *daxa-b*.[40]

The kind of linguistic after-life that is exemplified here is very relevant to the subject of this book. If some knowledge passes from language to language, along with a specialized vocabulary that classifies the local environment and traditional local skills, perhaps after all the loss of languages is not such a serious issue? Perhaps we retain everything that we need? Let's investigate the scale of this phenomenon, and let's focus first on the languages that have contributed to English. British Celtic of the English lowlands is gone beyond recall. No one will ever again hear Anglo-Norman spoken. Anglo-Norman survives in written texts, but British Celtic (in common with many hundreds of other languages of the past) does not. All we have are the words (and perhaps sound patterns, and perhaps features of grammar and idiom) that these languages have left behind them embedded in English. As a second example we shall look at survivals of lost languages in the Latin and Greek of the Roman Empire.

In some cases we can no longer identify the sources on which English has drawn. It is equally true of all the modern languages of Europe that a certain proportion of their vocabulary is simply unexplained: no one has discovered how these words originated, or how they came to mean what they do. The English word *basket*, first recorded in the thirteenth century, might have a connection with the early Celtic word *bascauda* (possibly 'washing-tub') mentioned in passing by a Latin poet; this same Celtic word was definitely borrowed into old French and survives as modern French *bâche* 'cold-frame'. But any links between *bascauda* and *basket* are lost. Some even more difficult cases: *boast* can be traced back to Norman times and not before. *Coarse* seems to go back no further than the fifteenth century. *Curse*, also, has no known cognates in other languages. The idea of *darning* appeared about 1600, and no one knows where that word came from either. Here we have five important words that were once brand new in English, all five probably recording a fruitful contact with another language – because very few words are simply invented out of nothing – but we can no longer read the record.

However, the work of etymologists over the last two centuries has ensured that much of the record of the contact of English with other languages – and of the disappearance of those other languages – can be read with confidence.

Let's begin at the beginning, with the long-forgotten languages (we do not even have a name for them) that were spoken in Britain before the Celts arrived. This was somewhere between 2,750 and 5,500 years ago: this sounds vague, but it all depends on what view you take of the spread of the Indo-European languages, which included early Celtic. That is at present a very contentious issue. But, whenever the Celts came, there were people in Britain and Ireland already. We can be fairly sure that English contains a few words from one or other of their languages (as do the Celtic languages themselves). These will be words that came to English from Celtic, yet did not come to Celtic from proto-Indo-European or from one of the languages (such as Germanic) with which Celtic speakers were in contact on the continent of Europe. Because we cannot now trace all early Celtic words to their source, the best chance of finding words like this is to look for concepts that would not have been relevant to the Celts till they reached Britain. Among them will be the proper names of rivers and other natural features of the landscape; and the names of animal or plant species that the Celts would not have met or found useful before they came to Britain.

The rivers called *Wey* and *Wye* – four rivers in total – have names that cannot easily be explained in Celtic. The same is true of the river-names *Tarrant* and *Trent*, *Neen* and *Nene*. The likely answer is that these names were taught to the Celtic-speaking inhabitants of early Britain in contact with even earlier peoples. So were the names of the rivers we know as *Granta, Humber, Itchen, Kennet, Ouse, Severn, Tees, Test, Tweed, Tyne, Ure, Wear, Welland* and some others. It was from earlier peoples, too, that Celtic speakers learnt to call the common crab *partan* (now a regional word in Scots English, also known in Irish and Scottish Gaelic). It may be ultimately from pre-Celtic peoples that we inherit the name of the familiar English lake fish *char*, and the regional name *cammock* of the medicinal plant better known as rest-harrow and wild licorice. Beside these there is another interesting family of words that comes to English from Celtic and cannot be traced further back. The basic modern word is *curd* 'coagulated milk', though an older form *crud* is familiar colloquially and in dialects; *curdy, cruddy* and *curdle* are all linked. This, like the river-names, might possibly go back to the pre-Celtic language of Britain.

Just as interesting are the words that may have first become part of Celtic and Germanic in the period before those languages came to Britain. A number of possible candidates are to be found, shared by Celtic and Germanic languages, and sometimes by other groups too, yet not apparently part of proto-Indo-European. These words seem to record a very ancient language of western Europe, which might or might not be the same as a pre-Celtic language of Britain. From that now-forgotten language both Celtic and Germanic speakers learnt the words. They include *apple*, *yew* and *pool*, three familiar features of the landscape of the north European plains as well as of the British Isles. In all three cases it is usually said that the words reached English from Germanic, not from Celtic, but one cannot be certain, because the Welsh forms (*afal*, *ywen*, *pwll*) are so similar to the English. A fourth familiar feature of the landscape, *pig*, may have been so named in an ancient non-Germanic language of northern Europe, but this word is found only in some Germanic languages, not in Celtic, from which English borrowed the parallel term *hog*. The name of the island group, *Britain*, and the name of its inhabitants, *Brits* or *Britons*, also belong here. This group of words was first recorded in writing when used by the Greek author Aristotle, in the fourth century BC, in the form *Brettanikoi nesoi* 'British isles'; the name was presumably picked up indirectly from Celtic speakers, who at that time occupied the Channel coasts. The Celts themselves had perhaps originally used this word as their name for the Picts.[41]

Skipping Latin – which has modern descendants such as Italian and French, and so isn't truly extinct – what other examples can be found of words that survive in English, having begun their life in a now-extinct language?

Without even looking beyond the British Isles we can find English evidence of the vocabulary of Cornish, Manx and Norn, all three of which have left their mark in local dialects, such as the Isle of Man word *carval* 'carol' and the West Country *mort* 'pig's fat'. The Celtic speech of Cornwall contributed not only *mort* but also *bludgeon* and *bugaboo* to English, as well as some technical terms in tin-mining.

Norn gave English several useful words. Remember *Sheltie* 'Shetland or other small pony': in origin the word must be the Norn version of the Old Norse word *Hjaiti*, which meant 'Shetlander'. Then there is *tang*, bladder-wrack and related seaweeds, and *tangle*, two particular seaweeds that are good to eat; and *loom* (the North Atlantic name of the red-throated diver and Brünnich's guillemot) which in turn gave us *loon* (the American name of the great northern diver). Fishermen around the Scottish coast know plenty of other words that once belonged to Norn: *skerry*, a rock concealed at high tide; *voe*, a bay or inlet; *sillock*, one of a range of words identifying that useful fish the saithe (from which we get coley) at various sizes and ages.

As English speakers began to settle in New England, on the eastern seaboard of North America, they found that they had much to learn from the existing inhabitants. Most of these spoke what are now classed as Algonquian languages. Since the Amerind languages of the northeast have almost all disappeared, the English of New England represents a priceless record of the way the speakers of those languages named and used the natural world. *Moose*, like several other words that we shall encounter, comes from Narragansett *moosu*. Narragansett was the first local language studied by the New England colonists, described by Roger Williams in *A Key into the Language of America*, published in 1643. The word *moose* is first recorded in English in 1613. Even earlier, in 1608, the word *raccoon* (sometimes seen as *rattoon* and *coon*, along with an astonishing range of other forms) had been borrowed from Powhatan, an Algonquian language once spoken in Virginia.[42] *Skunk* was borrowed from Abenaki, a language of Maine and adjacent regions of Canada, in which the word is *sakonkwa*. *Caribou* was borrowed from Micmac, spoken in the Canadian Maritime provinces.

Native American knowledge of plants and their uses gave us the English word *squash* 'pumpkin', from Narragansett, and *pecan, hickory* and *persimmon*, all from Powhatan or a neighbouring language. Then there is an important group of names of foods made from maize or Indian corn, names that are familiar to many American speakers of English but not understood elsewhere, including *pone* 'cornmeal bread shaped into ovals, then fried', *hominy* 'hulled and coarsely ground maize', *samp* 'coarsely ground maize; porridge made from it' and *succotash* 'dish of maize and lima beans'. All four of these terms are borrowed from Algonquian languages of the eastern seaboard, the first two from Powhatan, the last two from Narragansett.

Most of the fish of North American coastal waters were unfamiliar to English speakers. From Narragansett they learnt their names for the *porgy*, which they also called *scup* and *scuppaug*: all three words are extracted from the Narragansett *mishcuppâuog* 'the thick-scaled ones'. Narragansett speakers also taught them names for the *squeteague*, *tautog*, *mummychog*, *quahaug* and *menhaden*: the original of this last name, Narragansett *munnawhatteaûg*, seems to have meant 'the fertilizing ones'. That is an instructive term, because this fish was used locally as a fertilizer and source of oil – and it still is. Across the continent, on the shores of Puget Sound, guidance to English-speaking settlers came by way of another now-forgotten language, Chinook Jargon, once a lingua franca of Native travellers in this multilingual region. Chinook Jargon was the source of the local English words *chum* and *quinnat*, both of them names of species of salmon; also *skil* or *skilfish*, known more widely as black cod.

Tupí or Lingua Geral, a language that was once spoken by millions across Portuguese Brazil and now has no more than a few hundred remaining speakers, is surely destined to disappear as a living language. It will survive in its loanwords in Portuguese and English. It is the source of several familiar English words, including *jaguar*, *tapir*, *macaw*, *piranha* and the highly important medicinal plant *ipecacuanha*, whose name meant 'creeping plant that causes vomiting'. Also from Tupí are *manioc* and *tapioca*, two further clues to the importance of the cassava plant in Central and South America; and *cayenne*, another name for the valuable chilli.

Taino, the Cariban language of the Antilles, continued to be spoken by small numbers of the original inhabitants of the islands until the beginning of the nineteenth century. One of the first Taino words recorded was *ashi*, which (in the form *ají*) is today the usual term for chilli in the Spanish of South America. Taino words now to be found in English include *maize*, *cassava*, *yucca*, three terms for two highly important food plants (*yucca* and *cassava* were synonymous in earlier English). The Arawakan languages of the Caribbean, also long since extinct, are the sources (by way of Spanish) of general English *iguana*, of Jamaican *green guana* and of Australian English *goanna*. The name that was given in the Arawakan of Cuba to the neighbouring Cariban speakers of the Antilles was (depending on dialect) *Kariba* or *Kaniba*:

thanks to Columbus's reports these words are both familiar in modern English, as *Caribbean* and *cannibal*.

In the same way, out of more than a hundred Australian languages that have already ceased to be spoken, perhaps twenty continue to exist in the tenuous form of loanwords in English: they may still do so even when the very last Australian language has fallen out of use as a mother tongue.

One of the first Australian languages encountered by Europeans, 'the Sydney language', now known as Dharuk, was spoken by a coastal people near Sydney and an inland tribe near Campbelltown. 'Today there are still Dharuk descendants in the Sydney region and some use a few words from this language in the English they speak, although the language ceased to be actively used many years ago.' From Dharuk English has borrowed over fifty words, including some of the best-known of Australian terms. These include *dingo* and *warrigal*, two names for the Australian race of dogs, kept as a domestic animal there for the last four thousand years. Dharuk speakers distinguished the feral *warrigal* from the domestic *din-gu*, but English speakers were less precise. Other Dharuk loanwords include the familiar *koala* (Dharuk *gula*); *wallaby*, originally a small black kangaroo of the Port Jackson district; *wallaroo*, from a name in the inland dialect for a large kangaroo of the hill country such as *Macropus robustus*; the burrowing *wombat* (Dharuk *wambad*, originally written *whom-batt* in English); the bird *boobook* or *mopoke* (Dharuk *bug-bug*, an imitation of its call), the fibrous plant known as *black kurrajong* (Dharuk *garrajung* 'fishing line'), used for making fishing lines and with an edible root; the beautiful tulip tree or *waratah*, whose flowers Aborigines once sucked for their sweet nectar; and then the *boomerang*, an implement which Australians have made for at least ten thousand years, the *woomera* or throwing-stick, and the dance ceremony or *corroboree*; and the now-opprobrious term for an Aboriginal woman *gin*, originating in Dharuk *diyin* 'woman, wife'.

Wiradhuri was spoken in southeastern New South Wales, southwest of Sydney, in the region of modern Canberra. A few Wiradhuri still know some words of the language, but it is no longer spoken. From Wiradhuri English has borrowed twenty-five or more words. These include several names of birds, the white cockatoo *corella*, the grey cockatoo *gang-gang* (the name in Wiradhuri originated as an imitation of its call), and the laughing jackass or *kookaburra* (Wiradhuri *gugub-arra*, again an imitation of its call). Names of trees borrowed into English include an Australian sandalwood species, the *quandong* or native peach, whose fruit can be eaten fresh or dried; and a familiar feature of the Australian landscape, *billabong*. 'In early summer each year,' we are told, 'people travelled from all over Wiradhuri country into the territory of the Ngarigo people in the Snowy Mountains to partake of the bogong moth amid festivity and ceremony.' Ngarigo, a long-forgotten language of which little was ever recorded, was spoken to the south of Canberra. Its only bequest to English is the name of the *bogong* moth, tasty, nutritious, and sufficiently important locally to have given its name to the town of Bogong, Victoria, and to several geographical features.[43]

Inland to the north of Sydney Kamilaroi and the related dialects Yuwaalaray and Yuwaaliyay were spoken over a wide area in northern New South Wales and southern Queensland. It ceased to be spoken fairly recently, and a few old people remember some words of it. From Kamilaroi and its dialects twenty-five or more words were borrowed into English, including the name of the burrowing rabbit-eared bandi-coot *bilby*; four birds, the crane *brolga*, the red-breasted cockatoo *galah*, the parrot *bullan-bullan* also known as mallee ringneck, and the *budgerigar* (Kamilaroi *gijirrigaa*), now known world-wide; also some tree names, the eucalyptus *coolibah* and the acacias *gidgee* and *mulga*: the latter is of use for its yellowish timber and is the host of a parasitic edible swelling known as *mulga apple*. And then there is the *bumble tree* (Kamilaroi *bambul*), a species of capers whose fruit is a summer delicacy rich in vitamin C.

The language spoken where Perth now stands was Nyungar. Some old people remember a few words, but the language is no longer in use. It recorded local knowledge of the rich forest vegetation of the southwest corner of Australia, and over fifty loanwords from Nyungar are now to be found in English. They provide names for several trees of genus *Eucalyptus* – details in Chapter 7. Nyungar loanwords also include the *bardie grub* (Nyungar *bardi*), a beetle larva said to be good to eat raw or roasted; and the names of several Western Australian mammals, the cat-like *chuditch*, which once ranged widely over the continent but is now restricted to the neighbourhood of Perth, the mouse-like *dibbler* (Nyungar probably *dibala*), the termite-eating *numbat*, the short-tailed wallaby *quokka* and the rat-kangaroos *boodie* and *woylie*.

In 1961 Luise Hercus, a Sanskrit teacher in Melbourne, heard by chance that there were a few people who still remembered some words of the Australian languages of Victoria. She was 'able to record a few dozen words said to be Wuywurung but there was no one left who could construct a complete sentence' of this language once spoken where Melbourne now is, a language whose death knell was sounded by the gold rush of the 1850s. Wuywurung now survives only in about ten loanwords in English. Hercus went on to record – just in time – all that could still be discovered of all the languages of Victoria. In western Victoria the major language was Wemba-wemba, spoken in several dialects. She found a few fluent speakers from whom she recorded texts and compiled a grammar. Wemba-wemba people had a local staple food, the seeds or rather spores of the perennial *nardoo* fern (the name is borrowed from an unspecified language of southern Australia). These spores are large enough to be ground into pulp to make porridge or a baked cake, *nardoo damper*. They also had a summer delicacy, the sweet secretions of insects (thus a local form of manna) called in English *lerp* (Wemba-wemba *lerab*). Other Wemba-wemba loanwords denote the small, bushy eucalyptus trees called generically *mallee* – on some of whose leaves lerp is found – and the freshwater crayfish or craybob known as *yabby* and *lobby*.

Gaurna, the 'Adelaide language', ceased to be spoken many years ago: speakers succumbed to venereal disease, smallpox and forced migration in the first half of the nineteenth century. The ten Gaurna loanwords to be found in English include *condolly* 'whale blubber' (from Gaurna *gandali* 'whale') and a local name for the bilby or rabbit-eared bandicoot, *pinkie* (Gaurna *bingu*).

The 'Brisbane language' was Yagara, for which all surviving records come from the nineteenth century. Yagara territory was rich in produce: the rainforest provided birds and vegetation as well as honey from the nests of native bees; there was seafood, too, and land animals. English has about sixteen loanwords from Yagara, including the names of the *bunya* pine and the *piccabeen* palm (*bigi* in Yagara: no one knows where the -*been* comes from). The palm heart used to be eaten. The immature cone and the big ripe nut of the bunya pine were favourite foods; people from far afield gathered in early January in the Bunya Mountains, near Dalby in southeast Queensland, for bunya nut feasts and ceremonies.[44]

Just as English preserves a record of lost languages, so did the Greek and Latin of the Roman Empire. More than from any other language, Greek adopted loanwords and loan-translations from Aramaic and Biblical Hebrew, a development that went alongside the spread of Christianity. Loanwords include *amen*, used in Greek (and now in many other languages) as a liturgical response 'so be it'; also such crucial Christian terms as *Messias* 'Messiah, the anointed one'. Loan translations include *Khristos* 'Christ, the anointed one', a direct translation of *Messias*. However, the presence of loanwords from the other languages of the Empire is a far more pervasive feature of later Latin than it is of Greek. Thanks to our survey of the languages of the Empire we know exactly why: more speakers in the western Empire than in the eastern were ceasing to use their traditional language. There was more contact, more interference, between these languages and Latin than there was between the languages of the eastern Empire and Greek.

The oldest influences on Latin were those of Oscan and other Italic dialects – bordering on the territory of Latin in central Italy – and of Etruscan and Greek, both of which were not only neighbours but also (in the earliest years of Rome) culturally superior. From other Italic dialects (which include the 'Sabine' and 'Praenestine' listed by Quintilian in the quotation below) Latin borrowed everyday words like *popina* 'cookshop', *olla* 'cooking pot', *lupus* 'wolf', *bos* 'ox, cow', *robus* 'red-brown' (used of oxen and of wheat), *scrofa* 'sow'. From Venetic to Latin came a feature of written style which we cannot now pin down, but which was obvious to the contemporaries and admirers of Livy (the great Latin historian born in the Venetic town of Patavium, modern Padua) and which they labelled *Patavinitas*. From Etruscan there were words of cultural or religious significance. Among these Etruscan loanwords is one of special interest, *persona*: in the languages that have adopted this word from Latin it has such varied senses as are evidenced by English *person* 'human individual' and *parson* 'priest' and French *personne* 'nobody'. The Latin word originally meant 'mask used in drama': its original was an Etruscan loanword from Greek *prosopon* 'face'. In due course Christian terminology also found its way from Greek to Latin, including *Christus* and *Messias*, the two titles mentioned above that both in origin mean 'the anointed one'.

Meanwhile Latin was spreading far beyond Italy, and interacting with the other languages of western Europe. Even writers who confine themselves strictly to classical, written Latin show an awareness that their language was adopting loanwords from many of these others. Here is the educator Quintilian once more, this time attempting a classification of the Latin vocabulary by its origins.

Words are either Latin or foreign. Foreign words have come to us from practically all peoples, as indeed have the things they denote. I say nothing of Etruscan, Sabine and Praenestine expressions; . . . I will allow myself to count all Italian terms as Roman. These apart, we have a great many Gaulish terms, as *reda* 'coach' (already in Cicero) and *petorritum* 'open coach' (in Horace). *Mappa* 'napkin', also as a racing term 'starting signal', is claimed as Punic; I am told that *gurdus*, the colloquial word for 'stolid', originates in Spain. But in this section I am bound to focus on Greek speech, on which Latin so largely depends. We use Greek words wherever we have none of our own, and they in return borrow a good many of ours.[45]

Quintilian elsewhere lists another word that had reached Latin from Spain, *cantus* 'dressed ashlar', and he is proved right by the fact that the word occurs in modern Spanish and Basque. He could have listed still other words, such as *ballux* 'nugget' and *paramus* 'bare plateau'. He could have found many other Gaulish words, including several to do with horses and carts: *ploxenum* 'cart', *esseda* 'chariot', *caballus* 'horse'. Each region of western Europe had its own style of beer, and he could have listed several local words for this interesting beverage: from Gaulish *cervisia* and *corma*, from an Iberian language *caelia*, from Pannonian and Illyrian *camum* and *sabaium*. As to Punic and Greek, he could easily have mentioned the everyday salutations used in the Roman street. When greeting people in Latin one said *ave* (apparently a word borrowed from Punic) or *chaere* (from Greek); when saying goodbye you said *vale* (a native Latin word meaning 'be healthy!').

All those are words that can be found in Latin texts of the period of the Empire. You might not feel quite sure whether they were appropriate to a correct classical Latin style. Quintilian in fact talks about this problem more than once, and he has it at the back of his mind in the quotation just given: by citing those model authors Cicero and Horace he means us to understand that foreign words had reached the highest level of Latin writing. In any case, whatever the thoughtful Latin writer might decide about the loanword issue, such words were certainly spoken and written in current colloquial Latin. And all of them (not counting those from Greek) are precious evidence of languages now extinct and otherwise largely unrecorded.

Now we must look at the negative side – and there is a negative side. We found words of the pre-Celtic language of Britain still surviving in modern English – but very few, most of them place-names, and we can get no meaning out of them. The British Celtic and British Latin words adopted by the Anglo-Saxons were few enough. We have listed most of the words that English speakers took over from Narragansett, Powhatan and Chinook Jargon, and a good many of those that came from the Taino of the Caribbean. They are interesting words, but the total numbers are small. So what about the languages that have been wiped off the map, in areas where English is now spoken, without leaving any identifiable trace in English at all? They are only recorded – if indeed they are recorded – because an enlightened observer noted some details down before the last speaker died.

Eight languages were spoken in Tasmania when English-speaking settlers and convicts began to colonize the island in the nineteenth century. Every last speaker of these languages was dead by 1876. They leave a genetic inheritance (see pp. 217–18) but no linguistic inheritance except for some short wordlists, none of them made by a skilled linguist. There are just three loanwords in English that appear to derive from the eight Tasmanian languages, and all three of them are words confined to Tasmanian and southern Australian usage. There is a derogatory term for 'aboriginal woman', *lubra*. There is the name of a local vegetable of which the fruit can be eaten raw and the leaves cooked, *canagong*. And there is a shrubby tree whose purple berries were eaten by Aboriginal peoples, *boobyalla*.[46]

Of the thirteen Australian languages spoken in what is now the state of Victoria, only two (Wuywurung and Wemba-wemba, listed above) contributed any loanwords to English. In Australia as a whole it is thought that over two hundred and fifty languages were spoken when British settlement got under way. Half of them have already ceased to be spoken, and few if any will survive the twenty-first century. Just over fifty Australian languages, in total, survive in the form of a few loanwords in English. Most of these are not familiar words like *boomerang* and *kangaroo*, but words known only in local Australian English like *conkerberry* (from the Mayawarli variant of Palku, once spoken in southwest Queensland). Fully four-fifths of the vanished languages of Australia have left no such mementoes, and very few indeed were fully recorded before they disappeared.

Lost without trace? the languages of California

California, once the field of activity of the Spanish missions, seized by the United States in 1846 in the Mexican War, might have formed an unrivalled laboratory for the linguist. It would be exactly that, if such a high proportion of its languages were not already lost or on the way to disappearance. Their variety was almost unmatched elsewhere in the world. Perhaps as many as 98 languages were once spoken here – and by that is meant 98 mutually unintelligible languages, many of them with several sharply distinct dialects. Not one of them is likely to survive the next generation.[47] We began this chapter with the example of a single language; we conclude it by observing the loss of nearly a hundred of them in a single US state. Of those 98 languages '45 (or more) have no fluent speakers left at all, 17 have only one to five speakers left, and the remaining 36 have only elderly speakers. Not a single California Indian language is being used now as the language of daily communication.' How did it happen?

Today, the few remaining native speakers of the languages of California are members of a differently privileged group – if I may borrow from the language of political correctness. They are privileged with knowledge, yet underprivileged socially and economically. Why? As children, these few people had a quite exceptional degree of exposure to their languages – and that happened to them because they were successfully kept away from boarding school by their families, or because they successfully escaped as soon as they could, or because they lived with grandparents who spoke no English. At the time of which we are speaking, parents would themselves have attended boarding school and would certainly have spoken English. Unfortunately, these survivors will themselves not have been able to pass on the language to their own children, or, even if they were able, they will not have had the motivation to do so. Practically none of them will have found a husband or wife who spoke the same language: there were so few such people around. Even if they happened to marry a speaker of a different Amerindian language, English would still be the only practical choice as everyday language of the home. Often 'there was simply no one left in the world for the speakers to talk to' in the language that had been their mother tongue. Indeed, after the treatment they had received at school, 'some people consciously chose not to put their children through the same agony . . . but given the lack of context, the loss of function, and the omnipresence of English, even had they chosen to try to pass on their language it would have been exceedingly difficult to do so.'[48]

Linguists and anthropologists have for many years been able to foresee that all the California Indian languages would soon disappear. There has been a concerted effort through the twentieth century to document them. So it is that some of the languages that are no longer spoken do survive on the printed page, in grammars and dictionaries. But as far back as 1978 Robert F. Heizer reached the following conclusion in his survey of research on the North American Indians of California: 'The old-style ethnographic work has ended because the aboriginal cultures are extinct. Many languages are no longer spoken, and the number of surviving tongues is steadily decreasing as the last speakers die.'

This made linguistic research in California all the more urgent; but it did not make it any easier. 'Folklore', Heizer added, 'has shifted to interests other than recording myths, but a large and essentially unstudied body of tales exists for examination by scholars. A strong reaction to archeology by Native Americans may . . . lead in future to a severe reduction of this kind of investigation.'[49] One can hardly blame the few remaining people with real and deep knowledge of the indigenous cultures of California if they have become somewhat possessive of the knowledge that they were under such pressure to abandon, and if they are no longer very keen to see it locked in a glass case. The linguists and anthropologists sometimes seem to jostle one another to gain time with the few people still able to teach them the grammar and the oral literature of one dying language or another. Meanwhile, the languages die. Will there be time to study the ethnobotany of Numic peoples such as the Shoshoni? Most linguists do not double as botanists, so dictionaries are often not sufficiently specific. There is a need for many more studies such as the brief collection of Shoshoni medicinal plants reported in 1972, which highlighted such potentially useful drugs as the bark of Oregon grape, *sokoteheyampeh*, used as an eyewash; milkweed, *me'eppeh tepuhi*, to stimulate lactation; snakeweed, *kwitaweyampeh*, for intestinal bleeding (and now under investigation as a possible anti-cancer agent); and desert parsley, *tootsa*, as a drug with actions comparable to penicillin. This is not even to mention yellow evening primrose, *tukohaya*. It had long been regarded as a powerful drug locally, but its investigation by Western scientists had not even begun when the 1972 survey was made.[50]

To put names to the statistics, the table on the next four pages shows the number of separate language families represented in California, it lists the languages that belong to each, and alongside each language it shows how many dialects are known with certainty to have existed.[51] The language list is probably nearly complete (but see the Yokutsan group of Penutian languages for one area where it is not now possible to give an accurate count of languages). The dialect list is certainly incomplete: there were many more than this, and their existence will never now be known. I have hinted at the disappearance rate among California's languages with the help of symbols attached to the language names (I have not done this for the dialects: even where a language survives, most of its known dialects may well have disappeared from use). An asterisk marks the languages that are known to have existed but no longer have any known speakers; a dagger marks those whose speakers can be counted on the fingers of one hand. I leave you to put a skull and crossbones beside all the others as you look through the table; because not a single one of these languages is now being spoken among children or even taught to children, except in one or two cases in a conscious act of revival (we shall see more of that later). Within about thirty years, they will all be gone.

Family	Branch	Language names	Recorded dialects
Hokan		Chimariko*	
		Esselen*	
		Karuk	
		Salinan*	Migueleño, Antoniaño, Playano
		Washo	
	Shastan	Shasta*	Oregon Shasta, Scott Valley Shasta, Shasta Valley Shasta, Klamath River Shasta
		New River Shasta*	
		Okwanuchu*	
		Konomihu*	
	Palaihnihan	Achumawi (Pit River)	
		Atsugewi (Hat Creek)†	Atsuge and Apwaruge
	Yanan	Yana*	Northern Yana, Central Yana, Southern Yana
		Yahi	
	Pomoan	Northern Pomo†, Northeastern Pomo*, Eastern Pomo†, Central Pomo†, Southeastern Pomo†, Southern Pomo†, Kashaya Pomo	
	Yuman	Quechan	
		Mojave	
		Maricopa	
		Diegueño	Kumeyaay, Ipai, Tipai

Family	Branch	Language names	Recorded dialects
Hokan (cont.)	Chumashan	Obispeño*, Barbareño*, Ventureño*, Purisimeño*, Ynezeño*, Island	
Penutian	Costanoan (Ohlone)	Karkin*, Chochenyo*, Tamyen*, Ramaytush*, Awaswas*, Chalon*, Rumsen*, Mutsun*	
	Wintun	Wintu	McCloud River, Trinity County, Shasta County, Upper Sacramento, Blad Hill, Hayfork, Keswick, Stillwater, French Gulch
		Nomlaki*	two or more
		Patwin†	Hill, River, Cache Creek, Lake, Tebti, Dahcinci, Suisun
	Maiduan	Maidu†	
		Konkow†	Otaki, Metsupda, Nemsu, Eskewi, Pulga, Feather Falls, Challenge
		Nisenan†	Valley Nisenan, Oregon House, Auburn, Clipper Gap, Nevada City, Colfax, Placerville
	Miwokan	Lake Miwok†	
		Coast Miwok†	Bodega, Marin
		Bay Miwok*	
		Saclan*	
		Plains Miwok*	

Family	Branch	Language names	Recorded dialects
Penutian (cont.)	Miwokan (cont.)	Northern Sierra Miwok East Central Sierra Miwok West Central Sierra Miwok Southern Sierra Miwok	
	Yokutsan	Choynumni, Chukchansi, Dumna†, Tachi†, Wukchumi, Yowlumni, Gashowu† and others	A dialect continuum which might be analysed as more than a dozen languages and at least 40 dialects
	Klamath-Modoc	Klamath, Modoc†	
Algic		Yurok Wiyot*	
Na-Dené	Athabascan	Tolowa†	
		Hupa	Hupa, Chilula, Whilkut
		Mattole*	Bear River and one other dialect
		Wailaki*	
		Nongatl-Lassik-Sinkyone*	Nongatl, Lassik, Lolangkok Sinkyone, Shelter Cove Sinkyone
		Cahto*	
Uto-Aztecan	Numic	Mono	Eastern Mono, Western Mono (Monache): each with sub-dialects
		Owens Valley Paiute Northern Paiute Southern Paiute Shoshoni Kawaiisu Chemehuevi	

Family	Branch	Language names	Recorded dialects
Uto-Aztecan (cont.)	Takic	Serrano	
		Cahuilla	Desert, Mountain, Pass
		Cupeño†	
		Ajachemem* (Juaneño)	
		Luiseño	
		Tongva* (Gabrielino)	
		Tataviam*	
		San Nicolas*	
		Kitanemuk*	
		Vanyume*	
		Tubatulabal	
Yukian		Yuki*	Yuki, Coast Yuki, Huchnom
		Wappo*	Clear Lake and 3 other dialects

The linguistic relationships among these language families were terribly complicated, providing evidence of a whole pattern of long-term interaction among them about which it is now very difficult to learn much. Bilingualism and multilingualism were certainly common among the peoples of what is now California, and so the borrowing of sounds, words and structures from language to language was happening all the time. Patwin, a language that is marked with a dagger in the table – all but one of its seven dialects have disappeared from use – once had as many as 6,000 speakers, and was a dominant language in central California, lending words to many neighbouring languages. But also, probably ever since California was first settled perhaps eleven thousand years ago, migrations of one group and another have contributed to the astonishing language patchwork. Then, when Spanish appeared on the scene, most of the Californian languages borrowed liberally from Spanish too. 'Hundreds of Spanish words, linked with diffused elements of Spanish culture, invaded the aboriginal tongues in the nineteenth century.'[52]

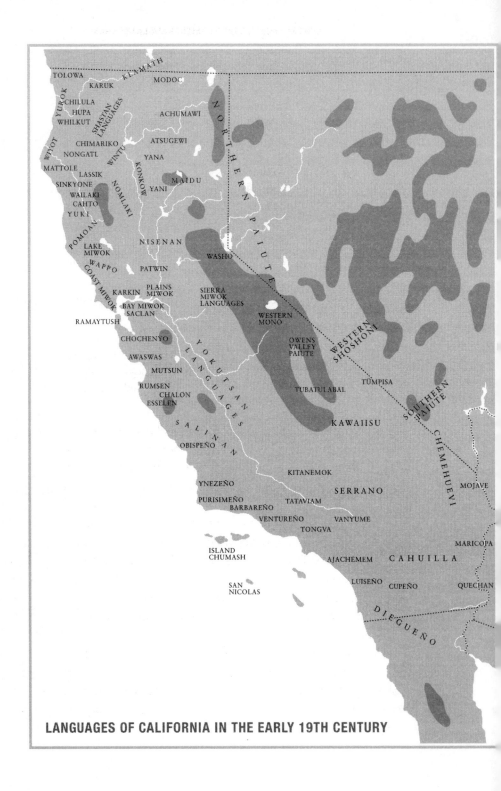

LANGUAGES OF CALIFORNIA IN THE EARLY 19TH CENTURY

The Spanish settlement of California began in 1769 at San Diego, though the mission there was destroyed in 1775. The native population of what is now the state of California is thought to have declined from 310,000 at that date, when mission settlement of the coastal strip from San Diego to San Francisco got under way, to about 150,000 in 1845. What caused this terrifying fall in numbers? The Spanish system was to enrol the Indians as serfs, gathering them forcibly in mission stations, *misiones*, and 'giving' them to Spanish citizens as labourers. Many died from a combination of chronic malnutrition – slave rations made a disastrous contrast with their former varied diet – and epidemics of European diseases. There were particularly disastrous sicknesses in 1833 and 1844. With Mexican independence, from 1821 onwards, the Indians were theoretically counted as 'citizens' but were still in practice subject to forced labour, enslavement and massacre. Throughout the period of Spanish-speaking rule there were numerous revolts, some of which were very dangerous. Death in warfare contributed to the population decline, as did the abortions and infanticides practised by Indian women who had been raped by Spanish priests and soldiers. It is clear that the eighteenth-century Spanish and nineteenth-century Mexican interpretations of civilization were not good for Californians.

Worse was to follow after 1845. Under a second, far more barbarous, wave of invaders and settlers – the Anglo-Americans – who now began to arrive in force, the population of Native Americans, locally known as 'Diggers', fell catastrophically in the next fifty-five years, to about 20,000 (one estimate is even lower, at 15,500) in 1900. In the single decade 1845–55, the first ten years of United States rule, the indigenous population probably dropped from 150,000 to 50,000. 'This desolation', writes S. F. Cook, 'was accomplished by a ruthless flood of miners and farmers who annihilated the natives without mercy or compassion. The direct causes of death were disease, the bullet, exposure, and acute starvation. The more remote causes were insane passion for gold, abiding hatred for the Red man, and complete lack of any legal control.' Previous practice had been to reduce whole communities to servitude. Now, by contrast, any surviving communities were broken up. To focus briefly on the effect of these events on a single tribe:

when gold was discovered along the rivers of northwestern California in the 1850s, traditional Karuk village and family life as known and carried out for generations abruptly ended. As gold miners poured into Karuk territory searching for the richest mining prospects, Karuk villages were systematically burned and villagers forced to leave their traditional homelands. Some were enslaved as labor for the miners. Volunteer militia units . . . assisted home-steaders in forcibly removing Karuk populations.

A fairly general aim was to kill adult males. Mass murders organized by miners and farmers, as private enterprises but with government support, were at their most frequent in 1845–55, and this is reflected in the estimated population figures. Spanish and Mexican practices were not entirely abandoned: the kidnapping and enslavement of children continued, as did the enslavement and rape of young women. This was now slavery in earnest, however, children fetching 50 to 60 dollars on the market, young women as much as 100 dollars.

Conditions in western North America in the late nineteenth and early twentieth centuries were so unfavourable to indigenous cultures that the stage of bilingualism – which is usually, as we have seen, a regular part of the shift from one language to another – scarcely existed at all or was confined to a single generation. Population losses were so huge that in some areas it must have been difficult to find any intact nuclear family, and very difficult to find a suitable wife or husband. In order to marry at all, survivors had to marry outside the tribe. But this meant that the language of the marriage would have to be English, and children would be brought up to speak English. One can find in California today language communities such as those of Serrano and Cupeño, where the last few speakers appear to be fully fluent elderly people, and no one younger knows more than a few words of the language; also examples such as Shoshoni, in which a more gradual disappearance is in progress and rural communities are dominated by fluent elderly speakers and younger semi-speakers, rather as is the case in some areas of Gaelic speech in Scotland – semi-speakers, in the jargon of language death, being people who know only a little of the traditional language.

Enslavement was ruled illegal under California law in 1867, but 'it was not until the 1870s that the atrocities began to decline enough for

Indian survivors to begin establishing settled families again' and the small surviving population had meanwhile been further weakened by diseases, including syphilis and gonorrhoea, which are reported to have been almost universal. By the 1870s the vast majority of people had no land base and no means of livelihood in their traditional territories (it is still, even now, difficult for Native Americans to make a living without moving away from home). In California no treaties were made with Indian tribes, though many were drafted. From 1869 onwards various religious groups were invited by the US Government to take charge of Indians, and in California the task was allotted to Episcopalians, who did not massacre indigenous peoples but forbade their ceremonies and their religion. The general United States policy of extermination was now gradually shifting to one of forcible assimilation, as defined under what was boastfully called the 'Civilization Act'. The objective was stated in 1887 by J. D. Atkins, Commissioner of Indian Affairs, as being 'to blot out the boundary lines which divide them into distinct nations, and fuse them into one homogeneous mass. Uniformity in language will do this – nothing else will.' Military boarding schools, some of them located at the forts that had previously been used in military campaigns against the tribes, were set up in the 1880s and continued until well into the twentieth century. School attendance was made compulsory in 1891, and after that it was only a fortunate few who escaped it – even though some of the day schools and some of the boarding schools were burnt down. Native American tribes are a federal responsibility – as sovereign but dependent nations – and through this period, from about 1880 to 1990, it was primarily federal policy, rather than state policy, that aimed at eradicating their languages and cultures.[53]

From 1900 onwards language eradication was going so well that the figures for ethnic population no longer tell us much about how many language speakers there still were. In fact there were 90,000 'Indians' by 1970, and the number is still growing – but there are only a few thousand speakers of Amerindian languages. To quote again from Leanne Hinton's survey, 'Not a single California Indian language is being used now [in] daily communication. The elders do not in actuality speak their language – rather, they remember how to speak their language.' Occasional attempts by linguists to encourage the speaking and transmission to children of the traditional languages of California can arouse bitter tensions in Native American communities. The history is too painful, the emotional implications too searing, and in any case 'California Indians are now immersed in English. There is little or no space in the present-day way of life for the use of indigenous languages.'[54] Ironically enough, 'Interest in Native Californian cultures is high among the public, and college courses in the subject are well attended.' If this interest is sustained, Robert Heizer observes, future generations of scholars will be making good use of the collected works of twentieth-century linguists and anthropologists,[55] even when the languages themselves are no longer spoken. It might be taken as a final expression of the victory of English over Amerindian languages that majority approval was gained by referendum in 1988 for making English the official language of California. Oddly, that had not been the intention. The policy was not aimed at Amerindian languages at all. They are so insignificant in Californian politics that in the history of the 'US English' movement in California written by a leader of the campaign, Stanley Diamond, for an academic conference volume published in 1990, they are not even mentioned.[56]

There is now – all too late – an enthusiasm for teaching their traditional language to children among some peoples who have practically ceased to use it themselves. In boarding-school times a few Karuk children had grown up in isolated Karuk-speaking settlements along the Klamath River, unable to go to school because of the problems of travel in these rugged mountains. Those children are now the last native Karuk speakers, a fragile resource for those of their tribe who now want to teach the language to modern schoolchildren.[57] Louise Hinton reports that Yuchi elders run language camps for children every summer. Elsewhere in California there are 'immersion camps' for language learning. 'Most of all, people are simply trying to use the language again in any way they can. In the Wiyot tribal council, for example, the chair has instructed the members to vote "yes" or "no" in Wiyot, not English ... People try to greet each other in their language.'[58]

Interesting as these developments are, their limited scope is all too evident. If the only words of Wiyot that you use are *yes* and *no*, and only in a particular semi-ceremonial context, this is no longer a language, any more than musicians are speaking Italian when they say *andante* and *fortissimo*. These are simply loanwords used in a special context, and so are the Wiyot *yes* and *no* at tribal councils that are otherwise conducted entirely in English. As for the new language classes, it has to be admitted that Karuk and Yuchi as now spoken by learners are no longer the Karuk and Yuchi of the past. Modern child and adult learners have an English accent and their grammar is very strongly influenced by English, their dominant language. From their own point of view, even a pidgin Karuk and Yuchi, and even a few words of Wiyot, are much better, as markers of tribal identity, than no language at all. From the perspective of this book, unfortunately, these three languages – even should they continue to be used at all – have to be counted among those that have converged with English: they are three more signs of our reduced linguistic diversity.[59]

7
THE LOSS OF DIVERSITY

Talking about the world

In a new survey of North American Indian languages Marianne Mithun gives an admirably clear statement of what is lost as each language ceases to be used. 'Speakers of these languages and their descendants are acutely aware of what it can mean to lose a language,' she begins – and this is perfectly true, although these speakers must have taken the decision themselves not to teach the language to their children. It happens all too often – people regret that their language and culture are being lost but at the same time decide not to saddle their own children with the chore of preserving them.

When a language disappears [Mithun continues] the most intimate aspects of culture can disappear as well: fundamental ways of organizing experience into concepts, of relating ideas to each other, of interacting with other people. The more conscious genres of verbal art are usually lost as well: traditional ritual, oratory, myth, legends, and even humor. Speakers commonly remark that when they speak a different language, they say different things and even think different thoughts.

These are very interesting assertions. They slip by in a book on anthropological linguistics, where in a book on linguistic theory they would be highly contentious. Is it true that 'fundamental ways of organizing experience into concepts [and] of relating ideas to each other' are specific to individual languages and are therefore likely to be lost when a language ceases to be used? This very statement has been argued among theoretical linguists for most of the twentieth century, and I don't think a majority of them believe that it has been proved. Is it true that when speakers speak a different language they 'say different things and even think different thoughts'? Again, the extent to which thought depends on language is very controversial. These questions must now be faced, because only when we have reached an opinion on them will we be able to accept or reject Marianne Mithun's conclusion: 'The loss of a language represents a definitive separation of a people from its heritage. It also represents an irreparable loss for us all, the loss of opportunities to glimpse alternative ways of making sense of the human experience.'[1]

When I began to work on this book, my agent reminded me that I had a perfect example of the way that different languages map the world differently in the famous case of the Eskimo words for snow. I restrained my enthusiasm, knowing already that I was in the presence of a myth. British English, language of a people who have occasional bad-tempered encounters with snow, provides several words for familiar variations on the concept: *snow, flake, sleet, slush, drift, blizzard* in addition to a number of compounds such as *snowfall, snowstorm* and so on. Eighty years ago the anthropologist Franz Boas showed that Eskimo (Inuit) was similar to English in the number of different words available, but was different in the way that meanings were shared out among them. He offered as examples four terms, *aput* 'snow on the ground', *qana* 'falling snow', *piqsirpok* 'drifting snow', *qimuqsuq* 'drift'. Plenty of later linguists and anthropologists used Boas's example. But nearly all of them wanted it to show that Inuit had a larger number of words for the concept than English had. Actually it does not show that, so they had to misrepresent it or exaggerate it, and, starting with Benjamin Whorf, they all did. Laura Martin, who has done the forensic work on this series of academic and journalistic crimes, noted claims in print that ranged from 'five words for snow' (Whorf) to 'one hundred words for snow' (a *New York Times* editorial).[2]

Putting this example aside, however, it is quite easy to show that people find the words they need and can make all the fine distinctions they need. Whereas a British English speaker and a French speaker have only one word apiece for trees of genus *Eucalyptus* – and those words are *eucalyptus, eucalypte,* borrowed from botanical Latin – a forester speaking the English of Western Australia can call to mind eight or more different words. Here are the eight. He may have to distinguish the *jarrah* or native mahogany, the tall, straight *karri*, the *mallett* (the indigenous word was probably *malard*), the *marlock*, the *marri* or red gum (the resin was once used for tanning), the *morrel*, the *tuart* (used for wooden railway carriages) and the *wandoo* (used for wooden wheels). Because he has to distinguish all these species, he has words for the purpose: and so had the nineteenth-century speakers of Nyungar, the local language of the Perth district, from whom English borrowed all these words and from whom local foresters acquired some of their local knowledge.

Geoffrey Pullum, in a paper based on Laura Martin's work, swept aside the slush from the Eskimo snow question: 'Even if there *were* a large number of roots for different snow types in some Arctic language, this would *not*, objectively, be intellectually interesting: it would be a most mundane and unremarkable fact. Horsebreeders have various names for breeds, sizes, and ages of horses; botanists have names for leaf-shapes.' Pullum writes as a linguist, and one must admit that to the average theoretical linguist, focusing on his speciality, the fact that a snowbound language like English or Inuit has several words for snow, or that a language spoken in eucalyptus and kangaroo country has several different words for species in these groups, is not very challenging. 'Utterly boring' is Pullum's final evaluation.[3] This is fine for a theoretical linguist, but it goes too far for humanity as a whole. It is really interesting to the anthropologist, wishing to understand a culture, to explore how the world is classified (and, as a single example, how snow is classified) in the language spoken by those who share that culture. It is really interesting to the ethnobotanist to find out the names of plants that are important to a particular people, to get clear what range of genera, species, varieties or non-genetic differences is covered by each name, and to relate this information to the uses of these plants. It is really interesting to pharmacologists to learn of plants or other products that appear to be effective in traditional medicine; that enquiry, also, involves exploring local terminologies, whether in local languages or in local forms of a national language such as the English of Western Australia.

We can be almost sure that there will be differences between any

language and any other in its classification of the world. One of the
very earliest linguistic discussions of this point happens to relate to a
dialect difference within ancient Greek. The commentator, Apollonius
'the Sophist', quoted below, is discussing six lines by the early Spartan
poet, Alcman, in which Alcman by chance provides an example of an
interesting five-way categorization of the animal kingdom: apart from
the 'family of bees', which stand for insects, and the 'swift-winged
birds', on which Apollonius does not comment, we have *theres* 'beasts',
herpeta 'creeping things' or reptiles, and *knodala* 'sea-creatures'.

Some people use *theres* or *theria* 'beasts' for lions, leopards, wolves and the
like, *herpeta* 'creeping things' as a general term for the kinds of reptiles,
knodala 'monsters' for sea creatures including whales and so on. This is
Alcman's classification in the following:

> εὕδουσι δ᾽ ὀρέων κορυφαί τε καὶ φάραγγες
> πρώονές τε καὶ χαράδραι
> φῦλά τ᾽ ἑρπέτ᾽ ὅσα τρέφει μέλαινα γαῖα
> θῆρές τ᾽ ὀρεσκῷοι καὶ γένος μελισσᾶν
> καὶ κνώδαλ᾽ ἐν βένθεσσι πορφυρέας ἁλός·
> εὕδουσι δ᾽ οἰωνῶν φῦλα τανυπτερύγων.

(*Asleep are the mountain crests and valleys, the ridges and ravines, and all the
tribes of creeping things that the black earth feeds, and mountain beasts, and
the family of bees, and monsters in the depths of the purple sea; asleep are the
tribes of swift-winged birds.*)[4]

Now it was all very well for me, in translating the story of Babel in
Chapter 1, to say that the world before Babel was 'of one language and
of few words'. Without an explanation, you as reader would not have
known what was meant by 'of few words'. Is it that the pre-Babel language had fewer words than any single modern language? Or is it rather
that since there were fewer languages, there were also fewer words in the
world, in total, than there would be after Babel? In Hebrew, parallelism
made the answer clear: what was said about words, in the second phrase,
must correspond logically with what was said about languages, in the
first phrase. Such parallelisms are not a feature of English, so the modern
English reader is not helped towards a conclusion.

It's all very well for me, in translating these lines by Alcman, to give pseudo-literal equivalents of his various terms for animals: 'creeping things' for *herpeta*, 'beasts' for *theres*, 'monsters' for *knodala*, 'birds' for *oiones*, and 'the family of bees' for *genos melissan*. What you will not get from my translation, though you can gather it from Apollonius' commentary, is the fact that by giving this curious list Alcman intends to name 'the whole animal kingdom' (as we might call it). Alcman had no word for that concept – in fact no such word is to be found in any of the earliest Greek texts.[5] However, he has words for four of the 'orders of animals' (as we might call them) and they correspond roughly with 'reptiles and amphibia', 'mammals', 'birds' and 'sea creatures'. But he hasn't finished: what about insects, spiders and other small flying and crawling things? He has no overall word for these (nor have we, unless it's 'creepy-crawlies') so he groups them in 'the family of bees'. And now I've explained precisely what he's doing and roughly what his orders of animals consist of – but how could I ever manage to get it all into a neat English translation of those six beautiful lines of Greek poetry?

Now this is not a unique problem of archaic Greek, or of ancient languages in general; nor is there anything specially easy or difficult about English as the target language of a translation. Every language offers its own classification of living things, natural phenomena and cultural concepts: and the proof of it is that translators from any one language to any other are always stumbling across such problems.

Let us take a few simple classification differences between English and French. English has a generic term *nut* which includes a number of large seeds that are usually eaten without preparation. It would be correct and normal to group walnuts, hazelnuts, filberts, brazil nuts, almonds, peanuts, pecans, cashews and macadamia nuts as *nuts*: not so many people, I think, would count sweet chestnuts (which are cooked before eating) or horse chestnuts and acorns (which are not usually eaten at all) as *nuts*, but you may disagree. No single seed is always unambiguously named simply *nut*, but in Britain the simple word rather suggests 'hazelnut' (as in the proprietary *Fruit and Nut*) while in the United States the simple word suggests 'peanut' (as in *nut allergy*). Now French has a superficially similar word *noix*, but its range of meanings is very different. Without further specification *noix* in French means 'walnut', and it is not normal in French to use the word generically to include any of the other species listed. So French has no easy and accurate equivalent for the English word *nut*; the temptation to translate French *noix* by English *nut* must nearly always be resisted.

The standard French of Quebec has a large number of words and phrases that differ from Parisian French, because Canada has a different form of government and different products and services. An example is *escalier de feu* for 'fire escape': Parisian French has *escalier de sauvetage*, literally 'safety stairs'. What is wrong with this Quebec term *escalier de feu*, literally 'fire stairs'? The answer is that there's more than one French word that corresponds to English 'fire'. Fire, as a general concept, is *feu*, but 'a fire' that breaks out in a building is *un incendie*. Somebody, perhaps an English-speaking builder or insurance agent in Quebec, made a thoughtless use of a dictionary equivalent, *fire = feu*, in inventing the term; it stuck, and it now neatly exemplifies interference between Canadian English and Quebec French. Just as there's more than one French word corresponding to English *fire*, so there's more than one English word that corresponds to French *feu*. When a French speaker, giving directions, tells you to turn right *aux feux*, this doesn't mean 'at the fires' but 'at the traffic lights' (the speaker might have said *au feu rouge* 'at the red light' or even *aux feux tricolores* 'at the three-coloured lights', the official technical term, but almost certainly didn't).

With the last two examples, the difficulty of translation is not very great (though misunderstandings as to the meaning of *nut* may be deadly in a case of peanut allergy). But then in addition, adjectives and adverbs are difficult to match between the two languages: French *infiniment*, literally 'infinitely', may turn out to be best translated by English *rather*; French *ravi*, literally 'ravished', may equate to English *glad*, and yet solutions of this kind do not solve everything, and no one who has translated an eighteenth-century French novel or memoir into twentieth-century English has been perfectly satisfied with the tone of the resulting text. Could I find a happy equivalent for that brief and expressive clause, *faire parler la langue [française]*, in the Revolutionary text quoted in Chapter 4? 'To ensure that the [French] language will be spoken' was my best try, several words longer than the original and not nearly as decisive. Aulus Gellius, quoted in Chapter

2, had a similar difficulty over the title of that Greek volume, *Peri Polypragmosynes* 'On Meddlesomeness', which he needed to translate into Latin. 'I racked my brains for a Latin word that would match the Greek,' Gellius wrote. 'I could not think that I had ever come across one, and any word I might invent out of *multitudo* "large number" and *negotium* "business" would be an absurd and ugly expression.' Amusingly, he showed not only that no single word could be found or devised as an equivalent, but even that a long sentence intended to explain the idea in Latin might fail to get it across.

All this comes as no surprise to translators or interpreters: they know very well how difficult their job is. So those theoretical linguists who have been in the habit of dismissing such observations as Marianne Mithun's at the head of this chapter – 'speakers commonly remark that when they speak a different language, they say different things and even think different thoughts' – face a real problem over translation and its complexities. Let me repeat, the last few examples are easy ones. English and French have interacted for so many hundreds of years that ways around most of the difficulties of translation have been found. Greek and Latin were in a similar symbiosis, and in Gellius' time there was much bilingualism among speakers of the two. When it comes to translation between languages that have *no* shared culture, the problems become almost insurmountable at times. Look at any three modern English translations of a short classical Chinese poem and you will think you are looking at three different poems. Sanskrit and classical Arabic poetry are just as hard to handle. Each word will have a range of possible meanings different from those of any English equivalent that might be chosen. The collocations of words evoke associations that the English translation cannot. Certain details, for example identifying the subject of a clause or the time-reference of a verb, must be stated in correct English – in English you are forced to choose between *goes* and *went* and *has gone* and in good English it is difficult to avoid stating who it is that goes – yet those details may be optional in Chinese. The translator is continually compelled to be either more precise or less precise than the original.

Lin Shu's classic nineteenth-century Chinese translation of Dumas's *La Dame aux camélias* was the first Chinese version of any work of Western literature. His task was to get a strange story from a totally unfamiliar culture across to an eager audience, and to do it in good stylish literary Chinese (which is something none of the modern translators of the same novel have managed to do). With continual departures from the original, both omissions and additions, Lin Shu succeeded. The result of his success was the beginning of a new literary genre in Chinese.[6] There is an earlier and more surprising case. Zen Buddhism is notable for its pursuit of sudden enlightenment, and in its earliest forms this sudden enlightenment came through contemplation of a Buddhist sutra – that is, a narrative of the Buddha's teaching. The philosophy arose in China in the sixth century AD. According to legend, it was implanted there by successors to an earlier Indian lineage of the same school of thought – but in early records no such preceding Indian lineage can be traced. In fact, Zen appeared, new-born, in China at the time that Buddhist sutras were being translated from Sanskrit into Chinese. The difficulties of translation between the two languages were so great at first that the logic of the texts simply did not come across.[7] They seemed to make no connected sense. Zen (it has been argued) came into existence because its early practices of long contemplation and sudden enlightenment appeared to be the only way in which these impressive texts could be put to spiritual use. Thus the genre of the Zen koan, those marvellous stories of master–pupil interaction and the sudden enlightenment that might with luck result from it, might never have existed at all but for the near-impossibility of translating Sanskrit into meaningful early medieval Chinese. The completely incomprehensible 'Hidden Language', supposed to be the language of the thirty-two heavens, used in some medieval Taoist scriptures of China, has a similar origin: it is written in a Sanskrit-like alphabet, has a Sanskrit-like sound, and is evidently meant to have a Sanskrit-like mystical power.[8]

Several examples closer to home could be found of attempts to translate literary texts whose result has been to create, in the 'target culture', a new literary genre – not closely resembling anything previously existing in either culture. The typically Latin genre of *satura*, 'satire', which has had such a lot of descendants and was in its original form inexplicably obsessed with food, may well have grown out of a bad early translation into Latin (by Ennius) of a light-hearted Greek gnomic poem (by Archestratus) which was all about food.

Language and thought

File away, for future reference, this astonishing creativity that arises – an unexpected and unintended side-effect – out of attempts to translate from one language to another. Meanwhile, focus on the problems of getting the original meaning across. Ennius was a skilful and forceful writer, a considerable linguist and a founder of Latin narrative and dramatic poetry: but in attempting a translation in this minor genre of gnomic verses to quote at dinner, he just could not turn Archestratus' highly quotable Greek into quotable Latin. The early translators of Sanskrit Buddhist sutras into Chinese were dedicated scholars with long experience of both languages, but they could not turn the logic of Sanskrit into logic in Chinese. If translation is so very difficult, there may well be some truth in that view reported by Marianne Mithun from bilingual speakers of Amerindian languages, that when they switch to another language, they say different things and even think differently.

There is, of course, nothing new about these observations. It was obvious to later Latin writers that Ennius and Lucilius had failed in some of their attempts to get Greek poetry across into Latin. Successors such as Horace went back to the sources and made new attempts to do what their predecessors had failed to do; meanwhile they also developed the new 'indigenous' genre of satire which had perhaps been created in an accident of translation. Later translators from Sanskrit into Chinese made more skilful attempts to get across the meaning of the sutras, aided by the fact that some of the new word-meanings and new phrases coined by their predecessors had found their way into the general consciousness in the interim; meanwhile Zen Buddhism continued to thrive from its starting-point in the older and imperfect translations.

In each case, those who had an insight into both the languages that were involved were well aware that translation had so far failed to work. They knew perfectly well that the difficulty was caused by the fact that in different languages one makes different choices of what to say – and possibly also what to think.

The unsophisticated, particularly those who do not themselves speak any languages very different from their mother tongue, often put the problem down to the 'poverty' of whatever language is not familiar to them. About the Arawakan language of seventeenth-century Dominica, Mathias du Puis wrote thus in 1652:

Il n'y a pas de langue plus disetteuse que celle-là, ils n'ont point de mots pour exprimer ce qui ne tombe pas sur la grossiereté de nos sens corporels. Ils ne sçavent ce que c'est d'entendement, de volonté, et de mémoire, parce que ce sont des puissances cachées, qui ne se produisent au dehors que par leurs effets. Ils ne peuvent nommer aucunes vertus, parce qu'ils n'en pratiquent pas.

There is no language poorer than this. They have no words for anything beyond what relates to our gross physical senses. They do not know what 'understanding' or 'will' or 'memory' are, because these are unseen faculties, only visible externally by their effects. They cannot list any virtues, because they practise none.[9]

Not many years later, the German philosopher G. W. Leibniz lamented that German had the same faults ascribed by du Puis to Arawak. 'Our language is inadequate in expressions referring to morality, emotion, social intercourse, the business of government, politics and public life,' Leibniz asserted in 1697, though I doubt if, even so, he would have put German and Arawak on a level.[10]

At the stage when anthropologists and linguists were beginning to take an informed interest in the different ways in which the world is viewed and classified in different languages, it was still possible to write about the issue as though it were one of superiority versus inferiority: but in W. J. McGee's 1895 view, modern English (which he calls Anglo-Saxon: evidently he disapproved of the Norman conquest) is better *because* it lacks complexity: 'The Anglo-Saxon language is the simplest, the most perfectly and simply symbolic that the world has ever seen . . . By means of it the Anglo-Saxon saves his vitality for conquest instead of wasting it under the juggernaut of cumbersome mechanism for conveyance of thought.'[11]

A more sophisticated approach to the subject is indelibly associated with the names of Edward Sapir and Benjamin Lee Whorf, and most often with that of Whorf alone.

Whorf had several predecessors in his particular line of thought, including J. G. Herder and Franz Boas, but it is the 'Sapir–Whorf hypothesis' that has been the focus of controversy among linguists ever since it was formulated in the 1930s.[12] We need to look at a couple of Whorf's examples, and then to consider the hypothesis which he derived from them, which is that the structure of individual languages maps different views of the world, and for that reason affects the way that speakers of those languages think about the world. The hypothesis is crucial to the argument I have developed in this book.

The first example is very simple. It is often said that Chinese is a monosyllabic language, meaning that Chinese words always consist of only one syllable. How did this idea arise? It is because, as Whorf puts it, 'There is no word for "word" in Chinese.' He goes on to explain how the mistaken view that Chinese is a monosyllabic language arises from the fact that the nearest Chinese term to English 'word', *ci*, actually means 'syllable' – and from the fact that the Chinese script presents each syllable as a separate unit. His conclusion is of quite general relevance: 'We are no nearer to understanding the types of logical thinking which are reflected in truly Eastern forms of scientific thought or analysis of nature. This requires linguistic research into the logics of native languages, and realization that they have equal scientific validity with our own thinking habits.'[13]

Whorf's use of the 'Eskimo words for snow' has already been mentioned in this chapter. He was inaccurate, but Boas's original example was a good one: it demonstrated, in English and Inuit, quite different ways of dividing up the general semantic area 'snow' among the several words available in each language. Like this one, most of Whorf's examples were taken from languages of Native America, on which he had done some original work himself. His most famous case is that of Hopi (a language still spoken in Arizona): particularly of how concepts of time are embedded in the structure of Hopi verb forms, differing totally from those that are seen in the verb tenses of most European languages.

As a preliminary, in verbs in European languages a typical distinction of 'voice' is between active (*I love*) and passive (*I am loved*); a typical distinction of 'aspect' is between punctual (*I went*) and continuous (*I was going*); a typical distinction of tense is between present (*I am going, I go*), past (*I was going, I went*) and future (*I will be going, I will go*). Well, Hopi verbs may have nine voices (intransitive, transitive, reflexive, passive, semipassive, resultative, extended passive, possessive and cessative), nine aspects (punctual, durative, segmentative, punctual-segmentative, inceptive, progressional, spatial, projective and continuative), and three tenses (factual or present-past, future, and generalized or usitative). Whorf promises, in treating this example, to deal only with the punctual and segmentative aspects (thank goodness) and he proceeds to explain the meaning of these two. Now read carefully: you'll be tested on this . . . And notice how different is Whorf's approach from that of, say, Mathias du Puis, whose focus was on the relative poverty of the unfamiliar language. Whorf is looking at how the wealth of Hopi differs from the wealth of English.

The segmentative aspect is formed by final reduplication of [the] root plus the durative suffix -*ta*, and produces a change in the meaning of the simplex[14] of the following character: the phenomenon denoted by the root, shown in the punctual aspect as manifested about a point, becomes manifested as a series of repeated interconnected segments of one large phenomenon of a stretched-out segmental character, its extension usually being predominantly in one dimension, indifferently of space or time or both. The nature of the change can best be shown by examples.

    pa''ci it is notched; *paci'cita* it is serrated

    pï'va it is gullied out; *pïva'vata* it extends in successive gullies and gulches

    nö'nga several come out; *nönga'ngata* it is coming out in successive multitudes, it is gushing or spraying out (applied e.g. to a fountain)

    tï'ri he gives a sudden start; *tïrï'rïta* he is quivering, trembling

    yo''ko he gives one nod of the head; *yoko'kota* he is nodding

All this has a wider interest than the mere illustration of an aspect-form. It is an illustration of how language produces an organization of experience . . . We have observed how, with very thorough consistency and not a little true scientific precision, all sorts of vibratile phenomena in nature are classified by being referred to various elementary types of deformation process. The analysis of a certain field of nature which results is freely extensible and all-in-all so harmonious with actual physics that such extension could be made with great appropriateness to a multiplicity of phenomena belonging entirely to the modern scientific and technical world – movements of machinery and mechanism, wave processes and vibrations, electrical and chemical phenomena – things that the Hopi have never known or imagined, and for which we ourselves lack definite names. The Hopi actually have a language better equipped to deal with such vibratile phenomena than is our latest scientific terminology.[15]

Du Puis had been concerned to show that certain concepts were lacking from the Arawak vocabulary as compared with French. The twentieth-century linguist notes the existence of a whole category of phenomena, easily denoted and naturally related with one another in Hopi, yet not consistently described and apparently unrelated when viewed through English. If we want to understand these things better, Hopi might help us. If we are going to translate into English a text from Hopi that depends on these concepts, we shall find it difficult. If a Hopi–English bilingual wants to discuss these concepts, it will be easier to do it in Hopi.

It would not be fair to Whorf, or to his many critics, to omit to quote a later passage in which he attempts to boldly describe the space–time continuum through the window of Hopi and its verb forms. Here we go.

As the objective realm displaying its characteristic attribute of extension stretches away from the observer toward that unfathomable remoteness which is both far away in space and long past in time, there comes a point where extension in detail ceases to be knowable and is lost in the vast distance, and where the subjective, creeping behind the scenes as it were, merges into the objective, so that at this inconceivable distance from the observer – from all observers – there is an all-encircling end and beginning of things where it might be said that existence, itself, swallows up the objective and the subjective. The borderland of this realm is as much subjective as objective. It is the abysm of antiquity, the time and place told about in the myths . . . the Hopi realize and even express in their grammar that the things told in myths or stories do not have the same kind of reality or validity as things of the present day, the things of practical concern . . . So the dim past of myths is that corresponding distance on earth (rather than in the heavens) which is reached subjectively as myth through the vertical axis of reality via the pole of the nadir – hence it is placed below the present surface of the earth, though this does not mean that the nadir-land of the origin-myths is a hole or cavern as we should understand it. It is *Palátkwapi* 'At the Red Mountains,' a land like our present earth, but to which our earth bears the relation of a distant sky – and similarly the sky of our earth is penetrated by the heroes of tales, who find another earthlike realm above it.

It may now be seen how the Hopi do not need to use terms that refer to space or time as such. Such terms in our language are recast into expressions of extension, operation, and cyclic process provided they refer to the solid objective realm. They are recast into expressions of subjectivity if they refer to the subjective realm – the future, the psychic-mental, the mythical period, and the invisibly distant and conjectural generally. Thus, the Hopi language gets along perfectly without tenses for its verbs.[16]

Whorf was not mad, just somewhat ahead of his time. His youthful attempt to deconstruct the tri-consonantal roots of Semitic languages failed – but Afroasiatic linguists such as Christopher Ehret have now just succeeded in doing it after all, by showing that these three-consonant forms embody ancient two-consonant roots and one-consonant suffixes. Whorf's attack on the undeciphered Maya hieroglyphs, attempting to read them as a phonetic script, persuaded few other scholars at the time; thirty years later it was dismissed thus by J. Eric S. Thompson in his 1972 book *Maya Hieroglyphs without Tears*: '[Whorf] failed to prove his case, and his views were not endorsed by any other student of the subject.' But Thompson is now discredited, and the basic correctness of Whorf's phonetic approach to Maya decipherment is generally recognized.[17] Whorf's observations on the Hopi world view were to be attacked at great length by Ekkehard Malotki, who knew the Hopi language well, and yet Peter Whiteley, one of the best anthropologists now working on Hopi, treats Whorf's views with respect.[18]

What, then, of 'Whorfianism' or 'the Sapir–Whorf hypothesis', the view that the structure of individual languages establishes different views of the world? Although Whorf has become a legend (so Joshua Fishman concludes in a seminal paper), a legendary hero to some, a legendary failure to others, that has not helped to clarify Whorf's line of thought in others' minds.

Clarification of 'what Whorf really meant' is no easy matter. It is complicated
by the fact that Whorf died in 1941 at the regrettably early age of 44 . . .
During his own lifetime he was aware of some doubts and misunderstandings
– even in the circle of his friends and admirers, including Sapir – and began to
revise, restate, and reinterpret his own views and the inconsistencies that were
inevitably to be found among them, given the fact that they were always
evolving rather than fixed and final in his own mind. Nevertheless, he was
granted very little time for such revisions and emendations.[19]

The Sapir–Whorf hypothesis is best stated not as a single hypothesis.
There are two. The first is generally called *Linguistic Relativity*: it is
the hypothesis that different languages embody different world views.
The extent of the difference will vary, depending on cross-language
links including long-term bilingualism and shared culture. The second
is *Linguistic Determinism*: the hypothesis that different languages steer
or impel their speakers to different ways of thinking about the world.
'Whorf did entertain both of the hypotheses,' Fishman concludes,
'although he was considerably less certain and less consistent with
respect to the latter than the former.'[20] Joshua Fishman's own evaluation is that the Linguistic Relativity hypothesis 'has been confirmed
over and over again, not only by Whorf and since Whorf, but prior to
Whorf'; the Linguistic Determinism hypothesis is regarded by Fishman
as 'contested or unconfirmed'.[21]

We must notice the extent to which Whorf's claims are oversim-
plified and misrepresented. Many of his writings, left scattered and
unfinished by his sudden death, were eventually gathered by John B.
Carroll in a book he called *Language, Thought and Reality: Selected
Writings of Benjamin Lee Whorf*.[22] I shall soon be quoting a couple of
sentences from Carroll's introduction to that book, sentences that are
intended to outline Whorf's views of 'the Hopi mind' – yet that is a
phrase that Whorf never used, and it is a concept that I (and many
linguists) would regard as invalid and unacceptable. In opposing
Whorf's views on the Hopi language and its treatment of time, Ekkehard Malotki claimed in his 1983 volume *Hopi Time* to have conclus-
ively disproved 'Whorf's widely publicized contention that "the Hopi
language contains no reference to "time", either explicit or implicit"'.
Malotki continues: 'For decades, while Whorf's startling findings

about a "timeless language" . . . have stirred the imagination of many minds, scholars have . . . deplored the absence of the necessary evidence to verify or falsify his claim . . . It is my hope that the evidence presented will eliminate the myth of Hopi being a "timeless language" once and for all.'[23]

Malotki has done much more work on Hopi than Whorf did, and Whorf did much more than most other people. The scholarly consensus, I believe, is that six hundred pages on *Hopi Time* are enough, so, if Malotki concludes that Hopi is not a timeless language, we must defer to him, but at the same time we must look suspiciously at those quotation marks. Did Whorf really ever say that it was a timeless language? Certainly not in the passages that I have quoted: in fact he says the opposite, that Hopi deals with both time and space in a wholly unfamiliar way. As if conscious that he has been tilting at windmills, Malotki finally admits that 'one can probably concede to Whorf that linguistic differences may result in different thought worlds' but that these thought worlds 'are limited to the lexical level'.[24] I'm worried about the 'thought worlds' too: it is a metaphor which Whorf did not use. You may think I'm quibbling, but you'll soon see why. However, after all of his six-hundred-page conclusive disproof, Malotki has in this concluding sentence conceded a version of Whorf's Linguistic Determinism hypothesis after all.

In general, theoretical linguists who considered Whorf's views between the late 1950s and the 1970s reacted to them critically or dismissively. Those who tried to test them experimentally, as some did, found that the tests either showed nothing, or at any rate failed to prove the Linguistic Determinism hypothesis. A late and very strong statement of the negative position is in Steven Pinker's *The Language Instinct*. After a survey of Whorf's hypotheses he concludes: 'No one is really sure how Whorf came up with his outlandish claims, but his limited, badly analyzed sample of Hopi speech and his long-time leanings towards mysticism must have contributed.'[25]

The relatively few linguists who favoured Whorf's views, over this same period, included Dell Hymes and others who (I quote a roundabout characterization by Joshua Fishman) 'obviously did so in conjunction with more holistic and nonquantitative "poetic" perspectives than the empirical tradition of American hypothetico-deductive science is either accustomed to, comfortable with, or impressed by.[26'] They seemed unsound, in other words.

So why can't linguists leave Whorf alone? The reason, Fishman argues in the paper already cited, is that the differences between languages are at least as exciting to linguists as to anybody else; linguists, as well as other people, feel it deeply when a language ceases to be spoken and when a historic culture is assimilated and forgotten. 'Convictions such as these are among the very ones that brought many of us to linguistics.' Such views were expressed two hundred years ago by J. G. Herder – 'he did not wince at their romanticism, as many of us do now' – and modern linguists are attracted to Whorf's views 'on some prerational, intuitive level' because Whorf is a Herderian too. By the hypotheses associated with his name, of Linguistic Relativity and Linguistic Determinism, Whorf sought 'to control and tame or discipline the Herderian passions within him. But the passions are there nonetheless.'[27]

Linguists who feel this way – as many certainly do – know perfectly well, whatever the current view on Whorf's hypotheses, that 'when a language disappears, the most intimate aspects of culture can disappear as well: fundamental ways of organizing experience into concepts, of relating ideas to each other, of interacting with other people.' I am not quoting Whorf here, but Marianne Mithun again. Many, even as they coldly dismiss Linguistic Determinism, know in their hearts that 'the loss of a language [is] an irreparable loss for us all, the loss of opportunities to glimpse alternative ways of making sense of the human experience.'[28] So how to explain this in terms of linguistic theory? There is, or ought to be, a softer insight into the human nature of language lurking beyond those two hard hypotheses that theoretical linguists find it so hard to accept.

Our need for linguistic diversity

Well, while the theoretical debate, for and against Linguistic Relativity and Linguistic Determinism, has sputtered on, anthropological linguists and ethnobotanists, not all of them very interested in contributing to that debate, have gone on collecting evidence of the way the world is classified in different languages. Their findings are very interesting, and suggest a more nuanced answer to the Whorf question. These researchers are now quite sure that there are certain universals of linguistic classification. For example, Malotki claims to have shown in *Hopi Time* that languages always have to deal with time in some way, and no doubt he is right: that is a universal. Numerous investigations of colour terms show beyond a doubt that you can predict, from the number of colour terms a language has, which particular colours will be named: that also is a universal. Ethnobiologists find that there is a similar predictability about the levels of biological classification a language will have, and also about the high-level classes that will be named: it is exactly in accordance with this, in the early Greek list quoted above, that Alcman has no general word for insects and the like but simply lists 'bees'. These linguistic universals go along with many others, gradually being collected and recognized by linguists, most of which have less to do with the classifying of the world and more to do with the way that grammar works. These universals stand in opposition to the Whorf hypotheses; and they are the part of language that is built into our brains. They are essential to us – they provide the basis on which our originality, our creativity, is founded – but in themselves they are the same for everybody. I would say, though Geoffrey Pullum (quoted on p. 254) might say the opposite, that these universals are 'utterly boring': our individual human creativity begins one step beyond.

Once we have got beyond those linguistic universals, which are apparently the same for every language and in every human mind, further relevant evidence, from whatever language it may come, always favours the Linguistic Relativity hypothesis. As Fishman rightly said, this has been confirmed 'not only by Whorf and since Whorf, but prior to Whorf'. A proportion of the newer evidence seems to come close to confirming the Linguistic Determinism hypothesis, at least to the extent stated by Marianne Mithun in her survey of North American Indian languages: 'Languages differ not only in what they permit speakers to say easily, but also in what they require them to specify in order to speak grammatically.'[29]

Mithun herself provides an example from Yupik, an Eskimo-Aleut language of Alaska, of cross-linguistic differences in vocabulary, some of which reflect aspects of the natural environment while others grow out of separate cultural traditions. Yupik 'contains nouns like *qelta* "fish scale, bark of tree, eggshell, peel" and *ella* "world, outdoors, weather, universe, awareness and sense", which seem quite general in meaning from the vantage point of English. Yup'ik also contains nouns like *qellukaq* "aged seal flipper" and *alrapaq* "back-to-back sitting partner" which seem quite specific.'[30] It is interesting (and not too surprising, perhaps) that while the Yupik world for 'world' encompasses additional meanings such as 'outdoors' and 'weather', several European words for 'world' encompass meanings such as 'people, crowd, inhabitants'. Here are some examples: French *le monde* 'the world'; *du monde* 'a lot of people, a crowd', literally 'some of the world'; *tout le monde* 'everybody [who matters to us]', literally 'all the world'; classical Greek *he oikoumene* 'the world', literally 'the settled zone'; and old-fashioned English *all the world* meaning 'everybody we can think of', an expression I quoted from Matthew Arnold in Chapter 1 note 2.

We noticed the different semantic ranges of French *feu* and English *fire*. I might have mentioned English *clock*, which has no single equivalent in French: *réveille-matin* 'alarm clock' is a quite different thing in French from *pendule* 'striking clock', and you will never get one by asking for the other. In English you can *fetch* or *bring back* or *pick up* or *go and get* a package or a person; in French *ramasser* is what you must do with a package while *ramener* is what you must do with a person, and you will be thought odd if you use the wrong word. Very many such differences will be found between any pair of languages you care to choose. Here's one more example, from the Australian language Dyirbal, of a word *gunga* which at first sight seems to have the same meaning as English *raw*:

There is in Dyirbal an adjective *gunga* which has three related senses: used of a fruit or nut that ripens naturally in the sun it means 'unripe, green' (and here the opposite is *dungun* 'ripe'); used of meat or of any vegetable food that requires cooking it means 'raw, uncooked' (here the opposite is *nyamu* 'cooked'); used of a human or animal it means 'alive' (being here the opposite of *buga* 'dead, stinking') . . . The English word *raw* just means 'uncooked' and can refer to something that is edible. The Dyirbal word *gunga*, used of food, may be roughly translated by 'raw' but it means 'not yet ready to be eaten'.[31]

So if you mean to ask a Dyirbal speaker whether a plant can be eaten raw, and the word you use is *gunga*, you are asking a silly question: to the Dyirbal speaker *gunga* equates with unripe and not ready to be eaten, and to say that any such plant should be eaten would be a self-contradiction. The sensible question would have to be 'Can it be eaten when ripe, or must it be cooked?'

You can find a lot of these things written down in books. Many of the linguistic details used as examples in this book have already been in one or two others, and some of them can be picked up from standard dictionaries, though you might be surprised at how many there are that can't. Most dictionaries will give English *nut* as a translation for French *noix*, and only a very good dictionary will warn you of the mismatch between the two words. If you want to translate *dinner*, *tea* and *supper*, from an English novel, into French or German, your dictionary will not guide you very much: an awful lot depends on social and regional factors, and few reference books are around to help you. You might find almost as much trouble with French *déjeuner*, now 'lunch' but formerly 'breakfast', or German *Jause*, sometimes 'elevenses' and sometimes not.

You can't ever go directly from one language to another in translating, nor even from one to another by way of a dictionary. You always have to go from one to another by way of the real world, because it is the real world that each language is a map of. Dictionaries are not good enough because they can't ever include the world. Computers can't translate properly because they don't understand the world.

People have to be aware, for themselves, of the fact that no one language directly matches any other. For people who live in monolingual communities and have never themselves learnt more than one language this is quite a difficult concept to grasp. However, many people, in many parts of the world, are aware of language issues. When an English ship visited the Caribbean island of Dominica in 1597, the inhabitants were immediately interested in learning the newcomers' language, 'for some of them, pointing to the limbs of their body one after the other, told us the names in their language and desired to know what they were called in English. This they then kept repeating till they were able to pronounce it well, or what seemed to them well enough and was fairly well indeed.'[32] When French explorers were on their way up the St Lawrence river, half a century earlier, they were addressed in a strangely familiar language which they at first assumed to be local; they were astonished when it turned out to be Basque. The local people (although, as they said, they did not ask to be visited) had none the less thought it worth while to learn something of the language of the Basque fishermen who had been there in advance of better-known European voyagers.

While the world was full of strange languages, and English speakers and Europeans had not yet visited every square mile of it, we badly needed people like these, people who were sufficiently motivated to learn a strange language spoken by outlandish visitors, who might or might not ever return, for no other reason than that it might turn out useful some time in the future. Just to show that in the sixteenth century the intellectual curiosity was not all on one side, we should mention the Spanish explorer of the Amazon in 1541, Francisco de Orellana, who impressed local peoples with his knowledge of their language. Whether it was Tukánoan or Tupían, he had had no chance to learn it before his one-way voyage began, and he must have picked it up very quickly. People with this much intellectual curiosity (I wonder whether their genes survive?) bode well for our future.

Humanity certainly needs bilinguals as much as ever, and not only for the reason that international understanding is (so recent research claims to demonstrate) more likely to make progress where there is a significant degree of multilingualism.[33] We need bilinguals because, even in the generally accepted weaker form of Whorf's hypothesis, each language is a different way of looking at, mapping and classifying the world. Bilinguals are those who grow up speaking two languages, or who afterwards learn to handle a second language well, perhaps as well as if it had been a mother tongue. It is only a bilingual who can really show us what there is to learn from the way the world is mapped and classified in another language.

This is why Whorf's faithful editor, John Carroll, goes astray in introducing Whorf's thesis regarding Hopi. You may still think I'm quibbling, but read it in full:

The Hopi mind automatically separates the 'occupancy' or spot of ground or floor on which the occupancy occurs from the use to which the occupancy is put, whereas the speaker of English tends to merge these, as where 'school' is thought of as both an institution and a building. (Indeed, do we not instinctively feel that an institution must of necessity be housed in some kind of building?)[34]

It's a good illustration. But if you now look at Whorf's paper carefully – it is reprinted in full, later in the same book – you realize that Whorf never uses the phrase 'the Hopi mind'. He insists throughout that this is a 'linguistic' phenomenon and that he is talking about 'the Hopi language'. More than that: he is not saying that 'the Hopi language' as a whole does not merge such concepts as English does: rather, he says that 'if they [the speakers of Hopi] do this, they have begun to do it only recently, and few terms of this sort have accumulated'. Whorf is correctly speaking of what the users of a language do, and making it clear all the time that their practice may vary and change. Carroll has evolved out of Whorf's observation the idea of a 'Hopi mind'. But human beings don't share a mind. It is surely true that a particular language presents a particular world view (Linguistic Relativity), and it may or may not be true that speakers of a language are steered or impelled by that language to think in a particular way (Linguistic Determinism): but to deduce that our thinking is *limited* by our language goes beyond Whorf's views and is quite certainly wrong, because many of us are brought up bilingual and we can any of us speak as many languages as we may trouble to learn. How does Carroll's idea of a 'Hopi mind' relate to bilingualism? It doesn't. With this phrase Carroll is buried in the anthropological past when it was possible to imagine a perfect, monolingual, original tribe, its language and culture uncontaminated by others, the kind of culture and language that anthropologists before Margaret Mead usually tried to reconstruct. For such a Hopi tribe, older anthropologists might indeed have reconstructed a 'Hopi mind'. But such a tribe never existed.

If we are multilingual, a common condition, perhaps the normal human condition, then each one of our languages presents us with a particular world view. To the extent that I am bilingual in English and French, I don't, as Carroll might have supposed, have an English mind and a French mind, while Malotki's idea of 'different thought worlds' may also stray from reality. I am sometimes speaking in English, sometimes in French, and I am often aware that something I am saying in one language would be easier or more difficult for me to say in the other. To the extent that Whorf was bilingual in English and Hopi (and he certainly was not fully bilingual) he was able to say that the world views presented in these two languages were very different: but many Hopi speakers were already as bilingual as he was – perhaps they are all bilingual now – and they are certainly not confined to one world view, any more than Whorf himself was.

The crucial fact for us is that only someone who is to some extent bilingual can make such observations. Whorf's expertise in Hopi permitted it. L. J. Watahomigie, bilingual in English and the Hualapai language of Arizona, is able to assert: 'There are concepts in Hualapai that can never be translated into English – concepts that must be experienced in Hualapai to be fully understood.'[35] Those who try to translate Chinese lyric poetry into English, or vice versa, say similar things. Still, they go on trying, and if we need different world views we need all the translators and all the bilinguals that we can get.

Do we need different world views?

In the first half of the twentieth century a lot of research was done on the effect of bilingualism on intelligence. Some studies showed that bilingual children were less able; the majority of studies found no correlation; some showed that they were more able. We are not far here from the German 1930s research, already mentioned on p. 130, on moral defects in bilingual children. The results always said more about the researchers and the test methods than about the children studied or about the real effects of bilingualism in children. In some states of the United States, to this day, bilingual children are automatically classified as having a learning difficulty; once more, a comment on the intelligence of the child psychologists, not on that of the children. For quite some time now it has been possible to demonstrate on the basis of serious scientific research, that of Wallace Lambert for example, that bilingual people show greater cognitive flexibility: they are better at lateral thinking. This is not at all surprising, and would follow very neatly from the Linguistic Relativity hypothesis, because if you are bilingual, you are familiar with two distinct world views as embodied in two different languages.[36] We have here a strong indication that individual bilingualism helps human beings to realize the full potential of their intelligence.

There's much more to it than individual intelligence. If we are to go on thinking and communicating our ideas to one another, our language needs to continue to change with us. It's because each of us can innovate linguistically that we can progress as a species. Now although language change can and does happen independently of interaction between languages, the examples in this book have shown that the more purposeful kind of language change – the adoption of new words, new forms of expression, even new types of literature – comes about when languages are in contact. Having explored the views of Whorf and others, we are better able to see why this is: if languages are in contact, world views are in contact. Let's put it straight back into real human terms. Languages are in contact and world views are in contact only if there is bilingualism: only if some people, at least, speak both the languages that are involved and are able to share both the world views that are involved. For our continued progress, that kind of interaction must continue.

Loss of languages, loss of bilingualism

Well, now that English and various other broadcast languages can be heard everywhere in the world, it is easy for lucky English speakers to take their own language for granted. We can just as easily take other people's bilingualism for granted. It no longer requires intellectual curiosity for people to decide to learn English as a foreign language: it calls for nothing more than a vague desire to be more prosperous, because it is obvious to hundreds of millions of people that English may quite possibly bring them greater prosperity. So English speakers, uniquely, can afford to be lazy about this: most of us have less need than ever before to learn a foreign language. There are bound to be bilinguals. So we need not worry.

But there is, after all, something of a problem here. As we saw in Chapter 1, the number of languages world-wide is in steep decline. This being so, the variety of world views embodied in those languages is also in steep decline. Will these trends continue and gather pace? And will the long term result also be a decline in bilingualism?

In practice this amounts to a question about English. Is it destined for permanent ascendancy, or could another language in the future spread internationally as Latin did and as English is now doing?

Up to now languages have spread with trade and conquest. Whatever barriers existed to prevent the spread of Indo-European languages in prehistoric Europe and northern India, or of Bantu languages in southern Africa, or of Tupí-Guaraní languages in eastern South America, or of Iroquoian and Algonquian languages in eastern North America, those barriers were insufficient. The languages spread, very widely and apparently very rapidly, in areas where previously quite different languages must have been spoken: whether the earlier speakers shifted to the new language, or moved away, or died, is in general not known. That's prehistory. When Aramaic spread across the Middle East, and Greek across the eastern Mediterranean, and Latin in the West, and Quechua along the Andes, and Spanish across most of Latin America, and Chinese across southern China, and English across North America and Australia and into India, they spread with conquering and migrating peoples, who for good reasons of their own took no account of earlier political frontiers.

Such conquests could happen again – but not in the present political state of the world. In the late twentieth century peace was more or less assured, for the time being, on the assumption that frontiers would not change and that nations were independent. Those who did try to change frontiers or reduce nations to subjection met with the strong disapproval of the international community, and most such people eventually wished they hadn't tried. Powerful interests are vested in current international frontiers. All that has been allowed has been the occasional episode of fragmentation within existing boundaries for ethnic or historical reasons, such as the secession of Eritrea from Ethiopia. As far as conquest is concerned, therefore, the time isn't ripe; and since the world is fairly full of people, it is difficult to imagine this situation changing without some catastrophic episode of depopulation.

As for peaceful migration, that can still take place, and it does. The current migration of Spanish-speakers from Latin America to the United States is probably one of the largest such movements ever recorded. However, for reasons discussed in Chapter 4, it is not likely to bring with it a permanent change of language. If it did, it would be a much smaller affair than any of the historical examples just given, affecting only the southern fringe of the United States.

It is important to remember that changes in language dominance of the kind that have affected Aramaic, Greek, Latin, Quechua, Spanish and now English do not come about simply because of the number of speakers. Which languages rival English in terms of their growing numbers of speakers? Chinese and Hindi. Chinese probably now has about 800 million mother-tongue speakers – over twice as many as English – and up to 200 million speakers as a second language. Hindi has 350 million mother-tongue speakers, about as many as English, and again perhaps 200 million second-language speakers. In another thirty years Hindi might, like Chinese, have over a thousand million current users. Both Hindi and Chinese are assured their statistical position by virtue of being the national languages of the world's most populous countries. Universal education means that hundreds of millions will learn these languages each generation. But Hindi and Chinese are dominant in a single well-defined geographical area, marked out by fixed national frontiers. There are indeed Hindi and Chinese-speaking communities in several other countries, but they are not about to become dominant in those countries. Therefore, numerically staggering as it is, the dominance of these languages is essentially a national phenomenon, not a world-wide one. They cannot be expected to grow beyond a certain point, or to spread geographically outside their region.

The immediate future is all too clear. National languages will continue to spread very rapidly within their frontiers, and minority languages will continue to disappear. English will continue to spread, as a national language in many countries, and as a second or third language for people across the world. Those who predict the future have a habit of being wrong; but that's how it looks now.

Will language loss eventually stop? A time will certainly come when English, French, Spanish and the other national languages of the world – somewhere around two hundred in total – are the only languages still in use, each dominant within its own borders. Will the situation then stabilize?

In fact, as we saw in Chapter 5, these national languages are already under pressure from English. Their fields of use are beginning to diminish in number. Their English loanwords are rapidly increasing. The attraction of neighbouring English-speaking culture is terribly strong.

Quebec, as one example, has English-speaking Canadian provinces on its eastern and western borders and, more crucially, it has the United States to its south. The effect is already quite noticeable in official and standard Canadian French: expressions like *escalier de feu* for 'fire escape' are rather evidently based on American English. However, young people in Quebec speak and write a language that is stuffed with North American English terms, and with turns of phrase imitating English. Perhaps it does not matter quite so much how effective the French-language lobby has been in Canada. How French will Canadian French be in another couple of generations?

Johann Gottfried Herder (1744–1803) was already worried about the convergence of European societies – under a French tide. The Slavonic languages and cultures, in particular, were under threat even as they strove for modernity – in fact they were all the more under threat, for the modernity they wanted, the nationalism they claimed, were French and west European. Noah Webster, writing in 1789 and quoted at length in Chapter 5, had the same view as Herder about the gradual convergence of European languages: 'The vicinity of the European nations, with the uninterrupted communication in peace, and the changes of dominion in war, are gradually assimilating their respective languages.'[37]

Webster, unable to predict the coming rapidity and ubiquity of world-wide communication, had thought that the Atlantic would be a sufficient barrier to ensure that an 'American language' would gradually separate from the English of Britain. By the twentieth century (in spite of Mencken's 1936 book *The American Language*) it was clear that Webster was wrong on that point. Whorf, therefore, writing at almost the same date as Mencken, was able to talk about a view of the world which was 'common European', in which term he included the North American (and Australian and other colonial) varieties of English. This 'common European' world view, the result of at least a thousand years of convergence among English, French, German,

Hungarian and all the other languages of Europe, Whorf quite rightly contrasted with the many different world views embodied in Amerindian languages.

All the evidence tells us that this convergence is continuing. Modern global communication involves not only the world-wide circulation of written and spoken material in English, but also an ever-increasing quantity of written and spoken material in other languages – notably Spanish and French – that is modelled on English or translated from English. All this is a vehicle for the spread of English ways of speaking and ways of thinking. The convergence is on several levels. In scientific and technical writing, in lecturing, in serious broadcasting, English is more and more involved: writers in other languages draw on material previously written in English, they may be called on to submit a text in English, they are aware of English readers and future English translation. They use English-like phraseology, styles and formats that will transfer easily into English. In popular writing, in the mass media, there is a persistent fashion for English words. Ordinary people find themselves reading more English words, hearing more English, using more English in everyday life.

Finally we return to the total number of languages and to the interaction between them.

The total number of languages remains high, at 5,000, even if many hundreds may have disappeared in the course of the last century. But the number is now falling very steeply: I will not draw a parabola, but will repeat that, a hundred years from now, the total is expected to be only 2,500. Assuming that the decline does not become even more rapid, the next milestone – when none but national languages survive, and the world total is around 200 – will be reached in under two hundred years from now.

Even during the present stage, when the 200 national languages of the world are in the process of superseding the 4,800 minority languages, English is meanwhile spreading extremely rapidly: I have just outlined some of the reasons. Unless world-wide travel and communications change so drastically that people no longer find English of any special use or interest – unless globalism itself is doomed – then English will continue to spread. It is already taking over more and more of the functions hitherto performed by the various national and regional languages: there is every reason to suppose that it will go on doing so, as global business and the global media monopolize more and more of people's lives. This means that even the national languages are threatened with disappearance in the long term.

At present there is very probably more bilingualism in the world than ever before, simply because the number of people in the world is far greater than ever before. Bilingualism can be maintained for a long time, as we saw in Chapter 3, and it has recently been argued that long-term 'stable bilingualism', as it is optimistically called, will prevent future language losses caused by the spread of national languages and of English. That may be so, but our historical examples do not support the idea; in fact they suggest the opposite. Bilingualism lasts as long as people find it useful. It may be one or two generations, as with nearly all the migrant languages of modern Europe; it may be some hundreds of years, as with speakers of Romani and some speakers of Yiddish. As long as people find it useful – and not a single generation longer.

In two hundred years or less, the minority languages of the world will mostly be gone. The national languages may at that point still be battling it out with English, but by then it will be easy to foresee the speed with which the last milestone will be attained, the point at which only English is spoken. It is closer than you think. And no more bilingualism then.

The losses we face

It's fair to say that linguists have been no slower than anyone else to grasp the seriousness of the increasing disappearance of languages: no slower, but also no faster. Indeed, for a while in the second half of the twentieth century research on exotic languages tended to be marginalized within linguistics: theory and universals were the fashion, and minor languages do not in practice feed much into these research areas, though they might. It is only in the last fifteen years or so that linguists have themselves been publishing significantly on the question of world-wide language loss.

People who are concerned about issues of minority rights, minority cultures and biodiversity tend to be active in the preservation of languages: some of these, in the right place at the right time, go as far as to learn a disappearing language and to bring their children up to speak it. Speakers of minority languages, on the other hand, very often want to switch to a national language and want their children to do the same. Linguists are well placed to see both sides of the question. Thus in a symposium on endangered languages published by the journal *Language* in 1992 there was a series of invited papers dealing with the phenomenon in various parts of the world, several of them giving some space to suggestions about how to stop or reverse the trend, but they were countered by a short, trenchant article from Peter Ladefoged, arguing that if people want to switch from their traditional languages, that's up to them, and it's no business of the linguist to try to change their minds.[38] It's true that when a language is lost, a culture may also be abandoned, but this also is something that people may decide for themselves that they want to do; and, on the other hand, cultures may occasionally and to a certain degree be maintained even though people have begun to speak a new language.

Ladefoged's case is perfectly well founded, then, and most published comments by linguists on the language disappearance question have not overbalanced it. It is a pity, from this point of view, that linguists' reasons for deploring the loss of languages are, in general, so very linguistic. They write that when a language is lost, some examples – phonetic, syntactic, semantic – of the possible features available to any language may also be lost. This is true: it is true for example that as each Khoisan language ceases to be spoken, one or two more of the click consonants so typical of that language group will probably never be heard again; but does it matter outside linguistics? James Crawford puts this well:

Linguists . . . have warned that the death of any natural language represents an incalculable loss to their science. No doubt few who are acquainted with this problem would disagree: from a scientific standpoint, the destruction of data is always regrettable. The loss of a language represents the loss of a rare window on the human mind. But from the perspective of the public and policymakers, this argument smacks of professional self-interest; it is hardly a compelling justification for new spending in a time of fiscal austerity.[39]

Recently, linguists have begun to write of some further reasons for deploring the disappearance of languages. Nicholas Ostler, editor of the newsletter *Iatiku*, lists two. First, some disappearing languages are disappearing because of political oppression, not because people have simply decided to switch to another instead:

Some languages (one thinks especially of those in California and Tasmania in the last century, Brasil and East Timor in this) have been actively stamped out with their last speakers; in other countries (Colombia might be an example, or the South West of the USA) the traditional minority populations often cling on fiercely to their languages and communities, while well-meaning members of the middle classes have attempted to educate them out of their old ways. In other countries again (Latvia in the 1940s and 1950s, Ethiopia in 1970s and 1980s) languages and traditional communities have suffered when large scale movements of population have been enforced.

In all such cases, many of them discussed in earlier chapters of this book, language loss is a symptom of ethnic inequality or of genocide, and anyone who opposes these will certainly oppose linguistic oppression too, at least to the point of winning freedom of choice for the speakers of the threatened language. But that doesn't take us very far, because so very many people, when free to decide, are still deciding against their minority language.

Secondly, language shift is a one-way process. People often begin it in their own families without realizing how many other families are doing the same, and once it has become general, it is too late to change. Ostler again:

At some points in their history, members of a community may opt to give up their language, and try to move closer to other communities by adopting a common lingua franca. Often, they are pursuing a perceived, reasonable, economic goal. The problem comes when that goal changes, or perhaps when the goal is achieved . . . There is no path back; an option or an identity which was given by the old language is no longer there.[40]

In many hundreds of language communities, at this moment, children are not being taught the traditional language, and parents honestly do not realize that, a generation later, it will not be there to be revived. Yes, linguists must make this as clear as possible wherever and whenever they can. But it may not change many minds. If people are shifting language because they want something better for their children, linguists and others will find it difficult to persuade them that their national language is not in fact better. Their national language does really offer to most people of today better chances of survival and prosperity than their minority language.

This book points towards three overriding reasons why we need to stop losing languages – reasons that are valid not just for individual communities of speakers but for all of us and our children. It is now time to set them out concisely.

First, we need the knowledge that they preserve and transmit. Human beings have been able to evolve cultures that make use of the natural resources of practically every square mile of this planet. We have done so by exploring and testing those resources, and each culture transmits the cumulated knowledge that has been gained from generation to generation through its language.

That's nothing very serious in itself, you may say. The information gets published. Selye published his research on the pituitary, and North Frisian no longer matters. We have quinine, and now we need not care if the Callahuaya abandon their medicine and forget their language. But unfortunately the great majority of the disappearing languages of the world are – if I can put it like this – not so lucky. There has been no one around to take such careful notes.

Never mind, you may say. When people change language, they transmit their knowledge in the new language. But all too often this does not happen. They change language because they want to assimilate to the majority culture – a culture in which (if you will allow the generalization) local resources are less and less valued while information, education, food and drink and medicine all come from somewhere distant, in a more standard and a more mass-produced form, in exchange for money. That's the modern way. Local cultures are simply being abandoned. 'There is some urgency to this work,' so Cox and Balick wrote concerning ethnobotanical discovery: 'many healers are elderly and lack apprentices. As they die, much of their knowledge of local vegetation dies, too.'[41]

That's still not very serious, you may say. If the line of transmission from expert to expert is broken, we'll gather the local knowledge all over again. Yes, we can do this, if we are interested. But it takes a long time. 'One should attend to what is old, and not allow it to be forgotten,' said a Sumerian poet five thousand years ago,[42] and he said this because once the knowledge is forgotten it is that much more difficult to reconstruct it.

Ethnobotanists looking for possible new sources of medicinal drugs have found that they need to be selective: they need peoples who have been resident in the same region for many generations. Thus 'aboriginal peoples who have populated Australia for many thousands of years would be a better choice than European settlers'.[43] The Polynesians have had 1,500 years – by no means as long, but it has given them time to test and prove a hundred-odd medicinal plants; far more than the Europeans of Hawaii or New Zealand. There's no magic about it: it takes a long, long time for a reasonable proportion of plants to be tested, and the longer the process continues, the better for all of us. There is so much still to be learnt!

Second, beyond the transmission of acquired and tested knowledge, we need other languages for the insights they give us into the way things may be – we need them for those alternative world views. We are now pretty sure that 'the Anglo-Saxon language' is *not* 'the simplest, the most perfectly and simply symbolic that the world has ever seen' and we no longer characterize all other languages clumsily as 'cumbersome mechanism for conveyance of thought'.[44] We are now prepared to allow Whorf his precisely worded statement, written in the 1930s, of what exactly would be wrong with a mono-lingual world.

Those who envisage a future world speaking only one tongue, whether English, German or Russian, or any other, hold a misguided view and would do the evolution of the human mind the greatest disservice. Western culture has made, through language, a provisional analysis of reality and, without correctives, holds resolutely to that analysis as final. The only correctives lie in all those other tongues which by aeons of independent evolution have arrived at different but equally logical, provisional analyses.[45]

This is Whorfianism of the third kind, the kind with which modern linguists such as Marianne Mithun readily agree: 'The loss of a language represents . . . an irreparable loss for us all, the loss of opportunities to glimpse alternative ways of making sense of the human experience.'[46]

The problem is exaggerated, you may say. It is all in books, or it soon will be. We have a hundred pages of Whorf and six hundred pages of Malotki on Hopi concepts of time: surely that pins it down?

No, it isn't enough. Books don't answer our questions. We have dictionaries of ancient Greek by the score, yet we still can't say for certain what colours the ancient Greeks called by what names. And the words of a language are not all. When a language is lost, Mithun observes, oral literature is lost as well – ritual of all kinds, oratory, lyric and narrative poetry, myths and legends.[47] Like the classification that is embedded in the lexicon and grammar of a language, but at a different level of consciousness, oral literature is also a way of making sense of the world and of our place in it. It is a realm that we have hardly begun to explore. With laudable exceptions, most of the oral literature in non-European languages that was collected in the course of the twentieth century was collected and published for scholars – if it has yet been published at all – in books that are none too accessible, and none too readable. And while I write this I know perfectly well that readable layouts for traditional oral literature can be difficult or impossible to devise. We do not quite know how to make oral literature cross the language boundaries in such a way that it will transmit knowledge and insight to others as compulsively as it does to its original audience. While we continue to try to do that, it is being forgotten – young people nowadays want to listen to American-style music or watch the television. Soon, all that will be left will be our video recordings and our scholarly transcripts.

Finally the *third* step. Beyond the transmission of knowledge, beyond the transmission of insights into the structure of the human world, we need a multiplicity of languages because it is interaction with other languages that keeps our own language flexible and creative.

We have seen, throughout this book, how English speakers have drawn on the resources of dozens of other languages to stretch the capabilities of their language and to increase its vocabulary. As far as English is concerned, the phenomenon was never more noticeable than it is today. The dictionaries of American English, Canadian English, Caribbean English, South African English, Australian English, New Zealand English, Bahamian English (and I could go on) are full of words you don't know but might one day, and words you never will know unless you travel to a remote corner of the English-speaking world, and turns of phrase that say it better than anyone has said it anywhere else. English is flourishing as never before and is packed with innovation, bursting with creativity, pullulating with new rhythms. All is for the best.

Not far ahead is the time when the number of languages English is drawing on for its new words, rhythms and ideas, a number still increasing up to that point, will equal the total number of languages currently spoken in the world. No problem so far: but I don't need to tell you what will happen after that. The total number of languages spoken in the world, having fallen very steeply to that point, will continue to fall very steeply, as we have already predicted. From that point, the speakers of English will have fewer and fewer other languages to draw on for new words and ideas. And within two to three hundred years from now they will have none.

The problem is imaginary, you will say. With its vast inherited resources, English will already have enough words; possibly too many.

No. They will be the wrong kind of words. There is already a vast mass of words in the English dictionaries, but many of them are lying dormant. Ordinary, innovative, creative people, when they want to express a new idea or spread a new thought, reach for words and rhythms from their own minds; they don't reach out for dictionaries. That isn't how creativity happens. And people don't usually invent a word out of thin air. For every *Kodak* (an invented name) there are several dozen *robots* (a word borrowed from Czech, though with a new meaning). People might do more in the way of pure invention of words, it's true: but it's an unfriendly business. Esperanto, in which nearly all the words suggest something or other to a hearer who knows European languages, is far and away easier to learn than the justly forgotten Volapük, the international language that reminds you of nothing on earth. If you invent your words out of nothing, you will be hard to understand. Natural language never has worked that way, and it's difficult to suppose it ever will.

It isn't just a matter of words. When Latin spread around the Mediterranean, not only did its speakers adopt a mass of new words from Greek and the other major languages with which Latin was in contact: the sound pattern and the grammar of Latin also entered a period of rapid change. Did the changes come somehow straight out of Latin, pre-programmed? Evidently not, otherwise there would have been no reason for them to happen at that moment and so comprehensively. They came, by way of bilingual speakers, during a period of language shift, in the interaction between Latin and the other languages of the region. Now although we are seeing English in the early stages of a similar process, and the perspective is foreshortened, it is still clear that similar things are happening: alongside numerous loans from other languages, English is fertile in new sound patterns and new, apparently simplified, grammar, and the changes are not coming out of the resources of standard American or British English but rather from the periphery, in the accents of non-standard and bilingual speakers. We can't yet see which changes will spread and stick, but the potential is rich enough. In both cases, classical Latin and current English, the changes are surely catalysed by interaction with other languages. As we have seen, even new literary genres sometimes arise in just this way. But as the other languages of the world, one after another, cease to be used, the potential for natural, fruitful innovation in the surviving languages – including English – inexorably shrinks to nothing.

The knowledge that we and our children need is being lost as we destroy the languages and cultures in which that knowledge has been recorded. The insights that we can gain from understanding the world views embodied in other languages will soon be beyond our reach. The creativity and flexibility that our descendants will need in their language, if they are to survive and prosper, will in due course wither away.

The purpose of this book has been to show why our long-term future is threatened by the disappearance of languages. Its aim is not to persuade those who are currently shifting to a new language: probably nothing can persuade them. Its aim is to persuade us –

writers, broadcasters, business people and the rest of us, pursuing our short-term prosperity and meanwhile spreading English and other national languages as fast and as far as we can – that our great-grandchildren need us to stop doing it and find another way.

NOTES

I LANGUAGE AND OUR SPECIES

1. This statement of the basis of linguistic change would not be universally accepted. For example, in *The Language Instinct*, Steven Pinker's explanation is almost completely opposed to mine: 'Some person, somewhere, must begin to speak differently from the neighbours, and the innovation must spread and catch on like a contagious disease until it becomes epidemic, at which point children perpetuate it.' He adds later that 'because speech can be sloppy and words and sentences ambiguous, people are occasionally apt to reanalyze the speech they hear' (Pinker 1994 pp. 243–4), not realizing, I think, that every child performs a complete reanalysis.

2. Matthew Arnold, *On Translating Homer*. Newman took offence, and Arnold had to add an explanation. 'I meant merely to convey, in a familiar form of speech, the sense of bewilderment one has at finding a person to whom words one thought all the world knew seem strange, and words one thought entirely strange, intelligible' (Arnold 1861, 1862).

3. Examples from Indian English: Nihalani and others 1979.

4. I originally wrote 'unconsciously', but not all linguistic innovation is unconscious. *Someone* has to be the first to use any new word or expression: someone had to be the first on Tristan to call it *berry time*. New expressions like this, if they are taken up by others, quickly become a part of everyday language, their originator forgotten.

5. Examples of the Tristan dialect come from Zettersten 1969.

6. It also became clear that a grammar of Sanskrit devised as long ago as the fourth century BC by Pāṇini was in transformational form. Chomsky 1968, 1986.

7. I owe the question, but not the answer, to Steven Pinker (1994 pp. 240–43). His answer begins 'No one knows, but here are some plausible hypotheses . . .'. Here is another.

8. Greuter and others 2000.

9. There are no limits: but if you overdo the innovations your language will be hard to understand and people may stop listening. Which is why *Finnegans Wake* has fewer readers than *Ulysses*, and *Ulysses* has fewer than *Animal Farm*.

10. Genesis 11: 1–9. Pre-Babel speech was, collectively, 'of few words' because it was 'of one language'; the parallelism, typical of biblical style, works on the assumption that the number of words in the world varies with the number of languages.

11. Some linguists regard this unrecorded dialect, and its modern descendants Frisian and English, as being roughly equally distinct from West Germanic and North Germanic. Traditionally, however, it is counted in the West Germanic group along with German, Low German and Dutch.

12. This is why linguists who try to date the splits between dialects or languages by counting the differences between them (a technique called glottochronology) are bound to fail (on this see Lees 1953; J. A. Rea in Sebeok 1973 pp. 355–68. For a more favourable estimate of glottochronology than mine, see Renfrew 1987 pp. 113–18).

13. Some are controversial; in some cases a Celtic and a Germanic word came together. On 'dual etymology' see Todd 2000.

14. These are among the most likely loans direct from British Latin to Old English. Jackson 1953 estimates the total of words in this category at two dozen. Some other Latin loanwords, found in several Germanic languages including English, might have been adopted by the Anglo-Saxons after their migration or might have been brought with them from the Continent. Some of these are listed on p. 71.

15. The Observatoire Linguistique, headed by David Dalby, is an independent research unit supported by Unesco, with the aim of tracking and enumerating the languages of the world. The Observatoire has its own standard way of naming languages and its own special punctuation.

16. David Crystal in *Language Death* (Crystal 2000 pp. 2–11) discusses these statistics in more detail. A specialist in Central and South America, Terrence Kaufman (see his contribution to the *Atlas of the World's Languages*, Moseley and Asher 1994 p. 33) regards the *Ethnologue* figures for the number of languages in those regions as considerably exaggerated; so does Willem Adelaar (in Robins and Uhlenbeck 1991 p. 53).

17. Goddard 1996 p. 8: varying but similar numbers would be given by other 'splitters'. 'Splitters' are linguists inclined not to believe in speculative large groupings of languages; 'lumpers' are their opponents.

18. On English: Crystal 1997 p. 61. For these statistics I have also used my own *Dictionary of Languages* (A. Dalby 1998), as well as D. Dalby 1998 p. 83, and Malherbe 1995 p. 21.

19. Crystal 1997 p. 13.
20. This is not to deny that the intervention of speakers of other languages has sometimes made things worse.
21. Cann and others 1987; Cavalli-Sforza and others 1994; Cavalli-Sforza 2000. Recent claims to have reconstructed 'Eve's language', or the language ancestral to all current human languages, are not to be taken seriously.
22. Dixon 1997 p. 148. He proposes a 'punctuated equilibrium' model of the evolution and split of languages, the same model that has recently been applied to the evolution of biological species.

2 LANGUAGE AND CHANGE

1. In particular, although people sometimes assert the opposite, Iberian and Basque were quite unrelated.
2. Acts of the Apostles 21: 37–22: 3. In the Greek text the term used for *tribunus militum*, the officer's official Latin title, is its standard Greek equivalent, *khiliarkhos* 'commander of a thousand'. The word for the language we know as Aramaic is *hebraike dialekte* 'Hebrew dialect', because Aramaic was the current language of the 'Hebrews' or Jews.
3. Aulus Gellius, *Attic Nights* 17.17.
4. Quoted in Jerome, *On Galatians* 3.2.
5. Seneca, *Letters to Lucilius* 56.2.
6. Aulus Gellius, *Attic Nights* 17.17.
7. Ausonius, *Memorial of my Father* 1–10.
8. Quintilian, *Education in Rhetoric* 1.1.12–14.
9. Aulus Gellius, *Attic Nights* 11.16.
10. Ulpian, *On Wills* 2 [Justinian, *Digest* 32.1.11.1].
11. Ulpian, *Comments on Sabinus* 48 [Justinian, *Digest* 45.1.1.6]. Assyrian means not the Assyrian form of Akkadian cuneiform, which had long ceased to be used at this period, but one of the forms of Aramaic currently spoken in Roman Syria and Palestine.
12. Josephus, *Jewish Antiquities* 20.12.263–4; quotation continued below.
13. Lucian, *Heracles* 4.
14. Caesar, *Gallic War* 6.13–14 (translation after S. A. Handford); quotation continued below.
15. Strabo, *Geography* 4.4.4.
16. Ibid. 3.1.6, 3.2.15.
17. Irenaeus, *Against the Heresies* preface.
18. Silius Italicus 8.495–501 (Loeb translation).

19. Hans Dieter Betz (ed.), *The Greek Magical Papyri in Translation* (Chicago: Chicago University Press, 1986), 174–6.
20. W. W. Weaver, personal communication.
21. Diodorus Siculus 5.31.1–5, perhaps deriving from observations by the 2nd-century BC scientist Poseidonius (translation after C. H. Oldfather).
22. Juvenal 7.147–9.
23. *Epitome de Caesaribus* 20.8; *Historia Augusta, Severus* 1.4 – unreliable and unscholarly compilations by unknown authors of the late Empire. I use them for these details because they happen to support one another convincingly.
24. Gildas, *Ruin of Britain* 34.6 (translation after Michael Winterbottom).
25. Cicero, *For Roscius of Ameria* 133.
26. Plutarch, *Life of Demosthenes* 2 (translation by Ian Scott-Kilvert).
27. Lucian, *On Paid Employment in Great Houses* 24.
28. P. Nigidius, *Grammatical Notes* [Aulus Gellius, *Attic Nights* 13.6].
29. Dillard 1985, pp. 51–65.
30. Cicero, *On the Orator* 3.12.45.
31. Horace, *Odes* 3.6.21–32; Propertius 3.9.43–6; Dalby 2000 pp. 120–24.
32. Weinreich 1953 p. 94, citing work by Th. Capidan and E.-H. Lévy.
33. Breton 1978 [compiled 1647] p. 55.
34. Breton 1978 [compiled 1654] p. 133.
35. It is interesting to read what a secondary source, Mathias du Puis, makes of Breton's report. Du Puis's narrative was published in 1652. He deals with the language of Dominica on pp. 195–7. Note especially this passage:

Les femmes ont un langage tout different de celuy des hommes: et comme ce seroit un crime entr'elles de parler autrement quand elles ne sont pas obligées de converser parmy les hommes, aussi elles se mocquent des hommes qui se servent de leur façon de parler. Les vieillards aussi usurpent une façon de parler tout autre de celle des jeunes gens. Enfin quand ils ont dessein de faire la guerre, ils ont un baragoüin pour la persuader à ceux de leur nation, qui est fort difficile à apprendre: 'The women have a form of speech wholly different from that of the men. Just as they would consider it improper, except when they have to talk to the men, for them to use any other language but their own, so they make fun of any men who address them in their own manner of speech. The old men have a manner of speech quite different from that of the youngsters. And finally when they determine on warfare they have a special jargon in which they urge their own people to make war, and this is a very difficult language to learn.'

Du Puis, rather obviously, drew on Breton's explanations but did not give them his full attention. That is how he makes the old men's language different from the young men's, when Breton merely meant that there was an oratorical style of speech used in formal debate, a style which youngsters would take some time to learn. That, again, is how Du Puis, conflating the 'enemies' with 'us French' (perhaps not unnaturally), creates a special jargon of military rhetoric out of what Du Puis had described as (1) bombastic war poetry and (2) a jargon or pidgin used when trading with the French. Later readers have not understood du Puis's ambiguous clause *qui se servent de leur façon de parler*, 'who address them in their own [whose own?] manner of speech': Breton is thus the only writer who makes it really clear that each sex used both registers depending on who was addressed.

36. Taylor 1977 pp. 89–99; B. J. Hoff in Bakker and Mous 1994 pp. 161–8, citing further work by Taylor.
37. Ellis 1974 pp. 115–30.
38. S. van Ness in Burridge and Enninger 1992 pp. 182–98.
39. M. L. Huffines in Dorian 1989 pp. 211–26.
40. C. Hoppenbrouwers in Deprez 1989 pp. 83–97.

3 LANGUAGE AND COMMUNITY

1. Bede, *Ecclesiastical History of the English People* 1.1. Bede, a Northumbrian, was the first historian of the English (the Angles, in which term the Saxons were already subsumed) but he wrote in Latin.
2. Ellis 1974 pp. 115–30.
3. Sahagún, *Historia general de las cosas de Nueva España* book 2 appendix 6 (ed. Garibay 1979 p. 172).
4. The 'one father' of the district of Guarocherí is the Inca god Pariacaca – and yet, for the 'faith' of the Ancients, the writer borrows a word from the Spanish missionaries, *fe*. See Salomon and Urioste 1991.
5. Arnold 1867. As Arnold commented, the views of *The Times*, if at all typical of Englishmen, explained why they were not very good at governing Ireland.
6. Krauss 1998 p. 16, quoted more fully on p. 160.
7. Dixon and others 1990 p. 7.
8. H. Batibo in Brenzinger 1992 p. 90.
9. Nicephorus Gregoras, *Roman History* 8.10.1–5 [1.348–351 Bonn edn.].
10. *Journal d'un bourgeois de Paris* sections 464–8 (Shirley 1968 pp. 216–19).
11. In this outline I have treated the distinction between Yiddish and German speakers as religious: I could equally have described it as ethnic (racial, in older terminology). To both formulations there were exceptions (there were non-believers on both sides, and there was intermarriage) but not so very many. My way is easier here because it means that I can treat 'German' simply

as the name of a language and 'Jewish' simply as the name of a religious group and not be troubled with the overlapping ethnic and political senses of the words.

12. Fishman 1981, 1985. His 1981 volume *Never Say Die!* is a rich collection of material on the history of Yiddish and its literature. Quotations in the text are from p. 4, p. 21 n. 10, and p. 23 of *Never Say Die!*

13. Fishman 1981 p. 5 n. 2.

14. Information and examples from A. P. Grant in Bakker and Mous 1994 pp. 123-150, citing work by I. F. Hancock and others.

15. For more on these: Weinreich 1953 p. 96 with references (Sarakatsani and 'Loshlekoydesh'), also Campbell 1964 (Sarakatsani); N. Boretzky and B. Igla in Bakker and Mous 1994 pp. 35–68, citing work by I. F. Hancock and others (Romani mixed dialects); A. P. Grant ibid. p. 124 on the 'language of the stonemasons'.

16. Dixon and others 1990 p. 14.

17. Girault 1984; Bastien 1987. For the quotation from Bernabé Cobo I am indebted to Girault 1984 p. 413. The language name is often spelt Kallawaya.

18. '. . . and the first came and stood before my father, and gave unto him a book, and bade him that he should read' (*1 Nephi* 1.11). Though grammatical, this is not Biblical English. In that variety of the language the construction 'bid him that he should . . .' does not occur.

19. Williams 1965 pp. 20–21: he uses the objective term 'female ritual specialists' for those whom others describe as priestesses. I don't know whether a botanical identification of the *kambaranun* root has been made.

20. Dum-Tragut 1997.

21. Because at that time there was little incentive to learn Irish later in life, and no incentive to claim greater knowledge of it than one really had. This is my reason for the estimate of 15 per cent native Irish speakers in 1922, given below. For the other facts and statistics in this section see Hudson-Edwards 1990.

22. Wardhaugh 1987 pp. 211–20.

23. Deprez 1989 pp. 11–79; Wardhaugh 1987 pp. 203–29; K. Deprez in Pütz 1994 pp. 239–54.

24. C. J. Daswani in Coulmas 1989 p. 83.

25. Marshall 1996. On the results of intermarriage, work is cited by Barbara Anderson and Brian Silver. On Estonia: Laitin 1996.

26. Marshall 1996.

4 LANGUAGE AND NATION

1. G. Nunberg in Adams and Brink 1990 p. 123.
2. G. W. Leibniz, *Ermahnung an die Deutschen.*
3. J. G. Fichte, *Reden an die deutsche Nation.*
4. Seen on an Austrian gravestone.
5. Technical term required in listing the ingredients of mass-produced orange juice.
6. For a survey of this school of research see Weinreich 1953 pp. 116–21.
7. Jespersen 1938 p. 121.
8. Ibid. p. 2.
9. B. Barère in *Gazette nationale ou Le moniteur universel* (9 Pluviôse an II = 28 January 1794).
10. Grégoire 1790.
11. Wardhaugh 1987 pp. 97–119.
12. Practically no one: but Rabbi Judah the Patriarch, born in AD 135 and son of the patriarch Simon ben Gamaliel II, was brought up to speak Hebrew as his mother tongue – an excellent training for his eventual task, for he was the compiler of the traditional Jewish law, the *Mishnah.*
13. J. D. Brown in Bender 1976 p. 311.
14. Seyoum 1988.
15. Day 1985 pp. 171–9.
16. Victor Clark, Commissioner of Education, quoted by Kachru 1986 p. 5.
17. G. Nunberg in Adams and Brink 1990 p. 123.
18. Atkins 1887 (as quoted by Crawford 1994).
19. Quoted by S. Diamond in Adams and Brink 1990 p. 111.
20. Reyhner 1995. In the past, too, Mexican immigrants and Native Americans have been treated alike in United States schools. 'When I was working on the Menominee reservation, several Menominee women told stories of how the boarding school teachers washed out their mouths with soap if they dared utter a word of Menominee . . . The same thing happened in my own high school in Milwaukee, Wisconsin, where at South Division High School I myself observed my classmates, Mexican-American students, being dragged by teachers into the bathrooms if they dared speak Spanish' (Boseker 1994 p. 151).
21. Adapted from Krauss 1998 pp. 9 and 11.
22. Goddard 1996 p. 3: he regards his total of 209 living languages of North America as 'perhaps roughly half the number that existed five hundred years earlier'.
23. Krauss 1998, with citation of work by Bernadette Adley-Santamaria. See

ibid. p. 20 n. 1 on the differences (which are minor) between Krauss's figures and those given in Goddard 1996.

24. *Iatiku*, 1 (May 1995), reporting work by M. Krauss.

25. The comparison can be seen in the North America maps in Moseley and Asher 1994, though these have been criticized for inaccuracy in detail.

26. Mithun 1984.

27. L. J. Watahomigie in McCarty and Zepeda 1998 p. 5.

28. As Tom Dutton remarks in the context of pre-colonial Papua New Guinea, a mistaken impression of monolingualism 'is perhaps created by the sheer number of languages spoken in the area and supported by linguistic maps which necessarily portray languages as discrete static entities' (in Pütz 1994 p. 236).

29. Haas 1968 p. 81, abridged.

30. M. Silverstein in Goddard 1996 p. 118, with references.

31. So M. Silverstein ibid. p. 121.

32. Brown 1999 p. 106.

33. Ibid. p. 112.

34. Quoted by M. Silverstein in Goddard 1996 p. 120.

35. Which supports Emanuel Drechsel's contention (Drechsel 1997) that a form of Mobilian Jargon was already in use when the Europeans arrived.

36. Quoted by Drechsel 1997 p. 218.

37. Haas 1968 p. 81.

38. In this book, North American languages are those whose territories lie north of the city civilizations of central Mexico. Columbus himself recorded some words of Caribbean languages, including *aji* 'chilli, Capsicum sp.'.

39. Mithun 1999 p. 3.

40. Goddard 1996 pp. 17–18 with references.

41. Siebert 1975.

42. Hill 1983 p. 261; Lanner 1981.

43. Quoted in Atkins 1887.

44. In the century that was to follow, nationalism of this irrational kind has spread even further across the world. It is because Afghanistan is thought by its government to be 'a Muslim nation' that ancient Buddhist images are being destroyed there as I write these words.

45. Krauss 1998 p. 16; G. S. Dick in McCarty and Zepeda 1998 p. 24; C. P. Sims ibid. pp. 98–9; L. J. Watahomigie ibid. p. 6; Reyhner 1995 p. 231; Crawford 1994, quoting A. H. Kneale.

46. As abridged in Reyhner 1995 p. 229.

47. Crawford 1994.

48. Krauss 1998 pp. 17–18.

49. McCarty 1998; L. J. Watahomigie in McCarty and Zepeda 1998 pp. 6–7;

D. Lopez ibid. p. 44; O. Zepeda ibid. pp. 47–57; G. McLean in Cantoni 1996 p. 125; Krauss 1998; Crawford 1994.
50. M. Linn in McCarty and Zepeda 1998 p. 66; A. Vera ibid. p. 78; Crawford 1994; Krauss 1998.

5 HOW TO BECOME A GLOBAL LANGUAGE

1. I am oversimplifying a very complex situation: see E. Adegbija in Pütz 1994 pp. 139–63; C. M. B. Brann ibid. pp. 165–80.
2. Laitin 1996 p. 57.
3. These details and quotations after V. Webb in Pütz 1994 p. 186; opinions mine.
4. After a report by Tatjana Tubic, AIA/Misanet, 25 April 1997.
5. Bec 1986 p. 120.
6. By A. M. Aurand; several editions in the 1930s.
7. Dalby 1996 pp. 180–83.
8. Dillard 1985.
9. Mencken 1936 p. 592.
10. Kachru 1986 p. 20.
11. Crystal 1997 pp. 55–61 for statistics and estimates of English speakers.
12. Pyles and Algeo 1993 p. 233.
13. Laitin 1996 p. 49.
14. Kachru 1986 p. 36.
15. C. M. B. Brann in Pütz 1994 p. 171.
16. Tatjana Tubic reporting for AIA/Misanet, 25 April 1997.
17. Coulmas 1988 pp. 15–16 and n. 11, source of the Gandhi quotations used in the text.
18. C. M. B. Brann in Pütz 1994 pp. 170, 178. Kanuri, local language of Borno state, is an old language of culture in northeastern Nigeria and Chad, now under threat of gradual decline under the pressure of Hausa, English and French.
19. Weinreich 1953 pp. 45, 51.
20. Orr 1962; Dillard 1985 p. 45.
21. Kachru 1986 p. 153.
22. For source references and for some of the original Hindi spellings see Kachru 1986 pp. 149–54.
23. C. Rabin in Coulmas 1989 pp. 26–38.
24. Kachru 1986 p. 151.
25. C. Rabin in Coulmas 1989 pp. 26–38.
26. Coulmas 1989 p. 18, citing work by Yanabu Akira and Kindaichi Haruhiko.

27. One of these journals, *English Today*, is particularly approachable.

28. M. Clyne in Laycock and Winter 1987 pp. 127–39.

29. For more on this see Kachru 1986 pp. 100–14.

30. Webster 1789 p. 22. See the comments by Kachru 1986 p. 130.

31. Dixon 1987. This is the language on which Dixon has done some of his best work.

32. Kachru 1986 p. 136; some other examples also from Kachru.

33. The Australian examples are from Dixon and others 1990. The South African examples are suggested by Silva 1997, Butler 1997 and Branford and Branford 1991. The Jamaican examples are suggested by Cassidy 1971.

34. These and some later examples suggested by Pyles and Algeo 1993 pp. 215–16.

6 WHEN WE LOSE A LANGUAGE

1. Lydecker 1918 p. 58 (as quoted by Day 1985 p. 167).

2. Day 1985.

3. Jespersen 1938 p. 3.

4. Some examples from Laudan 1996.

5. Paulsen 1981 p. 186.

6. Ibid. p. 188.

7. Cox and Balick 1994 p. 62.

8. Ibid. p. 60.

9. Silius Italicus, *Punica* 1.324–5.

10. Here, for the record, are the thirty-four Dacian plant names that can be identified with known species. Apart from proper names, this list represents most of what is now known about the Dacian language. They used *amolusta* 'camomile', *aurumetti* 'crowsfoot', *blis* 'blite', *budathla* 'bugloss', *guoleta* 'columbine', *duodela* 'mullein', *aniarsexe* 'cock's head', *arpopria* 'ivy', *aprus* 'yellow flag', *kinuboila* 'white bryony', *priadila* 'black bryony', *krustane* 'greater celandine', *usazila* 'hound's tongue', *kotiata* 'dog's tooth grass', *propodila* 'cinquefoil', *rathibida* 'blue daisy', *sipoax* 'small plantain', *skiare* 'teasel', *tulbela* 'lesser centaury', *khodela* 'ground-pine', *phithophthethela* 'maidenhair fern'. The list also includes some useful wild food plants, *mantia* 'blackberry', *mizela* 'thyme', *olma* 'danewort', *lax* 'wild purslane', *polpum* 'dill', *seba* 'elderberry', *sikupnux* 'eringo', *teudila* 'calamint', *dyn* 'nettle'. They also used some of the most effective poisons known to the ancient world, *zena* 'hemlock', *koikolida* 'deadly nightshade', *diellena* 'henbane', *prodiarna* 'black hellebore'.

11. Sydney *Bulletin*, 16 December 1920.

12. Did the large and venomous Jamaican lizard called *galliwasp* and the stinging mosquito called *gallinipper* get the first half of their names from Taino or some other Arawakan language? No one knows. Examples from Cassidy and Le Page 1967.

13. Cox and Balick 1994 pp. 61-2.

14. Dixon and others 1990 p. 5.

15. Ibid. pp. 55-6.

16. Dixon 1984 pp. 19-20.

17. Dixon and others 1990 pp. 8, 59.

18. Ibid. p. 29.

19. Crawford 1994, quoting H.-J. Sasse.

20. Dixon and others 1990 p. 5.

21. Prince 1910 pp. 459, 464; Dillard 1985 pp. 100-102.

22. Dixon 1984 p. 54.

23. Ibid. pp. 56-7.

24. Ibid. p. 107; see also pp. 127, 129.

25. Ibid. p. 220.

26. Ibid. p. 218.

27. The website is http://coombs.anu.edu.au/WWWVLPages/AborigPages/LANG/GAMDICT/GAMDICT.HTM. It was inaugurated on 19 January 1996: the news appeared in *Iatiku*, 2 (April 1996).

28. *Iatiku*, 1 (May 1995).

29. Dixon 1984 p. 328.

30. Haas 1968 p. 77.

31. Siebert 1967.

32. Dave Wells in *Iatiku*, 3 (August 1996).

33. Boseker 1994 p. 150.

34. Haas 1968 p. 77.

35. O. S. Andersen quoted in Crystal 2000 p. 2.

36. Reports in *Iatiku*, 2 (1996), 4 (1997).

37. David Crystal in the *Guardian* (25 October 1999).

38. The punctuation marks in these names are the standard system in South Africa for indicating click consonants, the special feature of Khoisan languages.

39. Nigel Crawhall in *Weekly Mail & Guardian* (Johannesburg, 25 October 1999) and in *Ogmios*, 6 (1997), 7 (1998).

40. Examples and quotation from Silva 1997. Old Dutch Medicines are a recognized branch of herbal knowledge in South Africa.

41. It is usually said that *Britain* is a Celtic word in origin, but no likely meaning in Celtic is available to explain why the islands or the people should have been so named. The balance of probability is that Celtic speakers borrowed the word from an earlier language.

42. For the Powhatan loans see Siebert 1975.

43. Dixon and others 1990 p. 28 (for quotation in the text) and pp. 106–7, citing work by J. Flood.

44. This section is based on material in Dixon and others 1990; compare Hercus 1969. One famous Australian loanword is excluded from the examples in the text because the language it comes from still has a few living speakers. Cooktown in Queensland is named after the famous explorer, who was forced to spend six weeks on shore at this point repairing the *Endeavour*, damaged in crossing the Great Barrier Reef. While he was here Cook recorded a few words of the local language, Guugu Yimidhirr, including the word *kangaroo* (Dixon 1984 p. 221). It is simply because no permanent settlement was established at this spot till long afterwards that Guugu Yimidhirr, one of the first Australian languages noted down by Europeans, has survived.

45. Quintilian, *Education in Rhetoric* 1.5.55–8.

46. Dixon and others 1990. Some other words originating from Tasmanian languages are listed in Brooks and Ritchie 1995, but they result from citations, in English reports and memoirs, of words used by Aborigines: the words were never taken into use in English, even locally.

47. W. F. Shipley in Heizer 1978 pp. 80–90; Hinton 1998.

48. Hinton 1998; quotations in the text from pp. 83, 85–6.

49. Heizer 1978 p. 14.

50. Smith 1972.

51. Table based on Hinton 1994 pp. 83–5; Hinton 1998 p. 84. The implication of this table, that all Californian languages belong to six families, might be an oversimplification. The Hokan and Penutian families have not been proved to be single families by comparative linguistics. 'There are many provocative resemblant forms among the languages, particularly among the Penutian ones, as well as certain general grammatical features that may be labeled Penutian or Hokan. In short, the terms Penutian stock and Hokan stock are names for unverified hypotheses . . .' (W. F. Shipley in Heizer 1978 p. 80). In addition, Wappo and Yuki are (or rather were) very different from one another – it might be wrong to group them in a single 'stock' or family. They might be isolates. Esselen might be not Hokan but Penutian, or it might be neither, and in that case it is another isolate. Scarcely anything was recorded of it; it is now long extinct and can only be classified – rightly or wrongly – on the basis of a few word resemblances.

52. W. F. Shipley in Heizer 1978 p. 80.

53. Hinton 1994, 1998; C. P. Sims in McCarty and Zepeda 1998 pp. 95–113; W. F. Shipley, E. D. Castillo and S. F. Cook in Heizer 1978 pp. 80–127; Crawford 1992 p. 48. Verbatim quotations in the text are by Cook, Sims and Hinton respectively.

54. Hinton 1998 pp. 83, 85; L. Hinton reported in *Iatiku*, 1 (May 1995).
55. Heizer 1978 p. 14.
56. S. Diamond in Adams and Brink 1990 pp. 111–19.
57. C. P. Sims in McCarty and Zepeda 1998 p. 99.
58. Hinton 1998 p. 91.
59. Ibid.

7 THE LOSS OF DIVERSITY

1. Mithun 1999 p. 2.
2. Martin 1986.
3. Pullum 1991.
4. Alcman fragment 58 Diehl [Apollonius the Sophist, *Homeric Lexicon* s.v. *knodalon*].
5. In later classical Greek the general word is *zoa* 'animals'.
6. Laurence Wong in *Babel*, 44/3.
7. Mizuno 1982 esp. pp. 52–5.
8. See for example Bokenkamp 1997 esp. pp. 385–94.
9. Du Puis 1652 pp. 195–7.
10. G. W. Leibniz, *Unvorgreifliche Gedanken*.
11. McGee 1895: I owe the quotation to Fishman 1982 p. 12 n. 4.
12. Benjamin Lee Whorf (1897–1941) spent his whole working life with the Hartford Fire Insurance Company, and by general consent he was 'as thorough and fast a fire prevention inspector as there has ever been'. His linguistic research was done in his spare time, but in contact with leading linguists including Edward Sapir (1884–1939).
13. Whorf 1941 quoted in Carroll 1956 p. 21. Whorf cites the linguist Yuen Ren Chao for work demonstrating that Chinese is not monosyllabic.
14. The basic form of the verb, or 'simplex', is used for the punctual aspect.
15. Whorf 1936.
16. Whorf 1950.
17. Coe 1999.
18. Malotki 1983; Whiteley 1998.
19. Fishman 1982 p. 3.
20. Ibid. p. 12 n. 2.
21. Ibid.
22. Carroll 1956 p. 18, summarizing Whorf 1953.
23. Malotki 1983 pp. 629–30.
24. Ibid. The seriousness with which Malotki tries to refute anything refutable is demonstrated by the following. 'A theory by White Bear Fredericks that the

Hopi kachinas were once preastronauts who traveled about aboard spaceships without engines or fuel but guided by magnetic fields . . . can easily be punctured because simply no Hopi linguistic equivalents relate to such technological concepts' (ibid. p. 631), or, briefly, the Hopi haven't got words for these things. Sadly, Malotki's argument fails: once the spaceships had been abandoned and forgotten, their names would have changed meaning or been forgotten too. I leave it to the reader to decide whether there is any non-linguistic way of proving that Fredericks' theory is false . . .

25. Pinker 1994 p. 63.
26. Fishman 1982 pp. 1–2.
27. Ibid. p. 7.
28. Mithun 1999 p. 2.
29. Ibid. p. 11.
30. Ibid. p. 10.
31. Dixon and others 1990 p. 13.
32. Report by Dr Layfield in Hakluyt's *Principal Navigations* (1598–1600).
33. Fishman 1982 p. 10.
34. Carroll 1956 p. 18, summarizing Whorf 1953.
35. L. J. Watahomigie in McCarty and Zepeda 1998 p. 6.
36. Fishman 1982 p. 10.
37. Webster 1789 p. 22.
38. Hale and others 1992.
39. Crawford 1994.
40. Nicholas Ostler in *Iatiku*, 3 (August 1996).
41. Cox and Balick 1994 pp. 61–2.
42. Black 1992.
43. Cox and Balick 1994 pp. 62–5.
44. McGee 1895, quoted more fully above.
45. B. L. Whorf in Carroll 1956 p. 244.
46. Mithun 1999 p. 2, quoted more fully above.
47. Ibid., quoted more fully above.

REFERENCES

Adams and Brink 1990: Karen L. Adams and Daniel T. Brink (eds.), *Perspectives on Official English: The Campaign for English as the Official Language of the USA* (Berlin: Mouton De Gruyter, 1990).

Arnold 1861: Matthew Arnold, *On Translating Homer* (London: Longman, 1861).

Arnold 1862: Matthew Arnold, *On Translating Homer: Last Words* (London: Longman, 1862).

Arnold 1867: Matthew Arnold, *On the Study of Celtic Literature* (London: Smith, Elder, 1867).

Atkins 1887: J. D. C. Atkins, *Report of the Commissioner of Indian Affairs* (Washington: US Government Printing Office, 1887).

Atran 1990: Scott Atran, *Cognitive Foundations of Natural History* (Cambridge: Cambridge University Press, 1990).

Bakker and Mous 1994: Peter Bakker and Maarten Mous (eds.), *Mixed Languages: 15 Case Studies in Language Intertwining* (Amsterdam: IFOTT, 1994).

Bastien 1987: Joseph W. Bastien, *Healers of the Andes: Kallawaya Herbalists and their Medicinal Plants* (Salt Lake City: University of Utah Press, 1987).

Bec 1986: Pierre Bec, *La Langue occitane* (Paris: Presses Universitaires de France, 1986).

Bender 1976: M. L. Bender (ed.), *The Non-Semitic Languages of Ethiopia* (East Lansing: African Studies Center, Michigan State University, 1976).

Berlin 1992: Brent Berlin, *Ethnobiological Classification: Principles of Categorization of Plants and Animals in Traditional Societies* (Princeton: Princeton University Press, 1992).

Black 1992: Jeremy Black, 'Some Structural Features of Sumerian Narrative Poetry' in Marianna E. Vogelzang and Herman L. J. Vanstiphout (eds.), *Mesopotamian Epic Literature: Oral or Aural?* (Lewiston, NY: Edwin Mellen Press, 1992), 71–101.

Bokenkamp 1997: Stephen R. Bokenkamp, *Early Daoist Scriptures* (Berkeley: University of California Press, 1997).

Boseker 1994: Barbara J. Boseker, 'The Disappearance of American Indian Languages', *Journal of Multilingual and Multicultural Development* 15 (1994), 147–60.

Branford and Branford 1991: Jean Branford and William Branford, *A Dictionary of South African English* (Cape Town: Oxford University Press, 1991).

Brenzinger 1992: Matthias Brenzinger (ed.), *Language Death: Factual and Theoretical Explorations with Special Reference to East Africa* (Berlin: Mouton De Gruyter, 1992).

Breton 1978: Raymond Breton, *Relations de l'Ile de la Guadeloupe* (Basse Terre: Société d'Histoire de la Guadeloupe, 1978).

Brooks and Ritchie 1995: Maureen Brooks and Joan Ritchie, *Tassie Terms: A Glossary of Tasmanian Words* (Melbourne: Oxford University Press, 1995).

Brown 1999: Cecil H. Brown, *Lexical Acculturation in Native American Languages* (New York: Oxford University Press, 1999).

Burridge and Enninger 1992: Kate Burridge and Werner Enninger (eds.), *Diachronic Studies on the Languages of the Anabaptists* (Bochum: Brockmeyer, 1992).

Butler 1997: Susan Butler, 'Selecting South-East Asian Words for an Australian Dictionary: How to Choose in an English not your own' in Edgar W. Schneider (ed.), *Englishes around the World: Studies in Honour of Manfred Görlach* (Amsterdam, 1997), ii. 273–86.

Cameron 1961: Kenneth Cameron, *English Place-Names* (London: Methuen, 1961).

Campbell 1964: J. K. Campbell, *Honour, Family and Patronage* (Oxford: Clarendon Press, 1964).

Cann and others 1987: R. L. Cann, M. Stoneking and A. C. Wilson, 'Mitochondrial DNA and Human Evolution', *Nature*, 325 (1987), 31–6.

Cantoni 1996: Gina Cantoni (ed.), *Stabilizing Indigenous Languages* (Flagstaff: Northern Arizona University Center for Excellence in Education, 1996).

Carroll 1956: John B. Carroll (ed.), *Language, Thought and Reality: Selected Writings of Benjamin Lee Whorf* (New York: Technology Press, Massachusetts Institute of Technology, 1956).

Cassidy 1971: Frederic Cassidy, *Jamaica Talk: Three Hundred Years of the English Language in Jamaica*, 2nd edn. (Basingstoke: Macmillan, 1971).

Cassidy and Le Page 1967: F. G. Cassidy and R. B. Le Page, *Dictionary of Jamaican English* (Cambridge: Cambridge University Press, 1967).

Cavalli-Sforza 2000: Luigi Luca Cavalli-Sforza, *Genes, Peoples and Languages* (London: Allen Lane, The Penguin Press, 2000).

Cavalli-Sforza and others 1994: L. L. Cavalli-Sforza and others, *The History and Geography of Human Genes* (Princeton: Princeton University Press, 1994).

Chomsky 1957: Noam Chomsky, *Syntactic Structures* (The Hague: Mouton, 1957).

Chomsky 1968: Noam Chomsky, *Language and Mind* (New York: Harcourt, Brace & World, 1968).

Chomsky 1986: Noam Chomsky, *Knowledge of Language, its Nature, Origin and Use* (New York: Praeger, 1986).

Coe 1999: Michael Coe, *Breaking the Maya Code* (London: Thames and Hudson, 1999).

Coulmas 1988: Florian Coulmas (ed.), *With Forked Tongues: What are National Languages Good For?* ([Singapore?] Karoma Publishers, 1988).

Coulmas 1989: Florian Coulmas (ed.), *Language Adaptation* (Cambridge: Cambridge University Press, 1989).

Cox and Balick 1994: Paul Alan Cox and Michael J. Balick, 'The Ethnobotanical Approach to Drug Discovery', *Scientific American*, 270/6 (June 1994), 60–65.

Crawford 1992: James D. Crawford (ed.), *Language Loyalties: A Source Book on the Official English Controversy* (Chicago: Chicago University Press, 1992).

Crawford 1994: James Crawford, 'Endangered Native American Languages: What is to be Done, and Why?' Paper presented at the annual conference of the American Educational Research Association, New Orleans, April 5, 1994. http://www.ncbe.gwu.edu/miscpubs/crawford

Crystal 1997: David Crystal, *English as a Global Language* (Cambridge: Cambridge University Press, 1997).

Crystal 2000: David Crystal, *Language Death* (Cambridge: Cambridge University Press, 2000).

Dalby 1996: Andrew Dalby, *Siren Feasts: A History of Food and Gastronomy in Greece* (London: Routledge, 1996).

Dalby, A., 1998: Andrew Dalby, *Dictionary of Languages* (London: Bloomsbury, 1998).

Dalby 2000: Andrew Dalby, *Empire of Pleasures: A Geography of Roman Luxury* (London: Routledge, 2000).

Dalby, D., 1998: David Dalby, *The Linguasphere: From Person to Planet* (Hebron, Wales: Linguasphere Press, 1998).

Day 1985: Richard R. Day, 'The Ultimate Inequality: Linguistic Genocide' in Nessa Wolfson and Joan Manes (eds.), *Language of Inequality* (Berlin: Mouton, 1985), 163–81.

Deprez 1989: Kas Deprez (ed.), *Language and Intergroup Relations in Flanders and the Netherlands* (Dordrecht: Foris, 1989).

Dillard 1985: J. L. Dillard, *Towards a Social History of American English* (Berlin: Mouton De Gruyter, 1985).

Dixon 1984: Bob [R. M. W.] Dixon, *Searching for Aboriginal Languages* (St Lucia: University of Queensland Press, 1984).

Dixon 1987: R. M. W. Dixon, 'Words of Juluji's World' in D. J. Mulvaney and P. J. White (eds.), *Australia to 1788* (Fairfax: Syme and Weldon, 1987), 147–65.

Dixon 1997: R. M. W. Dixon, *The Rise and Fall of Languages* (Cambridge: Cambridge University Press, 1997).

Dixon and others 1990: R. M. W. Dixon, W. S. Ramson and Mandy Thomas, *Australian Aboriginal Words in English: Their Origin and Meaning* (Melbourne: Oxford University Press, 1990).

Dorian 1989: Nancy C. Dorian (ed.), *Investigating Obsolescence: Studies in Language Contraction and Death* (Cambridge: Cambridge University Press, 1989).

Drechsel 1997: Emanuel J. Drechsel, *Mobilian Jargon: Linguistic and Sociohistorical Aspects of a Native American Pidgin* (Oxford: Clarendon Press, 1989).

Dum-Tragut 1997: Jasmine Dum-Tragut, 'Armenians in Austria', *Iatiku*, 4 (January 1997).

Du Puis 1652: Mathias du Puis, *Relation de l'establissement d'une colonie françoise dans la Gardeloupe, isle de l'Amerique, et des moeurs des sauvages* (Caen: Marin Yvon, 1652).

Ellis 1974: P. Berresford Ellis, *The Cornish Language and Literature* (London: Routledge, 1974).

Fishman 1981: J. Fishman (ed.), *Never Say Die! A Thousand Years of Yiddish in Jewish Life and Letters* (The Hague: Mouton, 1981).

Fishman 1982: J. A. Fishman, 'Whorfianism of the Third Kind: Ethnolinguistic Diversity as a World-wide Social Asset', *Language in Society*, 11 (1982), 1–14.

Fishman 1985: Joshua A. Fishman, 'The Lively Life of a Dead Language, or "Everyone Knows that Yiddish Died a Long Time Ago"', in Nessa Wolfson and Joan Manes (eds.), *Language of Inequality* (Berlin: Mouton De Gruyter, 1985), 207–22.

Garibay 1979: Fr. Bernardino de Sahagún, *Historia general de las cosas de Nueva España*, ed. Angel María Garibay K., 4th edn. (Mexico: Porrúa, 1979).

Girault 1984: Louis Girault, *Kallawaya: guérisseurs itinérants des Andes* (Paris: ORSTOM, 1984).

Goddard 1996: Ives Goddard (ed.), *Handbook of North American Indians, vol. 17: Languages* (Washington, DC: Smithsonian Institution, 1996).

Graddol and Meinhof 1999: David Graddol and Ulrike H. Meinhof (eds.), *English in a Changing World* (Oxford: AILA, 1999).

Grégoire 1790: *Rapport sur la nécessité et les moyens d'anéantir les patois et d'universaliser l'usage de la langue française* (Paris, 1790).

Grenoble 1997: Lenore A. Grenoble (ed.), *Endangered Languages: Current Issues and Future Prospects* (Cambridge: Cambridge University Press, 1997).

Greuter and others 2000: W. Greuter and others (eds.), *International Code of Botanical Nomenclature (Saint Louis Code)* (Königstein: Koeltz Scientific, 2000).

Haas 1968: Mary R. Haas, 'The Last Words of Biloxi', *International Journal of American Linguistics*, 34 (1968), 77–84.

Hale and others 1992: Ken Hale and others, 'Endangered Languages', *Language*, 68 (1992), 1–41; comment by Peter Ladefoged, 'Another view of endangered languages', ibid., pp. 809–11.

Heizer 1978: Robert F. Heizer (ed.), *Handbook of North American Indians, vol. 8: California* (Washington, DC: Smithsonian Institution, 1978).

Hercus 1969: Luise Hercus, *The Languages of Victoria: A Late Survey* (Sydney: Australian Institute of Aboriginal Studies, 1969).

Hill 1983: Jane H. Hill, 'Language Death in Uto-Aztecan', *International Journal of American Linguistics*, 49 (1983), 258–76.

Hindley 1989: Reg Hindley, *The Death of the Irish Language: A Qualified Obituary* (London: Routledge, 1989).

Hinton 1994: Leanne Hinton, *Flutes of Fire: Essays on California Indian Languages* (Berkeley, Calif.: Heyday, 1994).

Hinton 1998: Leanne Hinton, 'Language Loss and Revitalization in California: Overview', in T. L. McCarty and O. Zepeda (eds.), *Indigenous Language Use and Change in the Americas*, pp. 83–93.

Hudson-Edwards 1990: Alan Hudson-Edwards, 'Language Policy and Linguistic Tolerance in Ireland' in Karen L. Adams and Daniel T. Brink (eds.), *Perspectives on Official English: The Campaign for English as the Official Language of the USA*, pp. 63–81.

Jackson 1953: Kenneth Hurlstone Jackson, *Language and History in Early Britain* (Edinburgh: Edinburgh University Press, 1953).

Jespersen 1938: Otto Jespersen, *Growth and Structure of the English Language*, 9th edn. (Oxford: Blackwell, 1938).

Kachru 1986: Braj B. Kachru, *The Alchemy of English: The Spread, Functions and Models of Non-native Englishes* (Oxford: Pergamon, 1986).

Kay and McDaniel 1978: Paul Kay and Chad K. McDaniel, 'The Linguistic

Significance of the Meanings of Basic Color Terms', *Language*, 54 (1978), 611–46.

Krauss 1998: Michael Krauss, 'The Condition of Native North American Languages' in T. L. McCarty and O. Zepeda (eds.), *Indigenous Language Use and Change in the Americas*, pp. 9–21.

Laitin 1996: David D. Laitin, 'Language Planning in the Former Soviet Union: The Case of Estonia', *International Journal of the Sociology of Language*, 118 (1996), 43–61.

Lancelot and Arnauld 1660: [Claude Lancelot and Antoine Arnauld], *Grammaire générale et raisonnée* (Paris: Pierre le Petit, 1660).

Lanner 1981: Harriette Lanner, *The Piñon Pine* (Reno: University of Nevada Press, 1981).

Laudan 1996: Rachel Laudan, *The Food of Paradise* (Honolulu: University of Hawaii Press, 1996).

Laycock and Winter 1987: Donald C. Laycock and Werner Winter (eds.), *A World of Language: Papers Presented to Professor S. A. Wurm on his 65th Birthday* (Canberra: Department of Linguistics, Research School of Pacific Studies, 1987).

Lees 1953: R. B. Lees, 'The Basis of Glottochronology', *Language*, 29 (1953), 113–25.

Lydecker 1918: Robert C. Lydecker (ed.), *Roster, Legislatures of Hawaii, 1841-1918; Constitutions of Monarchy and Republic; Speeches of Sovereigns and President* (Honolulu: Hawaiian Gazette Co., 1918).

McCarty 1998: Teresa L. McCarty, 'Schooling, Resistance, and American Indian Languages' in T. L. McCarty and O. Zepeda (eds.), *Indigenous Language Use and Change in the Americas*, pp. 27–41.

McCarty and Zepeda 1998: Teresa L. McCarty and Ofelia Zepeda (eds.), *Indigenous Language Use and Change in the Americas* (Berlin: Mouton De Gruyter, 1998). (*International Journal of the Sociology of Language*, 132.)

McGee 1895: W. J. McGee, 'Some Principles of Nomenclature', *American Anthropologist*, 8 (1895), 279–86.

Malherbe 1995: Michel Malherbe, *Les Langages de l'humanité* (Paris: Laffont, 1995).

Malotki 1983: Ekkehard Malotki, *Hopi Time: A Linguistic Analysis of the Temporal Concepts in the Hopi Language* (Berlin: Mouton, 1983).

Marshall 1996: David F. Marshall, 'A Politics of Language: Language as a Symbol in the Dissolution of the Soviet Union and its Aftermath', *International Journal of the Sociology of Language*, 118 (1996), 7–41.

Martin 1986: Laura Martin, '"Eskimo Words for Snow": A Case Study in the Genesis and Decay of an Anthropological Example', *American Anthropologist*, 88 (1986), 418–23.

Maurais 1996: Jacques Maurais (ed.), *Quebec's Aboriginal Languages* (Cleve-don: Multilingual Matters, 1996).

Mencken 1936: H. L. Mencken, *The American Language*, 4th edn. (New York: Knopf, 1936).

Mithun 1984: Marianne Mithun, 'The Proto-Iroquoians: Culture Reconstruction from Lexical Materials' in M. K. Foster, J. Campisi and M. Mithun (eds.), *Extending the Rafters: Interdisciplinary Approaches to Iroquoian Studies* (Albany, NY: State University of New York Press, 1984), 259–81.

Mithun 1999: Marianne Mithun, *The Languages of Native North America* (Cambridge: Cambridge University Press, 1999).

Mizuno 1982: Kogen Mizuno, *Buddhist Sutras: Origin, Development, Transmission* (Tokyo: Kosei, 1982).

Moseley and Asher 1994: Christopher Moseley and R. E. Asher (eds.), *Atlas of the World's Languages* (London: Routledge, 1994).

Nihalani and others 1979: Paroo Nihalani, R. K. Tongue and Priya Hosali, *Indian and British English: A Handbook of Usage and Pronunciation* (Delhi: Oxford University Press, 1979).

Orr 1962: John Orr, *Old French and Modern English Idiom* (Oxford: Blackwell, 1962).

Paulsen 1981: Frederik Paulsen, 'The Recent Situation of the Ferring Language', in Einar Haugen, J. Derrick McClure and Derick Thomson (eds.), *Minority Languages Today* (Edinburgh: Edinburgh University Press, 1981), 182–8.

Pearl 1996: Stephen B. Pearl, 'Changes in the Pattern of Language Use in the United Nations', in Kurt E. Miller (ed.), *Language Status in the Post-Cold-War Era* (Lanham, Md.: University Press of America, 1996), 29–42.

Pinker 1994: Steven Pinker, *The Language Instinct* (New York: Morrow, 1994).

Prince 1910: J. Dyneley Prince, 'Jersey Dutch', *Dialect Notes*, 3 (1910).

Pullum 1991: Geoffrey K. Pullum, *The Great Eskimo Vocabulary Hoax, and Other Irreverent Essays on the Study of Language* (Chicago: University of Chicago Press, 1991).

Pütz 1994: Martin Pütz (ed.), *Language Contact and Language Conflict* (Amsterdam: Benjamins, 1994).

Pyles and Algeo 1993: Thomas Pyles and John Algeo, *The Origins and Development of the English Language*, 4th edn. (Fort Worth, Tex.: Harcourt Brace Jovanovich, 1993).

Renfrew 1987: C. Renfrew, *Archaeology and Language: The Puzzle of Indo-European Origins* (London: Cape, 1987).

Reyhner 1995: Jon Reyhner, 'American Indian Languages and United States Language Policy' in Willem Fase, Koen Jaspaert and Siaak Kroon (eds.),

The State of Minority Languages: International Perspectives on Survival and Decline (Lisse: Swets & Zeitlinger, 1995), 229–48.

Robins and Uhlenbeck 1991: R. H. Robins and E. M. Uhlenbeck (eds.), *Endangered Languages* (Oxford: Berg, 1991).

Ruiz 1990: Richard Ruiz, 'Official Languages and Language Planning', in Karen L. Adams and Daniel T. Brink (eds.), *Perspectives on Official English: The Campaign for English as the Official Language of the USA*, pp. 11–24.

Salomon and Urioste 1991: *The Huarochiri Manuscript: A Testament of Ancient and Colonial Andean Religion*, trans. Frank Salomon and George L. Urioste (Austin: University of Texas Press, 1991).

Sebeok 1973: T. A. Sebeok (ed.), *Current Trends in Linguistics, 11: Diachronic and Typological Linguistics* (The Hague: Mouton, 1973).

Seyoum 1988: Mulugeta Seyoum, 'The Emergence of the National Language in Ethiopia: An Historical Perspective' in Florian Coulmas (ed.), *With Forked Tongues: What are National Languages Good For?*, pp. 101–45.

Shirley 1968: Janet Shirley (tr.), *A Parisian Journal 1405–1449* (Oxford: Clarendon Press, 1968).

Siebert 1967: Frank T. Siebert, 'The Original Home of the Proto-Algonquian People', in *Contributions to Anthropology. Linguistics I: Algonquian* (Ottawa: Government Printer, 1967; *National Museum of Canada: Bulletin*, 214; *Anthropological Series*, 78), 13–47.

Siebert 1975: Frank Siebert, 'Reconstructing Virginia Algonquian from the Dead: The Reconstituted and Historical Phonology of Powhatan', in James Crawford (ed.), *Studies in Southeastern Indian Languages* (Athens: University of Georgia Press, 1975), 285–453.

Silva 1997: Penny Silva, 'The Lexis of South African English: Reflections of a Multilingual Society', in Edgar W. Schneider (ed.), *Englishes around the World: Studies in Honour of Manfred Görlach* (Amsterdam: Benjamins, 1997), ii. 159–76.

Smith 1972: Janet Hugie Smith, 'Native Pharmacopoeia of the Eastern Great Basin', in Don D. Fowler and Alma Smith (eds.), *Great Basin Cultural Ecology: A Symposium* (Reno, Nev.: Desert Research Institute, 1972; *Desert Research Institute Publications in the Social Sciences*, 8), 73–86.

Taylor 1977: Douglas Taylor, *Languages of the West Indies* (Baltimore: Johns Hopkins University Press, 1977).

Todd 2000: Loreto Todd, 'Where Have All the Celtic Words Gone?', *English Today*, 163 (July 2000), 6–10.

Wardhaugh 1987: Ronald Wardhaugh, *Languages in Competition: Dominance, Diversity and Decline* (Oxford: Blackwell, 1987).

Webster 1789: Noah Webster, *Dissertations on the English Language* (Boston: Thomas, 1789).

Weinreich 1953: Uriel Weinreich, *Languages in Contact: Findings and Problems* (New York: Linguistic Circle of New York, 1953).

Whiteley 1998: Peter M. Whiteley, *Rethinking Hopi Ethnography* (Washington, DC: Smithsonian Institution Press, 1998).

Whorf 1936: Benjamin Lee Whorf, 'The Punctual and Segmentative Aspects of Verbs in Hopi', *Language*, 12 (1936), 127–131; reprinted in Carroll 1956, pp. 51–6.

Whorf 1941: Benjamin Lee Whorf, 'The Relation of Habitual Thought and Behavior to Language', in Leslie Spier and others (eds.), *Language, Culture, and Personality: Essays in Memory of Edward Sapir* (Menasha: Sapir Memorial Publication Fund, 1941), 75–93; reprinted in Carroll 1956, pp. 134–59.

Whorf 1950: Benjamin Lee Whorf, 'An American Indian Model of the Universe', *International Journal of American Linguistics*, 16 (1950), 67–72; reprinted in Carroll 1956, pp. 57–64.

Whorf 1953: Benjamin Lee Whorf, 'Linguistic Factors in the Terminology of Hopi Architecture', *International Journal of American Linguistics*, 19 (1953), 141–5; reprinted in Carroll 1956, pp. 199–206.

Williams 1643: Roger Williams, *A Key into the Language of America* (London, 1643).

Williams 1965: Thomas Rhys Williams, *The Dusun: A North Borneo Society* (New York: Holt, Rinehart and Winston, 1965).

Yule and Burnell 1903: Henry Yule and A. C. Burnell, *Hobson-Jobson*, 2nd edn. (London: Murray, 1903).

Zettersten 1969: Arne Zettersten, *The English of Tristan da Cunha* (Lund: Gleerup, 1969).

INDEX